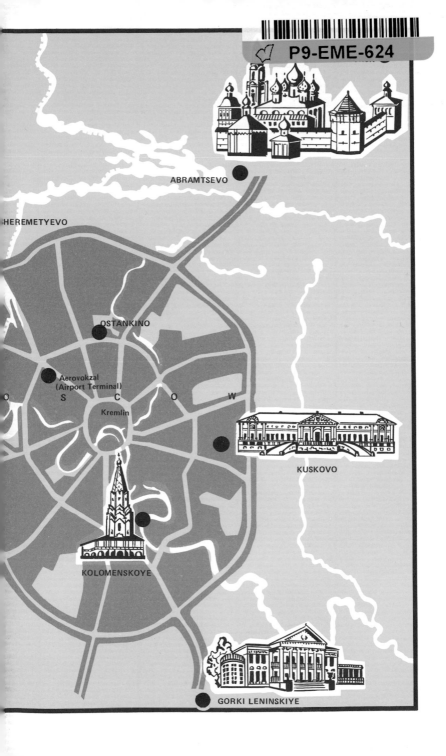

P9-EME-624

ABRAMTSEVO

SHEREMETYEVO

OSTANKINO

Aerovokzal
(Airport Terminal)

O   S   C   O   W

Kremlin

KUSKOVO

KOLOMENSKOYE

GORKI LENINSKIYE

Vladimir Chernov

Three Days in
MOSCOW

A Guide

PLANETA PUBLISHERS. MOSCOW

В. Чернов

ТРИ ДНЯ В МОСКВЕ

На английском языке

Translated from the Russian by *Cynthia Rosenberger*

Editor of the Russian text *Inna Rakhmanina*
Editor of the English text *Yekaterina Tabidze*
Designed by *Sergei Parkhomovsky*
Art editor *Vladimir Orlovsky*
Maps by *Lyubov Cheltsova*
Photos by *Sergei Parkhomovsky*

ISBN 5-85250-231-6

CONTENTS

TO THE READER

As its title suggests, this guide is written for the foreign tourist visiting Moscow for a limited period of time. It will acquaint you with the most important sights and places of interest including both monuments of history and culture and contemporary structures and landmarks. Not only will it serve as a source of interesting facts and information, this guide will offer helpful suggestions as to what best to focus attention upon, thus economizing both your time and energy. It is not necessary that you follow all the itineraries outlined in the guide — you may want to plan your own sightseeing tour of the city, selecting those things which correspond to your own personal interests.

To describe a city as vast as Moscow is difficult, especially within such a small compass. Those who would like a more comprehensive and detailed acquaintance with Moscow should turn to more substantial works. This English language edition of our short guide has been expanded and revised, taking into consideration many comments and suggestions received from readers. However, everything in this world is subject to change and Moscow is no exception in this respect. In the time that has passed since the guide went to press, Gorky Street has regained its old name of Tverskaya. There are plans to give back some twenty other Moscow streets their historic names. The Council for Mutual Economic Assistance has been reorganized to become an international organization for economic cooperation. Many new shops, restaurants, theatres and newspapers have appeared.

Few travel books are without errors, and no guidebook can ever be completely up to date. While every effort has been made to ensure that all information is accurate at the time of going to press, the publishers will be glad to receive any corrections and suggestions for improvements, which can be incorporated in the next edition. Please, write to 8/11 Petrovka Street, Moscow 103031, USSR.

Planeta Publishers

A BRIEF SKETCH OF THE CITY

Moscow is an extremely large city. It stretches approximately 30 kilometers from west to east, and 40 kilometers from north to south. Its **area**, as encompassed by the Circular Motor Road (109 kilometers long, radius from the center—17-23 kilometers), is about 1,000 square kilometers. In recent years new residential areas have spread beyond the Motor.Road.

Take a look at a map of the Soviet Union. The city in which you are now located is situated in the European part of the country, at an almost equal distance from the western borders of the USSR and the Ural Mountains which divide Europe and Asia. Moscow is at the center of the East European plain. For those who like exactitude, and for possible comparisons with the locations of other cities, its **geographical coordinates** are as follows: 55° 45' in latitude and 37° 37' in longitude from the Greenwich meridian. Moscow is bounded on all sides by coniferous and deciduous forests. The Moskva River flows through the city a distance of approximately 80 kilometers from the north-west to the south-east. To the north of the city the Moscow Canal joins the Moskva River to the great Russian river the Volga. In the southeast the Moskva River flows into the Oka, one of the largest tributaries of the Volga. Thanks to the canal, the Volga, and other rivers, Moscow is a port of five seas: the capital is accessible to vessels from the Baltic, White, Caspian, and Black seas, and the Sea of Azov.

Topographically speaking, Moscow lies primarily on an extensive plain, a factor which adds some measure of comfort to the tourist's excursions about the city.

Moscow is surrounded by a broad network of towns, settlements, and villages, whose residents make up a portion of the capital's work force. Up to one million people commute daily to Moscow from the outlying areas of Moscow Region. The **number of permanent residents** is about 9 million.

Muscovites are sociable, hospitable people. They love their city and take great pride in showing its sights to visitors.

And now some facts the tourist should know about the **climate**. Each season has its own special charm. The summer, spring, and fall are all good times to visit Moscow. And as for the winter—we believe it's an especially good time!

Moscow has a moderately continental climate. But in comparison with other major European cities, the yearly amplitude of temperature fluctuations is much higher, averaging 28 °C. The average winter temperatures over many years are as follows: −7.6 °C in December, −10.2 °C in January, and −9.6 °C in February. The first frosts begin towards the end of September, and the first snowfalls usually occur in the latter part of October or early November. The snow cover is generally established by late November, and begins to thaw in the first half of April.

As a rule, Moscow summers are warm and sunny. However, there can be hot spells, as in the summer of 1972 when the temperature remained above 30 °C for 23 days. The average summer temperatures over many years are: +15.8 °C in June, +18.1 °C in July, and +16.2 °C in August. In summer there are frequent thunderstorms, especially in July.

The weather in Moscow is usually quite pleasant in spring and early autumn. During this period it's dry and clear, with little or no wind and invigoratingly pure air. In May the average temperature is +11.6 °C, and in September, +10.6 °C.

People who take an interest in weather lore have compiled the following list representing many years of observations:

March 16	—snow begins to thaw;
April 12	—the ice breaks up in the Moskva River; drifting of ice lasts up to 18 days;
May 2	—Moscow has its first thunderstorm;
May 24	—the apples blossom;
August 26	—leaves begin to fall;
November 2	—the first snow;
November 18	—the Moskva River freezes.

Moscow is the main political, economic, scientific and cultural center of the country. It is the capital of the Union of Soviet Socialist Republics, the first socialist government in the world, created in the wake of the victory of the Great October Socialist Revolution in 1917. The Soviet Union is the home of over hundred various nations and ethnic groups. Among the 15 Soviet Socialist Republics enjoying equal rights, the RSFSR, or Russian Soviet Federal Socialist Republic, is the largest. Moscow is also the capital of the RSFSR.

The highest state, government and Party institutions are all based in Moscow: the Presidium of the Supreme Soviet of the USSR, the Soviet Government, the Central Committee of the Communist Party of the Soviet Union. The highest institutions of the Russian Federation are based in Moscow as well, and the capital is also the center of Moscow Region and local administrative bodies.

In Moscow are held congresses of the Communist Party of the Soviet Union, plenary meetings of the Central Committee of the CPSU, sessions of the Soviet Parliament—the Supreme Soviet of the USSR (and RSFSR), trade-union and Komsomol (Young Communist League) meetings, and various major conferences and meetings of public organizations and artistic and scientific unions.

From February 25 through March 6, 1986, the 27th Congress of the Communist Party of the Soviet Union was held in the Kremlin Palace of Congresses.

The Congress worked out a radically new strategic course aimed at comprehensive intensification of production based on scientific and technological progress, economic restructuring, effective forms of management, organization, and stimulation of labor, and further democratization of society.

The Congress approved an updated CPSU Programme, and an amended version of the CPSU Rules, as well as Guidelines for the Economic and Social Development of the USSR for 1986-90 and for the Period Ending in 2000.

Ensuring peace on the Earth is the most critical problem now facing mankind. The central task of the USSR's external policy in the forthcoming years is to implement the program set forth in the announcement of the General Secretary of the CC CPSU of January 15, 1986 to eliminate all weapons of mass annihilation and avert another world war.

The Congress elected the central organs of the Party. On March 6, at a plenary session of the Central Committee of the CPSU, Mikhail Gorbachev was elected General Secretary of the Central Committee.

At the 27th Party Congress representatives of 72 nations and nationalities of the USSR were elected. Among the 5,000 delegates elected, 1,352 were women.

Moscow is always in the center of world politics. Heads of foreign states, leaders of foreign political parties and prominent public figures are frequent visitors to the Soviet capital, and over 100 countries have accredited diplomatic representatives here. In February 1987 the International Forum "For Nuclear-Free World, for the Survival of Mankind" was held in Moscow and was attended by approximately one thousand foreign participants from over eighty countries. Renowned workers in the fields of science and art as well as representatives of religious groups— people of the most varied political views and convictions—came to the agreement that intelligent mankind has both the desire and the possibility of saving the precious gift of life on the Earth and that it is imperative that we learn the art of coexisting in the world. Delegates to 220 national organizations from 115 countries attended the World Congress of Peace Forces in 1973 and the World Forum of Peace Forces in 1977. In 1982 the World Conference "Religious Workers for Saving the Sacred Gift of Life from Nuclear Catastrophe" was held in the capital. In October 1983 a large anti-war rally of 800,000 Muscovites in support of the World Disarmament Campaign proposed by the United Nations was held.

In 1949 the Council for Mutual Economic Assistance (CMEA) was established to foster the systematic development of the national economies of socialist countries. Its secretariat is based in Moscow, and it is here that its sessions are held.

The USSR has trade connections with every major country of the world. Dozens of international scientific, industrial and economic exhibitions, fairs, business meetings, conferences, and symposiums are held in Moscow each year. Representatives of various foreign firms, banks, airlines, and tourist organizations have offices in Moscow. In 1980 the World Trade Center (WTC) was opened as a business center designed to facilitate trade, scientific and industrial cooperation between Soviet Union and foreign countries.

Each year the number of foreign visitors to Moscow increases. In 1987 over five million people from other countries visited the Soviet Union, and most of them spent some portion of their trip in Moscow.

The Moscow International Film Festival, the International Tchaikovsky Music Contest, the Moscow Stars festivals of Soviet art, the Russian Winter festivals, and the Moscow International Book Fair with its motto: "Books Serve Peace and Progress" have long become established events enjoying great popularity here. The International Folklore festival takes place in the middle of August every two years.

For many years Moscow has maintained traditional friendly ties with 75 foreign capitals and cities.

Every year dozens of major international competitions and world European championships in various fields of sport are held in the capital. In 1980 Moscow hosted the Olympic Games, in which over 6,000 sportsmen and women from 81 countries participated. Olympic competitions were attended by more than 4 million Muscovites and visitors.

The Moscow International Peace Marathon held each year in August has become a traditional event since 1981. Its course is 42,195 meters long and stretches along the capital's streets and embankments. Both Soviet and foreign sportsmen take part in the event. Among the participants are foreign

tourists to Moscow who are fans of this sport.

Moscow's policy of peace and friendship has in recent times gained much popularity and found an increasing number of followers in all countries of the world.

A BIT OF HISTORY

Moscow is over 800 years old. The first written mention of Moscow dates back to 1147.

In 1156 Prince Yuri Dolgoruky ordered a wooden fort to be built on a steep, wooded hill at the confluence of the Neglinnaya and Moskva rivers and surrounded it with a rampart, wooden walls, and a moat. The town that sprung up on this spot was called "Moskva" (Moscow) after the Moskva River.

At the beginning of the 13th century a 300,000 strong army led by Batu Khan invaded the Russian land, ravaging and burning towns and settlements. Although Moscow met the enemy with staunch resistance, it was seized and burned in the winter of 1237-38. Moscow recovered relatively quickly from the attack of the Mongol-Tatar hordes, and by the second half of the 13th century was already the center of an independent Moscow principality, which gradually assimilated other Russian lands. The strengthening and rise of Moscow was furthered by the fact that it was the center of an enormous territory where the Russian nation was being formed. Its rise was also facilitated by its advantageous geographical location at the crossing of river and land trade routes. The Moskva River and its tributaries were important routes of communication, along which merchant ships laden with furs, leathers, fabrics, grain, wax, honey, and other goods travelled to the West and the East.

At the beginning of the 14th century Moscow was established as the capital of the Great Moscow Principality, which emerged as the result of the annexation of a series of other Russian lands to the Moscow Principality. In 1326 the Russian Metropolitan Pyotr moved his residence from Vladimir—the major city of the Great Principality of Vladimir—to Moscow, which thus became not only the political, but the religious capital of Rus.

Moscow played a leading role unifying the Russian lands into a single state and in overthrowing the Mongol-Tatar oppressors. Under Prince Dmitry Donskoi (1350-89) Moscow became the center of the struggle against the conquerors. Russian forces led by Dmitry Donskoi marched from Moscow to battle against the enormous army of Mamai Khan. At Kulikovo Field on the upper reaches of the Don River Russian troops defeated the enemy hordes. This battle, which took place on September 8, 1380, had an enormous bearing on the fate of the Russian people, and marked the beginning of liberation of Rus from the Mongol-Tatar yoke. But the threat of destructive raids from the East hung over the Russian land for yet a long time. In 1382 Moscow was ravaged and burned to the ground by the hordes of Tokhtamysh Khan. Once again the city had to build anew.

In the last quarter of the 15th century the unification of all the surrounding Russian lands under the Moscow Principality was complete. Moscow, the capital of the Russian state, refused to pay the tribute to the Mongol-Tatars, and the Khan's army, after launching a campaign to suppress the unruly capital, backed down before the Russian armed forces. In 1480 Russians threw off the Mongol-Tatar yoke which had oppressed the country for more than 250 years.

With the formation of the Russian centralized state at the end of the 15th century Moscow became the country's most important political, economic, and trade center. There was a great burgeoning of trades, such as armour-making, founding, forging, jewel-making, chasing, tanning; pottery-making factories, and brickyards were built. In the 15th century Moscow became the focal point of Russian cultural scene. There the chronicles were compiled and outstanding works of literature, painting and architecture created. And in the middle of the 16th century it was in Moscow that Russian printing originated. In the 16th century the capital of the Russian state was one of the largest cities of Europe with a population reaching 100,000.

More than once Moscow was fated to play a decisive role in the country's struggle against foreign aggressors. In 1612 the people's volunteers, led by Prince Dmitry Pozharsky and rural council elder Kuzma Minin, liberated Moscow from Polish invaders and their foreign mercenaries.

In 1712 Peter the Great transferred the capital of Russia to St. Petersburg, now Leningrad, which he had founded nine years earlier on the banks of the Neva River. Although no longer the seat of power, Moscow remained the heart of Russia and its political, economic and cultural center.

Moscow played a vital role in the Patriotic War of 1812. Napoleon saw the capture of Moscow as the decisive factor in his battle against Russia. At the Battle of Borodino, near Moscow, Napoleon's Grande Armée suffered a blow from which it never recovered. But because of the heavy losses borne by the Russian Army, it was decided to surrender Moscow without a resistance. A mass exodus from the city followed in the wake of the army's withdrawal; of

Moscow's 275,000 citizens no more than 10,000 remained. The destruction of Moscow which followed aroused the people's hatred towards the interventionists. The popular resistance on the occupied territory of Russia gained force, and the invaders found themselves without food reserves or fodder. Much of Moscow was razed by fire. Within 39 days following the invasion of Moscow, after sustaining losses of 70,000 soldiers and officers, Napoleon's Grande Armée began to beat a hasty retreat. As one contemporary aptly remarked, in the beginning Napoleon was captivated by Moscow, then he took it captive and, finally, himself became its captive.

Moscow suffered enormous losses during the events of 1812. Of the city's 9,000 buildings, 6,500 were burned or seriously damaged in fires. Moscow had to build anew.

The growth of capitalism in Russia, which was especially accelerated after the abolition of serfdom in 1861, left its imprint on Moscow as well. Many new enterprises sprang up in the city, and metal-working factories appeared. The number of industrial workers quickly increased. By the late 19th century Moscow had become a major center of light industry and the country's main railway junction. The city's population at this time had grown to approximately one million.

In the 19th century Moscow strengthened its reputation as a major center of Russian national culture. The creative work of many great Russian poets and writers of the 19th and early 20th centuries are bound up with Moscow.

Moscow occupied an outstanding place in the revolutionary liberation movement in Russia. Major revolts by the city's poor, working people and artisans flared up during the 16th–18th centuries.

Moscow was closely linked with the Decembrists, the first Russian revolutionaries of the nobility, who took up arms against serfdom and autocracy in December, 1825. Moscow was the birthplace and home of Pavel Pestel and Nikita Muravyov, prominent ideologists and organizers of the revolutionary movement later to be known as the Decembrist. In the middle of the 19th century Moscow University became a center of the social movements in Russia.

In the 1870s and 1880s there was a significant surge of the working class movement in Moscow, and in the 1880s the first Marxist circles appeared. Upon his arrival in Moscow in August 1893 (his first visit was in 1890), Lenin established contact with the local Marxists. Under his influence and direct leadership the Moscow Marxist circles were united and in 1895 established themselves as the "Workers' Union". In the beginning of 1898 the Moscow Marxist organization became known as "The League of Struggle for the Emancipation of the Working Class."

In the spring of 1898 the Moscow Committee of the Russian Social Democratic Labor Party was elected immediately following the Party's first congress, the sponsors of which had included Moscow Social Democrats, members of "The League of Struggle for the Emancipation of the Working Class".

Moscow played a major role in the Revolution of 1905-07, the first people's revolution in Russia during the age of imperialism.

In February 1917, when Russia was in the throes of the second bourgeois democratic revolution, Moscow's workers again resolutely responded to the Bolsheviks' appeal to struggle against tsarism. (The *Bolshevik* political party was formed in 1903 as the result of the struggle of Russian revolutionary Marx-

ists, headed by Lenin, to create a genuine revolutionary party. Lenin's supporters received the majority of votes — *bolshinstvo*; their adversaries, the minority — *menshinstvo*.) The soldiers of a number of units of the Moscow garrison came over to their side, and the tsar's autocratic regime was overthrown. Together with Petrograd (St. Petersburg until 1914), Moscow became the country's most important center of preparation for the socialist revolution.

On October 25 (November 7 New Style), 1917, on receiving the first reports of the victory of the armed uprising of workers and revolutionary soldiers in Petrograd, Moscow Bolsheviks set up a center to direct the struggle to transfer power into the hands of the Soviets. On October 27-28 (November 9-10) counter-revolutionary forces started an armed uprising against the workers and soldiers. In Petrograd at the time, Lenin kept a close watch on the events taking place in Moscow. Addressing a detachment of sailors setting out to provide assistance to revolutionary Moscow, Lenin said: "Don't forget, comrades, that Moscow is the heart of Russia! And that heart must be Soviet, or the Revolution will be lost." After a week of battles, on the night of November 3 (16), the workers and revolutionary soldiers, under the leadership of the Moscow Bolshevik organization, crushed the counter-revolutionaries and established Soviet power in Moscow.

On March 12, 1918, the Moscow radio station broadcast the following address to the capitals of Europe and to Tokyo, Peking and New York: "... the government of the Soviet Republic has been established in Moscow. All diplomatic communications should be addressed to the Kremlin, Moscow."

In 1922 at the First All-Union Congress of Soviets in Moscow the Declaration and Treaty on the Formation of the Union of Soviet Socialist Republics was approved and Moscow became the capital of the Soviet Union. Big factories, research centers, and educational establishments were built here, and the reconstruction of the city was started on a grand scale.

In the summer of 1941 the peaceful work of all Soviet people was disrupted: on June 22, Nazi Germany treacherously, without declaration of war, attacked the Soviet Union. The Great Patriotic War against fascism began. Moscow became the organizational center of the country's counter-offensive effort. Hundreds of thousands of Muscovites joined the army in the field. During the first five months of the war 360,000 Moscow Communists and Komsomol members went off to fight against the enemy. Over 850,000 Muscovites in all fought at the frontlines. Moscow's machinery construction factories switched over to the production of weapons, ammunition, and equipment for the army.

By autumn of 1941 the enemy had reached Moscow's suburbs. The Nazis set themselves the task of taking the capital in the shortest possible time. In its attempt to surround and take the city, the fascist German command concentrated its main forces on its approaches. The enemy threw into action 1,800,000 soldiers and officers, 1,700 tanks, 14,000 guns and mortars, and approximately 1,390 fighter aircraft. From October 20 Moscow was declared in a state of siege. The front had reached the very approaches to the city. The fascist air force made more than 12,000 sorties on Moscow, and about 200 aircraft penetrated to the capital. These were trying days which would decide the course of World War II and the destiny of the country. The troops of the Soviet Army and the citizens of the capital displayed heroism in the battles. Some 450,000 of the city's inhabitants built defence works and over 168,000 Muscovites applied to join the ranks of the People's Volunteers. Moscow's citizens and its rural inhabitants operated valiantly in the rear of Hitler's troops.

"Russia is vast, but there's nowhere to retreat, Moscow's behind us." These words of the defence hero Vasily Klochkov became the motto of all the city's defenders. At the gates of Moscow the fascist troops suffered their first major defeat of World War II, and this victory marked the beginning of a radical turning point in its course.

On May 8, 1965, at the 20th anniversary commemoration of the victory of the Soviet people in the Great Patriotic War, Moscow was awarded the honorary title of Hero-City and decorated with the Order of Lenin and the Gold Star medal for the mass heroism, courage, and fortitude displayed by the people of the city in the struggle against the Nazi invaders. Over a million people were decorated with the Defence of Moscow medal, and more than 800 Muscovites were awarded the title of Hero of the Soviet Union for their battle feats during the Great Patriotic War.

SOME DATES FROM MOSCOW'S HISTORY

12th–early 13th centuries	Rise of Moscow
1237–38	Moscow sacked and burned by the Tatar hordes of Batu Khan
2nd half of 13th century	Moscow is rebuilt, becomes the center of the independent Moscow Principality
Early 14th century	Moscow established as the capital of the Great Moscow Principality
1326	First stone church built on the Kremlin territory
1367	The Kremlin walls of white stone erected
1380	Russian troops march from Moscow to defeat the Tatar hordes of Mamai Khan at the Battle of Kulikovo Field
1404	The first Moscow town clock installed in the Kremlin on one of the buildings near the Cathedral of the Annunciation
Late 15th century	Moscow becomes the capital of the centralized Russian state
1485–95	The present brick walls and towers of the Kremlin built
1564	The first dated Russian printed book published in Moscow
1612	Moscow liberated from Polish invaders by the people's voluntary levies led by Kuzma Minin and Dmitry Pozharsky
1648, 1662	Anti-feudal uprisings in Moscow: the "Salt Revolt" and the "Copper Revolt"
1653	At the request of the Ukrainian hetman Bogdan Khmelnitsky, leader of the liberation war of the Ukrainian people from the Polish-gentry yoke, *Zemstvo* Assembly *(Zemsky sobor)* in Moscow proclaimed the reunification of the Ukraine and Russia
1655	The first cotton mill built in the city
1687	The Slavono-Graeco-Latin Academy, the first higher educational institution in Russia, founded
1701	The School of Mathematics and Navigation opened in Moscow
1702	The first public theater in Moscow opened
1703	The first Russian newspaper *Vedomosti* (Gazette) published in Moscow
1712	On Peter the Great's edict the capital of Russia is transferred to St. Petersburg
1755	The first Russian University founded
1799	The great Russian poet, Alexander Pushkin, born in Moscow
September 2, 1812	Napoleon's troops enter Moscow
October 6–11, 1812	Napoleon's troops retreat from Moscow during the Patriotic War against French invaders

1817–25	The first revolutionaries of the Russian nobility (later called the Decembrists) active in Moscow
1824	The Maly (Little) Theater opened
1825	The Bolshoi (Grand) Theater opened (the date of its foundation is 1776, the year its first troupe was organized)
1831	The first all-Russia industrial exhibition opened in Moscow
1846	The first agricultural exhibition opened
1851	Arrival of the first train on the St. Petersburg–Moscow line
1866	The Moscow Conservatoire founded
1872	The Higher Courses for Women (the first higher educational institution in Russia for women) founded
1882	The first telephone lines operate in Moscow
1883	The first electric arc lamps installed
1880s	The first Marxist circles founded
1890	Lenin's first visit to Moscow
1891	The first workers' Social Democratic circles formed in the city's factories
1894	The Central Workers' Circle formed, which marked the beginning of the Moscow City Social Democratic organization
1895	The Moscow Marxist workers' circles unite to form the "Workers' Union"
1895	Moscow workers celebrate May Day, the day of international workers' solidarity, for the first time
1898	The Moscow Committee of the Russian Social Democratic Labor Party is formed
1898	The Moscow Art Theater founded
1898	The first trunk line between Moscow and St. Petersburg put into operation
October 1905	The general political strike
November 1905	The Moscow Soviet of Workers' Deputies formed (elected representatives from the city's mills and factories), the forerunner of Soviet power
December 1905	The armed uprising of the Moscow workers (during the first bourgeois–democratic revolution in Russia from 1905–07)
1913	The Bolshevik workers' daily newspaper *Nash put* (Our Road) published legally in Moscow (of the 16 published issues, 12 were confiscated by the police)
February 1917	The Moscow proletariat comes out against tsarism (during the second, February bourgeois–democratic revolution in Russia). The tsarist autocracy overthrown
October/November 1917	The October armed uprising in Moscow
November 3, 1917	Proclamation of Soviet power in Moscow

March 12, 1918	The Soviet government transferred from Petrograd to Moscow, and Moscow becomes the capital of Soviet Russia
April 12, 1919	The first communist *subbotnik* (voluntary working Saturday) of the Moscow workers
1920	The 8th All-Russia Congress of Soviets approves GOELRO, the plan for the electrification of Russia drawn up on Lenin's instructions
December 30, 1922	The First All-Union Congress of Soviets in Moscow adopts the Declaration on the Formation of the Union of Soviet Socialist Republics. Moscow becomes the capital of the USSR
January 21, 1924	Lenin's death at Gorki, outside of Moscow
1924	The first Soviet motor car produced in Moscow
1925	The 14th Congress of the All-Union Communist Party (of Bolsheviks), the VCP(B), (as the CPSU was called from 1925-52) meets in Moscow and adopts the policy of socialist industrialization of the country
1927	The 15th Congress of the VCP(B) meets in Moscow and adopts the policy of collectivization of agriculture
1931	The first sound film shown on Moscow screens
1933	Moscow's first trolleybuses put into operation
1934	Transfer of the Academy of Sciences from Leningrad to Moscow
1935	The first Metro line opened
1935	The first General Plan for the reconstruction of Moscow adopted
1936	The first color film shown on Moscow screens
1937	The first non-stop flights of Soviet aircraft across the North Pole from Moscow to the USA by the crews of Valery Chkalov and Mikhail Gromov
1937	The Moscow Canal, joining the Moskva and Oka rivers with the Volga commissioned
June 22, 1941	Nazi Germany invaded Soviet territory without a declaration of war
1941-42	Battle near Moscow during the Great Patriotic War of 1941-45 against fascist Germany: period of defence— September 30-December 4, 1941; period of offensive—December 5, 1941-April 20, 1942
June 24, 1945	The Victory Parade in Moscow
1947	The 800th anniversary of Moscow
1951	The second General Plan for the reconstruction of Moscow adopted
1952	The Moscow Committee for the Defence of Peace formed
1956	First flight from Moscow of the *TU-104* turbo-jet passenger aircraft

Lenin Mausoleum

Spasskaya (Saviour) Tower

Blagoveshchensky (Annunciation)
Cathedral

Rossiya *Hotel and Znamensky (Sign)*
Cathedral

Kremlin Towers
View of the Kremlin from Zamoskvorechye
Tsar Bell
Tsar Cannon

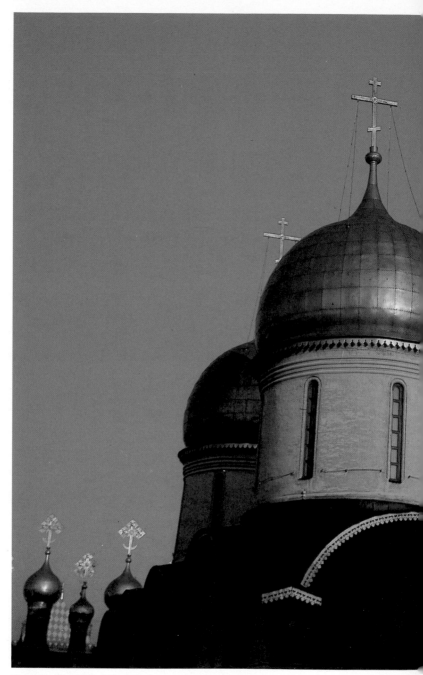

Uspensky (Dormition) Cathedral

Building of the Presidium of the Supreme Soviet of the USSR

Building of the former Arsenal

1957	The 6th World Festival of Youth and Students held in Moscow
November 1957, November 1960, June 1969	Meetings in Moscow of representatives of world Communist und Workers' Parties
1960	The Patrice Lumumba Peoples' Friendship University founded
April 14, 1961	Moscow welcomes Yuri Gagarin, the world's first cosmonaut
1961	The Kremlin Palace of Congresses opened
1963	Treaty Banning Nuclear Weapon Tests in the Atmosphere, Outer Space and Under Water signed in Moscow by the USSR, USA and Great Britain (the Moscow Treaty)
1965	The new international airport *Sheremetyevo* built
1967	Moscow workers together with the rest of the country celebrate the 50th anniversary of the Great October Socialist Revolution
1967	The Ostankino TV Tower built
1967	The *Rossiya* Hotel built, the largest in the USSR and one of the largest in Europe
1970	Centenary of the birth of Lenin celebrated in Moscow
1971	The General Plan for the Development of Moscow adopted
1971	The 24th Congress of the CPSU adopts the Peace Program actively and consistently implemented by the Soviet Government
1972	Moscow celebrates together with the rest of the country the 50th anniversary of the Formation of the Union of Soviet Socialist Republics
1977	The Supreme Soviet of the USSR adopts a new Constitution of the Union of Soviet Socialist Republics (the Fundamental Law)
1980	The 22nd Summer Olympic Games held in Moscow
March 11, 1985	Mikhail Gorbachev elected General Secretary of the Central Committee of the CPSU
1985	The 12th World Festival of Youth and Students held in Moscow
February–March 1986	The 27th Congress of the CPSU held in Moscow
August 23, 1986	The residents of Moscow appeal to the people of the world's capitals to join efforts in order to curb the arms race, free the Earth from nuclear testing, and preserve peace on the Earth
November 1987	Grand celebration of the 70th anniversary of the Great October Socialist Revolution
1988	Millennium of the Baptism of Russia
May 1989	First Congress of People's Deputies of the USSR held in Moscow

MOSCOW TODAY

Moscow's postwar development has been the most dynamic and widescale in her history. The city has become the most important industrial center of the country.

Before the Revolution Moscow was referred to as a "cotton" town (40 per cent of its workers were employed in the textile industry and only 9 per cent in the metal-working industries). Just before the war it became a center of production of means of production. Today the highly diversified engineering industry is the leading branch of the city's industry. Moscow produces motor vehicles, automation lines for machine building, electrical engineering and radio equipment, electronic devices and computers. It is very likely that most of the world's estimated 6,000 different trades and professions can be found in Moscow. To be more precise, over half the city's workers are employed in the engineering and metal-working industries. There are more than 1,000 industrial works in the city at present. The plants, factories, industrial complexes and warehouses are all situated outside the center, and for the most part on the city's periphery. Strict environmental measures with which the city's industrial concerns must comply ensure that the air remains clean.

Moscow is the scientific center of the USSR. The USSR Academy of Sciences, the USSR Academy of Medical Sciences, the All-Union Academy of Agricultural Sciences, the USSR Academy of Arts, as well as other specialized academies and a large number of research institutes are located here. The city has 76 higher education establishments with an enrollment of some 606,000 students. Qualified specialists with diplomas from Moscow University and colleges work throughout the Soviet Union and in many countries abroad, in the most varied professions. The Lomonosov Moscow University is the main institution of higher learning of Moscow, and the country.

In 1960 the Patrice Lumumba Peoples' Friendship University was founded in Moscow. This unique institution trains engineers, historians, philologists, physicists, mathematicians, doctors, agronomists, lawyers, economists, and teachers who become highly qualified national professionals for the developing countries of Asia, Africa, and Latin America. Around 7,000 students from 107 countries receive training in the University's seven departments.

Over the centuries Moscow has become one of the biggest cultural centers of the world. The city has a wealth of splendid architectural ensembles and cultural monuments of world significance. Moscow's museums and art galleries house collections of the works of old masters and outstanding contemporary artists. The city has more than 70 museums: history of the Revolution, historical, art, scientific and technical, literary, and theatrical museums (please refer to the Information section of this guidebook for a listing of the most prominent ones). Together with exhibitions they are visited by more than 25 million people a year. Moscow has over 30 professional theaters with permanent companies and large repertoires, many concert halls, and two circuses (three in summer).

Before the Revolution Moscow had only 12 public libraries. Now the number of general and specialized libraries is over one hundred times greater. In the All-Union State Foreign Literature Library there are books in 132 of the world's languages. Two hundred and six newspapers (including the newspapers of large enterprises and institutions) are published in Moscow. Among these, we can recommend *Moskovskiye Novosti* (Moscow News), which is published in nine languages.

In the Constitution of the USSR it is written that the "concern for the preservation of historical monuments and other cultural values is the duty of the citizens of the USSR".

The state institutions in charge of the preservation of these monuments are greatly assisted by the various volunteer societies for the preservation of monuments of history and culture. One such organization in Moscow is the local branch of the All-Russia Society for the Preservation of Monuments of History and Culture, with a membership of over 700,000 city residents.

Muscovites especially cherish everything connected with the memory of Lenin. In the city proper and the Moscow Region there are more than 180 buildings (state and public organizations, factories, mills, houses, and flats) which Lenin visited, spoke at, or worked in at various times.

Many foreign visitors to Moscow are interested in the overall organization of the public education system in our country, and the secondary school system in particular. Public education in the USSR is one of the most important achievements of the socialist society. The basic principles of public education are the equal rights of all citizens to receive education regardless of race, nationality, sex, religious preference, earnings, and social position; the freedom to choose instruction in one's native language or the languages of other nationalities of the country; compulsory education for children and adolescents; gratuitous education of every kind; and the collaboration of school, family, and society in the upbringing of children and young adults. In 1984 the Supreme Soviet of the USSR passed a resolution on the reform of the country's general education and professional schools. The reform is aimed at improving the methods of instruction and education, as well as the preparation of children for socially useful work; at helping schoolchildren realize their individual aptitudes in one or another subject, and guiding them in choosing a professison.

Muscovites, as all Soviet people, receive free medical treatment. There is a large number of hospital and out-patient clinics in the city staffed by a total of 90,000 doctors and specialists in every kind of medicine, 20,000 more than the number ten years ago. Prophylaxis has become the principal measure to protect citizens' health, and mass check-ups are carried out.

During its more than 800 years the appearance of Moscow has repeatedly changed, but the most striking changes have been since the Great October Socialist Revolution, and especially since the war. The city boundaries have been extended.

Before the Revolution Moscow used to be called the "big village" and contained many plain one- and two-storey wooden houses. Building was often carried on in an unplanned way. Crooked streets and remote side-streets were paved with cobblestone, and in the workers' districts they were not paved at all. The water supply system provided for less than half the city's residents and, with the exception of the streets and squares of the center, there was no street lighting. There were palaces and mansions where the aristocrats lived, and entire regions of slums and wooden huts where the working people were huddled.

But just look at Moscow now — broad, straight avenues and spacious squares, parks and gardens, modern apartment buildings, massive newly erected buildings in the city's developing regions, public buildings of striking architecture, bridges and granite embankments along the river, main thoroughfares, underpasses and flyovers, stadiums, recreation areas and, last but not least, protected zones. About the latter we would like to speak in more detail.

In accordance with the General Plan for the Development of Moscow, in order to preserve the historical appearance and layout of the city's center, its ancient core, nine zones have been designated as subject to special protection. Those which will be mentioned in this guide are *ulitsa Razina* (Razin Street), *ulitsa Arbat* (Arbat Street), *Kropotkinskaya ulitsa* (Kropotkin Street), *ulitsa Gertsena* (Herzen Street), and *ulitsa Petrovka—Kuznetsky most* (Petrovka Street—Smith's Bridge Street).

Construction in the capital relies on the city's own technical production base. In Moscow and its suburbs there are more than 100 factories and integrated plants with modern equipment which manufacture everything necessary for construction, from prefabricated structures to finishing materials. The pace and volume of construction increases with every passing year. An average of 160 new apartments are made available to Muscovites each day, and each year over 300,000 city residents better their living conditions. Now it's possible to say that Moscow has been renovated on a grand scale; over four-fifths of the city's housing space is located in buildings constructed after the war. Still, the housing problem has not been completely solved.

In recent times the city's population has grown by 65,000–70,000 each year. For this reason, Moscow continues its housing construction at an intensive pace.

New structures have enhanced the architectural appearance of the capital's central avenues such as Lenin, Komsomol, Kutuzov, Kalinin, Leningrad, Vernadsky and Olympic avenues. Among Moscow's architecturally unique new structures are the Kremlin Palace of Congresses, the Pioneer Palace on the Lenin Hills, the Children's Musical Theater, the Lenin Central Stadium at Luzhniki, the Borodino Panorama, the *Rossiya, Kosmos,* and *Izmailovskaya* hotels, the Council for Mutual Economic Assistance, the Television Center and TV Tower at Ostankino, the *Rossiya* and *Oktyabr* cinemas, the residential and office buildings on Kalinin Avenue, the Circus on the Lenin Hills, the *Sheremetyevo* Airport, the Olympic Village and Olympic sports complexes, and the large *Moskovsky* Department Store.

Despite the rapid growth and enormous changes, Moscow's unique, inherent features have remained the same. Let us look at the map of the city. The Kremlin is at the center of the city. Around it are five rings, consisting of broad streets, avenues, and highways. The first ring is actually a semi-circle abutting the Moskva River on both ends, and is composed of *prospekt Marksa* (Marx Avenue), *Staraya ploshchad* (Old Square), *Novaya ploshchad* (New Square) and Razin Street on one side and *Borovitskaya ploshchad* (Borovitskaya Square) on the other. This is the central portion of the city with a great number of historical and cultural monuments. The second ring, also a semi-circle, is known by Muscovites as *Bulvarnoye koltso* (Boulevard Ring). The third ring is *Sadovoye koltso* (the Garden Ring). But while the Boulevard Ring does actually appear as a long chain of picturesque boulevards along which Muscovites love to stroll, the name borne by the Garden Ring is based purely on tradition. It is the city's most important transport artery along which traffic flows from early morning until late evening. Yet another ring is the former Kamer-Kollezhsky Rampart, nearly 40 kilometers long, which some two centuries ago served as the city's customs boundary. The Moscow Circular Railway now runs along part of the original route of this rampart. Finally, there is the fifth, recently built ring, the Moscow Circular Motor Road, which, as we have already noted, marks the city's present boundary.

From the center a series of thoroughfares radiates out, cutting across these rings on all sides of the city. *Prospekt Mira* (Peace Avenue) leads north to the Exhibition of Economic Achievements and then becomes Yaroslavl Highway. *Leningradskoye shosse* (Leningrad Highway) stretches north-west in the direction of Leningrad. *Prospekt Kalinina* (Kalinin Avenue), which becomes *Kut-uzovsky prospekt* (Kutuzov Avenue), runs to the west, while *Leninsky prospekt* (Lenin Avenue) leads south-west toward *Vnukovo* Airport. The two old streets, Bolshaya Polyanka and Bolshaya Ordynka, join, opening the road to the south.

Beyond the Moscow Circular Motor Road stretch forests and meadows. This is the capital's forest park reserve zone, the so-called "Green Belt" where Muscovites can spend their weekends. It covers an enormous area of 1,800 square kilometers, and extends from 10 to 15 kilometers in width. Located within this reserve zone are small and fairly large-sized towns, workers' settlements and summer houses, and several hundred villages. In addition there are many rest homes, children's summer camps, boarding houses, tourist camps and recreation zones, easily accessible by public transport, where one can find places to eat, rent camping and sporting equipment, and enjoy various sports in specially designed areas.

MOSCOW'S FUTURE

What will the capital be like at the start of the third millennium? Already the technical and economic indices have been worked out and confirmed for a new General Plan for the Development of Moscow through the year 2010.

In 1987 the Executive Committee of the Moscow City Soviet of People's Deputies adopted a plan providing for the overall reconstruction of the historically evolved center of the city, specifically, that part in which two-thirds of all the historical landmarks are concentrated. The reconstruction and restoration of these historical buildings will be carried out in conjunction with the modernization and beautification of streets and squares. The center is envisaged as becoming an active hub of work, daily life and relaxation for both Muscovites and visitors to the capital. Also adopted was the "Architectural Legacy" program, which aims to increase the emphasis placed on the city's architectural legacy in urban planning considerations by the year 2000. This program has designated some 9,500 architectural monuments to be placed under state protection and calls for the restoration of 1,564 buildings of historical and cultural value.

In spite of the fact that the number of cars in the city will have almost doubled, pedestrians in the center of Moscow will be able to feel more at ease since certain streets will be turned into pedestrian malls (we will discuss the first of these, the Arbat, a bit later). The traffic on a series of thoroughfares cutting across the center will be funneled through underground tunnels. The Garden Ring and a 35-kilometer-long superhighway which will encircle the city at radius of 5-7 kilometers from the center together with a system of high-speed bypasses will be able to fully handle the inner-city flow of traffic.

It is assumed that the city will definitely stretch beyond the bounds of the Moscow Circular Motor Road. Moscow's territory will be divided into three sections (west, east, and south-west), each practically a town in itself with a population of approximately three million. These sections will in turn be broken down into 16 planning zones: 8 in the already developed regions of Moscow and the same number beyond the Circular Motor Road. Each zone will have its own center with stores and restaurants, parks, stadiums, cinemas and concert halls, consumer services establishments, and administrative institutions.

Particular attention is being directed towards the development of public transport system. The present Metro system will hardly be capable of providing for the speedy transport of passengers travelling long distances. For that reason plans are under way for the construction of an auxiliary, high-speed Metro. Its electric express trains will attain speeds of 100-120 kilometers an hour, and the distance between stations will increase by two or three times. The first two express lines, each 60 kilometers long, are scheduled to begin operation at the beginning of the next century, and will cross tangentially through

the city's center. When completed, the high-speed Metro will consist of four chordal and one circular line.

Aboveground electric commuter trains which run along 11 main lines have been assigned a large role in the city transport system. In density and speed the electric trains in the city limits will only be slightly inferior to the Metro trains. The tramway system will also undergo a change. New high-speed, four-car trams seating 500 passengers will service those regions where building a new Metro line would be inexpedient. Finally, the traditional modes of aboveground transport, such as buses, trolleys, and regular tramways, will flow to a new rhythm thanks to an electronic monitoring system which is already being put into effect.

In the north-east of Moscow within the city limits one of the largest natural parks in the country will be created.

By the end of the first decade of the next century it is expected that Moscow's population will have increased by not more than one million. A portion of Moscow's enterprises and organizations will be moved to other cities in the central part of the country. With these goals in mind, plans are being made to build three or four satellite cities at a radius of approximately 100 kilometers from Moscow.

On the threshold of the third millennium the capital of the USSR will be a beautiful and even more comfortable place to live.

That completes our brief introductory sketch of Moscow. Now we invite you to take a walk with us along its streets and squares. We will try our best to help you both take a good look at our city, and to learn many things of interest.

WALKING
AND MOTOR TOURS
THROUGH THE CITY

ГРАЖДАНИНУ МИНИНУ И КНЯЗЮ ПОЖАРСКОМУ
БЛАГОДАРНАЯ РОССІЯ, ЛѢТА 1818

FIRST DAY

We recommend that you begin your tour of Moscow in the morning with a visit to Red Square and a look round the Kremlin's historic monuments and museums. In the afternoon we recommend a walk along Gorky Street.

KRASNAYA PLOSHCHAD (RED SQUARE)

Everyone visiting Moscow for the first time probably begins their acquaintance with the city on Red Square. And they are correct in doing so. Red Square is the heart of Moscow, and crowds begin to stream here from early morning on. Here one can find visitors from every corner of the Soviet Union and from many different countries. Red Square, one of the most beautiful in the world stretches out broadly along the eastern wall of the Kremlin and occupies an area of more than 70,000 square meters. It is 695 meters long, and has average width of 130 meters.

At the central part of the Kremlin wall on Red Square is the **Lenin Mausoleum**, built of dark red granite and black labradorite. This fine example of Soviet architecture was designed by the architect Alexei Shchusev. Inside the Mausoleum, in a crystal sarcophagus, lies the body of Lenin, the great revolutionary and founder of the Communist Party of the Soviet Union and of the Soviet State, who died on January 21, 1924. Originally there was a wooden Mausoleum, which was designed in a

night and erected in two and a half days. In May 1924 it was rebuilt and stood until 1930, when it was replaced by the present granite Mausoleum, of exactly the same shape. The walls of the mourning chamber are faced with polished grey and black labradorite, with a bright red zigzag band of smalt. A large monolith above the main portal bears the inscription "Lenin", incrusted in dark red porphyry.

Posted at the entrance to the Mausoleum is a guard of honor. The first sentinels assumed their post here at 4 p. m. on January 27, 1924, when the coffin bearing Lenin's body was carried in.

On the days the Mausoleum is open to the public a long stream of people can be seen wending their way towards it from the *Aleksandrovsky Gardens*. In summer or winter, come rain or shine, there is always a line on Red Square.

The Lenin Mausoleum is open to visitors on Tuesdays, Wednesdays, Thursdays, and Saturdays from 9 a. m. to 1 p. m., and on Sundays from 9 a. m. to 2 p. m. Foreign tourists are admitted separately from 12 noon to 1 p. m.

on Tuesdays, Wednesdays, Thursdays and Saturdays, and on Sundays from 1 p. m. to 2 p. m., and assemble about 45 minutes prior to admission at the corner of the Historical Museum facing 50th Anniversary of October Square (ploshchad Pyatidesyatiletiya Oktyabrya).

Located behind the Lenin Mausoleum along the Kremlin wall is a revolutionary necropolis. Buried here in two communal graves are more than 300 revolutionary fighters who perished in the struggle for Soviet power. The names of 76 famous heroes are engraved on marble slabs. Tombstones have been erected on the graves of outstanding leaders of the Communist Party and Soviet statesmen. Immured in the Kremlin wall are urns holding the ashes of eminent Soviet figures, including Maxim Gorky, Nadezhda Krupskaya (Lenin's wife), Igor Kurchatov, scientist and organizer of work in atomic science and technology, Sergei Korolyov, the designer of Soviet spaceships, and World War II Marshal Georgi Zhukov. Here too are buried renowned workers of the International Communist movement: Clara Zetkin, Sen Katayama, John Reed and Fritz Heckert.

Red Square is first mentioned in the 15th-century chronicles. All the roads leading to Moscow from the largest Russian towns of that period—Vladimir, Ryazan, Smolensk and Tver—converged at Red Square. Even then it was already "a great market-place and what the Forum was for Ancient Rome", as artist Apollinary Vasnetsov (1856-1933), a great expert on Moscow who dedicated to it all his creative work, wrote. From morn to night it was thronged with idle and busy folk. It was the place to learn news, and the starting point of many riots and revolts of the working people against their oppressors. The square received its present name in the 17th century from the Russian word *krasny*, meaning "fair" or "beautiful".

This old square has witnessed many historical events, a few of which we will mention briefly here.

In late October 1917 there was a fierce battle on Red Square between a detachment of revolutionary soldiers and units rising up against Soviet power. Its cobblestones were stained with the blood of workers and soldiers devoted to the Revolution, and its name acquired a new and deeper meaning. On November 10, 1917 a ceremonial burial of the workers and soldiers who fell in October 1917 fighting for Soviet power took place at the Kremlin wall. "Through all the streets to Red Square the torrents of people poured, thousands upon thousands of them, all with the look of the poor and the toiling. A military band came marching up, playing the *Internationale*, and spontaneously the song caught and spread like wind-ripples on a sea, slow and solemn. From the top of the Kremlin wall gigantic banners unrolled to the ground: red, with great letters in gold and in white, saying, 'Martyrs of the Vanguard of World Socialist Revolution,' and 'Long Live the Brotherhood of Workers of the World' ... a river of red banners ... against a background of fifty thousand people ..."—thus the event was described by the American writer and publicist John Reed (1887-1920) in his book *Ten Days that Shook the World* which Lenin called truthful and extraordinarily vividly written.

On March 12, 1918, on Lenin's orders, a red banner was raised over the Kremlin: red became the color of the country's State Flag. Since that time, for over 70 years, it has fluttered above the cupola of the USSR Council of Ministers building, above the Kremlin wall and Red Square.

Lenin spoke on Red Square many times, passionately calling on the people to uphold the socialist Revolution and the freedom and independence of the Soviet land, to defend it against interventions, and to put an end to wars between nations.

On November 7, 1918, the first anniversary of the Great October Socialist Revolution, Lenin spoke on the occasion of the unveiling of a memorial plaque in the Senate Tower in memory of those "Fallen in the struggle for peace and brotherhood of nations". The memorial plaque was executed by Sergei Konenkov, who later became an outstanding, world-famous Soviet sculptor. In 1950, when the tower

was being restored, the plaque was removed and is now in the Russian Museum in Leningrad.

On that day Red Square was overflowing with people, and was illuminated by powerful lamps and spotlights. Giant banners were hung on the wall of the Historical Museum with the enormous figures of a worker and ploughman, and an inscription which proclaimed: "The peasant shall give the worker bread, and the worker shall give the peasant peace." "Along the enormous brightly decorated streets," wrote the newspaper *Pravda*, "waves of people move along in one continuous flow—twinkling lights are reflected gaily on clothing and faces, and everyone seems festive and dressed up in fantastic costumes. What enthusiasm, what exultation on the faces! They walk along, arm in arm, laughing and singing free and proud songs."

Lenin spoke again on Red Square on the sunny day of May 1, 1919. With excitement and joy he observed the festive demonstration of Moscow's working people. "His coat was thrown over his shoulders, and pinned on his jacket was a big red bow like the ones the other demonstrators wore," recalled one of the participants of the celebration. "The people greeted Lenin with enthusiasm, and his face shone with exultation and joy. He waved cordially to the gathering. Red Square, filled to overflowing with people and an enormous quantity of flowers, was beautiful at that moment." A festively decorated tramcar filled with children carrying red flags and singing in unison entered the square. Lenin then said: "Up to now the story of what our children would see in the future has sounded like a fairytale; but today, comrades, you clearly see that the edifice of socialist society, of which we have laid the foundations, is not a utopia. Our children will build this edifice with even greater zeal."

On November 7, 1941, when Nazi troops were on the approaches to Moscow and within 70–100 kilometers from the capital, a traditional parade was held on Red Square to mark the anniversary of the October Revolution. Planned in strict secrecy, the parade was a total surprise for the enemy command and demonstrated to the world the Soviet people's determination and confidence in victory. Soviet soldiers marching before the Lenin Mausoleum gave an oath to defend the capital to the last. One of the participants of the unexampled parade recalled:

"... The snowfall ceased, and thousands of soldiers looked upon the Lenin Mauoleum, until that day for over a month hidden from view inside a wooden pavilion. Today its polished granite shone brilliantly, and it appeared even more majestic than before... Hitler's propaganda was already shouting to the whole world about Moscow's imminent fall, and the *führer* was preparing to carry out a review of his hordes on

our Red Square. And although the enemy was at Moscow's gates, it was we, Soviet people, who were standing today on the main square of the capital of the USSR, demonstrating our strength to the whole world!... Tanks thundered along the paving blocks of Red Square in clouds of snow dust—light, medium, and heavily armored, equipped with high-calibre guns. The foreign military attachés looked on in amazement from the guest stands at the tanks camouflaged in white and counted them carefully, for Goebbels' propaganda had assured everyone that the Red Army had not a single tank left..."

On June 24, 1945, the triumphant Victory Parade was held on the square in commemoration of the defeat of Hitlerite Germany. To the roll of drums, Soviet soldiers back from the frontlines cast 200 enemy standards at the foot of the Mausoleum. Among these were standards of units considered at one time to be creams of Hitler's reich, standards which fluttered in European occupied capitals during World War II, and which signified death and slavery. Among the first cast onto the square was Hitler's personal standard.

Red Square is the site of Moscow's ceremonial demonstrations on the annual May 1 holiday commemorating the Day of International Workers' Solidarity and the traditional November 7 anniversary of the Great October Socialist Revolution.

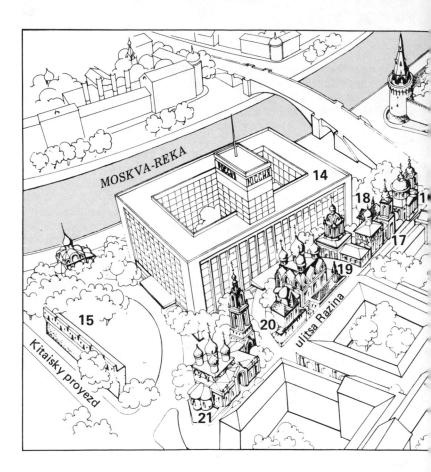

RED SQUARE

1. *Lenin Mausoleum*
2. *Cathedral of Vasily the Blessed (Cathedral of the Intercession)*
3. *Monument to Kuzma Minin and Dmitry Pozharsky*
4. Lobnoye mesto *(place of proclaimed tsar's edicts)*
5. *Spasskaya (Saviour) Tower*
6. *Senatskaya (Senate) Tower*
7. *Nikolskaya (St. Nicholas) Tower*
8. *Uglovaya Arsenalnaya (Corner Arsenal) Tower*
9. *Aleksandrovsky (Alexander) Gardens*
10. *Tomb of the Unknown Soldier*
11. *Historical Museum*
12. *Prospekt Marksa Metro Station*

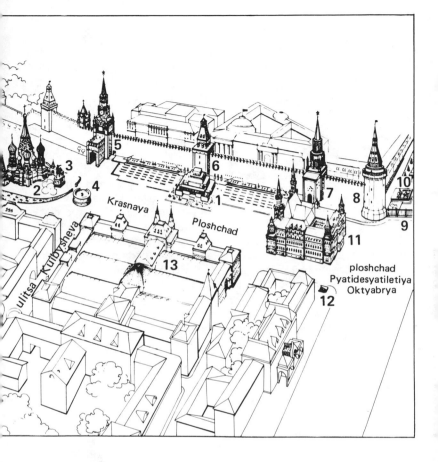

Krasnaya

Ploshchad

ulitsa Kuibysheva

ploshchad
Pyatidesyatiletiya
Oktyabrya

Lenin Mausoleum

The architectural ensemble of Red Square developed gradually, over the centuries. In 1555–61 the **Cathedral of Vasily the Blessed (the Cathedral of the Intercession)**, a unique creation of Russian national art, was built on the square. It was erected on the order of Ivan IV (the Terrible) to commemorate the victory over the Kazan khanate (a feudal state in the Central Volga Region). The names of the builders had been forgotten for over three centuries, and it was only in 1896 that some old manuscripts were discovered that mentioned "the Russian masters Postnik and Barma", by whose genius this architectural masterpiece was created. In 1957, however, other old sources were found that lead us to believe that "Postnik and Barma" were one person, the architect Postnik Yakovlev, nicknamed "Barma" (Mumbler). The Russian masters created a true architectural wonder—a cathedral consisting of nine pillar-like chapels united by a single artistic idea, yet each quite unlike the others. In the center the tallest chapel rises to a height of 47.5 meters and has a tent roof. Built into its walls is a steep white-stone staircase with narrow steps. Located in this chapel was the Church of the Intercession of the Virgin, the name given to the cathedral itself to commemorate the day the successful storm of Kazan (the main town and stronghold of the Kazan khanate) was begun—October 1, 1552, the day of the religious festival. In 1588 a small chapel was erected over the grave of a certain Vasily, a holy fool well-known in Moscow at that time. Ever since the Cathedral of the Intercession has been known as

Cathedral of Vasily the Blessed (Cathedral of the Intercession)

the Cathedral of Vasily the Blessed.

The cathedral is built of brick in traditional Russian style; at the same time it contains many elements of old Russian wooden architecture. Inside the cathedral some remarkable 16th-century frescoes are preserved. The inner gallery also contains fine wall and vaulted ceiling paintings (17th century) — stylized flower patterns of unique shapes in bright crimson and turquoise. One of the oldest works of Russian art preserved in the cathedral is the iconostasis in the Trinity Chapel with its 16th- and 17th-century painting. The tent-roofed bell-tower next to the cathedral was built in the 1670s and blends in organically with the entire ensemble.

The Cathedral of the Intercession has undergone repeated restoration in Soviet times. Most of the old Russian fresco paintings dating from the time of Ivan the Terrible, long concealed under later layers of oil paint, have already been restored to their original appearance. The beauty and splendour of the cathedral gave rise to a popular legend. Word had it that Ivan the Terrible asked the builders if they could build anything finer or duplicate what they had already done. When they answered that they could, in a rage he ordered that they be blinded so that there would never be anything more beautiful in the world than the Cathedral of the Intercession. A **branch of the State Historical Museum** has been opened in the cathedral with exhibits tracing the history of this remarkable monument of Russian architecture. Among the old books, one's attention is drawn to *A Guide to the Antiquities and Memorabilia of Moscow*, published in 1792. In it there is a description of the "cathedral of the Intercession or of Vasily the Blessed".

Next to the Cathedral stands the **monument to Minin and Pozharsky**, the first civil monument erected in Moscow. Up until 1930 it stood in the center of Red Square. The monument was sculptured in 1818 by Ivan Martos in high Classical style and depicts the historic meeting of Kuzma Minin and Prince Dmitry Pozharsky, under whose leadership the people's volunteers drove Polish invaders out of Moscow during the 1612 war of liberation and upheld the independence of the Russian state. No portraits of Kuzma Minin and Dmitry Pozharsky made in their lifetime had been preserved, so the sculptor gave them the typical features of the finest Russian people, strongwilled and courageous, reflecting in his work their readiness to fight for Moscow and drive the enemy from their native land. The inscription on the pedestal reads: "To Citizen Minin and Prince Pozharsky from a Grateful Russia, year 1818." The monument was erected with money raised by public subscription.

To the right of Vasily the Blessed is the **Spasskaya** (Saviour)

Tower, which has long become one of the symbols of Moscow. This majestic, graceful tower was built in 1491 by Russian craftsmen under the supervision of the Italian architect Pietro Antonio Solari of Milan (1450-93), who worked in Russia from 1490. It acquired its present appearance in 1624-25 when the Russian architect Bazhen Ogurtsov completed it with an oc-

Monument to Kuzma Minin and Dmitry Pozharsky

tagonal multi-storey spire. In those days ceremonial processions of the clergy passed through the Spasskaya Tower Gate, and tsars, emperors, and foreign ambassadors drove into the Kremlin through it. It was forbidden to pass through with covered head; even the tsars were required to remove their hats.

In 1625 the first **Kremlin chimes** were mounted on the Spasskaya Tower, and were replaced in 1851-52 by the present chimes, with ten bells cast in the 17th-18th centuries. The chime mechanism occupies three of the tower's ten storeys. The clockface is 6.12 meters in diameter and each figure is 72 centimeters high. The hour hand is 2,97 meters long, and the minute hand is 3,27 meters. The clock itself weighs 25 tons.

During the storming of the Kremlin in the October battles of 1917, the clock was damaged by artillery fire. In 1918, however, it was restored on Lenin's instructions. In 1974 the unique mechanism was completely renovated. The striking of the Kremlin chimes is broadcast daily by Radio Moscow at 6 a.m., noon, and midnight. The Spasskaya Tower Gates are the main gates of the Kremlin. In 1935 a luminous, five-pointed, ruby-red star was mounted on the tower. The height of the tower, together with the star, is 71 meters.

Not far from the Cathedral of the Intercession on Red Square is what is called the ***Lobnoye mesto***, a round platform of white stone approximately 13 meters in diameter, built in 1534. Here the tsar's edicts were proclaimed and religious ceremonies held. Up until the 18th century executions were sometimes carried out on the wooden scaffolds near the *Lobnoye mesto*.

Visible to the left of the cathedral, just beyond Red Square, is the ***Rossiya*** Hotel, which was built in 1964-67 and designed by Dmitry Chechulin. It contains

Lobnoye mesto *(place of proclaimed tsar's edicts). Detail*

3,070 rooms and can accommodate some 5,500 guests. The hotel occupies an area of nearly 10 acres, and stretches along the Moskva River for 250 meters. The 23-storey tower, known as the "Presidential block", is the compositional center of the hotel. It contains some extremely comfortable suites, ranging in size from one room to five.

The building of the hotel also houses the **State Concert Hall** (seating 2,600) and the ***Zaryadye Cinema*** (entrances on the Moskva River side). A number of small churches alongside the hotel were carefully preserved as rare cultural monuments during the reconstruction of this area. One of them, **Church of the Conception of St. Anna** (on the bank of the Moskva River), is the same age as the Kremlin walls (end of the 15th century).

To the left of the cathedral of Vasily the Blessed begins *ulitsa Razina* (Razin Street), formerly Varvarka (St. Barbara Street). It is the most ancient street in Moscow and

dates back to the 14th century. Situated between Razin Street and the Moskva River, is one of the capital's most interesting protected regions, the Zaryadye. A walk through this region is an excursion into the ancient past. Beginning in the 12th century it was the home of artisans, skilled craftsmen, and masters: carpenters and stonemasons, blacksmiths and gilding masters, potters and boiler-makers. The area from Varvarka Street to the Kremlin bustled with lively trading, stalls and ware-houses crammed Red Square, forming a solid wall around the Cathedral of the Intercession on all sides. The 15th and 16th centuries marked the beginning of Zaryadye's transformation into a region of the privileged nobility. Here boyars built their estates, foreign embassies took up residence, and overseas merchants settled. Varvarka Street

In the foreground, *Lobnoye mesto*

witnessed many popular uprisings and revolts. It was along this street that Stepan Razin was led to his execution, and the street was renamed in his honor in 1933.

A walk along this street will only require a short time. We recommend to those visiting Red Square to take a walk along Moscow's most ancient street. On the right-hand side are the gems of old Russian architecture, and to the left are the buildings of the former inns and trading rows of the 17th-19th centuries and monotonous multistorey buildings of the late 19th century.

At the entrance to the street on the right-hand side (No. 2) is the **Church of St. Barbara** (from which the street took its name in the 16th century) rebuilt in 1796-1801. A bit behind the church, closer to the *Rossiya* Hotel, is a striking building with narrow, asymmetrical window apertures and a steep wooden roof. This is the **Old English Court** or, as it is still known, the **English Town House**, where visiting English merchants and diplomatic envoys used to stay. Its role in Moscow's history dates back to 1556.

At No. 4 Razin Street is the **Church of Maximus the Blessed.** The original church building, which has not been preserved, was erected on the burial site of Maxim Blazhenny (holy fool) who died in 1434. The existing building was constructed in 1698-99, and is interesing as a monument of the transitional period in religious ar-

chitecture. The characteristic features of a 17th-century Moscow church are combined with decorative devices reminiscent of the Western European Baroque. The building now houses an exhibition hall. The bell-tower with a green cupola (1829) in front of the Church of Maximus the Blessed is a marvelous example of late Classical architecture. Beyond the overpass that connects Razin Street with the north entrance of the *Rossiya* Hotel, a stepped slope leads to the **Znamensky Sobor** (Cathedral of the Sign) at No. 8a—a massive structure of red brick. There is a concert hall in the cathedral with splendid acoustics where one can enjoy concerts of old Russian music. This cathedral is one of the structures of the former Znamensky Monastery ensemble, founded in the 17th century. Nearby at No. 10 is the so-called **Chambers of the Romanov Boyars.** Two of its storeys are visible from the street, while all three can be seen from the courtyard. This building houses the **museum "Chambers of the 16th-17th Centuries in Zaryadye"**, a branch of the State Historical Museum. Here, in small rooms with low, vaulted ceilings is recreated the décor of a boyar house of that period. Assembled here are household articles, needlework, cold steel and firearms, and books from a personal library. Among the most interesting exhibits are peasant rainwear of woven birchbark and a tile stove with a different scene painted on each tile. The last of the series of monuments of the Russian architecture on Razin Street is the **Church of St. George** at No. 12, which draws attention with its highly decorative and colorful appearance, gilded central cupola, and four surrounding cupolas with stars against a blue background. Built in 1657, today the church houses the **Exhibition Hall of the All-Russia Society for the Protec-**

Old English Court, or English Town House

tion of Monuments of History and Culture.

This ends our walk along Razin Street. At the end of the street is a descent which leads to the **Ploshchad Nogina** (Nogin Square) **Metro Station.** But we suggest that you return to nearby Red Square, and in doing so, walk along the other side of the street. Against the backdrop of the modern glass and geometrically strict exterior of the *Rossiya* Hotel, these already familiar 'strangers' from the distant past will reveal new facets of their beauty, bearing testimony to the

superb craftsmanship of the old Russian masters.

Now that we are back at Red Square, let us walk up from Vasily the Blessed to the opposite end, where facing us is a red brick building with four pairs of dissimilar towers. This is the **State Historical Museum**, founded on the initiative of many prominent progressive people of the 19th century. It was built in 1875-81 to the design of Vladimir Sherwood, on the site of the two-storey building in which Moscow University was founded in 1755 by Mikhail Lomonosov. Before the Revolution the museum was supported by private donations, and had around 300,000 exhibits. Today the State Historical Museum is a major depository of documents and relics relating to the history of the peoples of the USSR. It contains about 4,500,000 objects and there are tens of thousands of files in its archives. It houses the country's largest archaeological collection, a unique collection of coins and medals, a collection of precious ornaments and household articles, historical documents, ancient manuscripts and books, and a fine collection of works of art. Each year over two million people visit the museum.

The exhibits in the museum's 48 halls reflect the history of the peoples of the USSR from the earliest times to the present. The exhibits include letters written on birch bark by people of 11th-century Novgorod; clothes worn by Tsar

Ivan the Terrible; Peter the Great's carriage; a portrait of Yemelyan Pugachev, leader of the 18th-century Peasants' War, painted over a portrait of Empress Catherine II; Napoleon's sabre and field kitchen captured at Vyazma by a Russian cavalry detachment in 1812; a first issue of the revolutionary newspaper *Kolokol* (The Bell), published in the mid-19th century by Alexander Herzen and Nikolai Ogaryov, which played an immense role in the history of the revolutionary movement in Russia; and the first decree of Soviet power, the Decree on Peace, written by Lenin directly following the victory of the 1917 October Revolution.

To the left of the State Historical Museum stands the graceful three-tier **Nikolskaya** (St. Nicholas) **Tower** built in 1491 by Pietro Antonio Solari, and crowned with a spire at the end of the 18th century.

The architectural originality of the Nikolskaya Tower is to be seen in the Gothic decorations of the façade and its white-stone openwork elements and tall spire, erected at the beginning of the 19th century. The spire and part of the tower were destroyed by Napoleon's retreating troops in 1812, but were restored in 1816 to plans prepared by architect Osip Bovet. The tower was badly damaged again by artillery fire during the storming of the Kremlin in 1917, and was rebuilt on Lenin's instructions by Nikolai Markovnikov. Its height, including the ruby-red star, is 70.4 meters.

Opposite the Kremlin, along the whole length of Red Square, stretches the two-storey building with plateglass show windows of the **State Department Store** *(GUM)*. Originally known as the Upper Trading Stalls, the building was designed by architect Alexander Pomerantsev and erected in 1890-93. Before the Revolution it contained around 200 small shops. In 1953 the building was completely reconstructed.

To the right of the Historical Museum stands the former Provincial Government Building (No. 1 *Istoricheskii proyezd*—Historical Museum Passage), built in the late 17th and early 18th centuries. Situated in the courtyard of this build-

Historical Museum

ing was the *yama*, a debtor's prison, in which, in 1790 the great Russian writer and revoltutionary Alexander Radishchev (1749–1802) was held under guard on his way to exile in Siberia. Radishchev is the author of the famous pro-abolitionist book, *The Journey from St. Petersburg to Moscow*, which Pushkin called "an appeal for rebellion".

In 1974 extensive restoration and maintenance work was carried out on Red Square; the Lenin Mausoleum was restored and the granite visitors' stands renovated, and the stone paving blocks were relaid.

We leave Red Square through *Historical Museum Passage*. Before us are steps leading to the underground crossing and the **Prospekt Marksa Metro Station.** But let us turn to the left and walk through the Aleksandrovsky Gardens along the Kremlin wall.

Behind the iron grille gates of the Aleksandrovsky Gardens by the Kremlin wall, is the **tomb of the Unknown Soldier**, before which burns the Eternal Flame. On the gravestone at the site is a bronze sculptural composition consisting of a laurel branch and a soldier's helmet lying on a banner. The Eternal Flame illuminates the bronze inscription: "Your name is unknown, your feat immortal". The remains of the unknown soldier were brought here from the thirty-first kilometer along Leningrad Highway where, in the grim days of November 1941, the firing line of the front passed and where the So-

State Department Store (GUM)

viet soldiers halted the enemy. This monument commemorating the heroes which fell at the frontlines of the Great Patriotic War of 1941–45 was unveiled on May 8, 1967, on the eve of the 22nd anniversary of the victory. To the left of the tomb of the Unknown Soldier stands a block of red porphyry with the inscription: "1941—To Those Who Died for Their Country—1945". To the right is an alley with similar blocks with earth from the Hero-Cities of Leningrad, Kiev, Minsk, Volgograd, Sevastopol, Odessa, Kerch, Novorossiisk, Tula, Murmansk, Smolensk, and the Brest Fortress. These cities, just as Moscow, were given the honorary title of Hero-City for the mass heroism, courage and fortitude displayed by their inhabitants and Soviet soldiers in the battle against the fascist aggressors.

The Soviet people achieved victory in World War II at an enormous price. Soviet troops fought for victory for 1,418 days. Many Moscow families, just as many families throughout the country, suffered the loss of a loved one, a father, brother, sister, or son. Every year on May 9, Victory Day, the whole country honors the memory of those who died with a minute of silence, and flowers are laid on the soldiers' graves and memorials. This tradition is also observed by young married couples who come to the tomb of the Unknown Soldier on their wedding day or on the first day of their life together, to express their gratitude to those who died to defend their lives, their freedom, and their happiness.

Now let us walk along the Kremlin wall deeper into the **Aleksandrovsky Gardens.** They were laid out in 1819-22. It is interesting to note that the Neglinnaya River flows under them through a pipe. These gardens are a favorite spot with Muscovites and especially with visitors to the capital.

At the foot of the **Middle Arsenal Tower** is a grotto "Ruins"—a monument to the Patriotic War of 1812. To the left of the central alley on an open platform stands an **obelisk monument**, a four-sided spire of grey granite. Inscribed on it are the names of great revolutionaries and thinkers: Karl Marx, Friedrich Engels, Wilhelm Liebknecht, Ferdinand Lassalle, August Bebel, Tommaso Campanella, Jean Meslier, Gerrard Winstanley, Thomas More, Claude Henry

Saint-Simon, Edouard Vaillant, Charles Fourier, Jean Jaurès, Pierre-Joseph Proudhon, Mikhail Bakunin, Nikolai Chernyshevsky, Pyotr Lavrov, Nikolai Mikhailovsky, and Georgi Plekhanov. This, the first monument of revolutionary Russia, was unveiled in 1918. The obelisk was originally erected in 1913, in honor of the tercentenary of the Romanov dynasty, and bore the names of the Russian tsars. On Lenin's suggestion the names of the tsars were replaced by the names of great figures in the struggle for the emancipation of the workers.

The central alley of the Aleksandrovsky Gardens leads to Moscow's most ancient bridge, the **Troitsky Bridge**, embellished, like the Kremlin walls, with V-shaped merlons and loopholes. This bridge joins the Troitskaya and Kutafya towers, through which one may enter the Kremlin.

If you are tired or would prefer to explore the monuments and cathedrals of the Kremlin at another time, you can end your excursion here. A bit further from the Kutafya Tower is a passage leading to the *Biblioteka imeni Lenina* (Lenin Library) and *Borovitskaya*, or to *Kalininskaya* and *Arbatskaya* Metro stations.

THE KREMLIN

What is the best way to look round the Kremlin? How to start? You can, if you wish, walk right along the outside of its crenellated walls, which stretch along for 2,235 meters. Or you can begin by admiring the panorama from na-berezhnaya Morisa Toreza (Maurice Thorez Embankment); that is, from the opposite bank of the Moskva River, or from the Moskvoretsky or Bolshoi Kamenny bridges, which provide a good view of the ancient cathedrals, the Grand Kremlin Palace, and the Kremlin walls and towers. Alternatively, you may view it first from Red Square or from ploshchad Pyatidesyatiletiya Oktyabrya (50th Anniversary of October Square), or from the windows of the *National* or *Rossiya* hotels. In fact, it is worth viewing the Kremlin from all these vantage points so as to see its various perspectives. But nothing, of course, can equal a walk inside the Kremlin itself.

The Moscow Kremlin is open for tours from May 1 through September 30 from 10 a.m. to 7 p.m., and from October 1 through April 30 from 10 a.m. to 5 p.m., excluding Thursdays. The first structure we pass on our way is the white-stone **Kutafya Tower**, built at the beginning of the 16th century as a bridgehead watchtower. At that time it was surrounded by a moat and approached by drawbridges. From this tower we walk onto a stone bridge with a crenellated parapet (once spanning the Neglinnaya River) and proceed to the Troitskaya Tower.

The **Troitskaya** (Trinity) **Tower**, whose gates are hospitably flung open, was erected in 1495–99 by the architect Alevisio Friazine. It had five battle tiers and deep two-storey basements where ammunition for the Kremlin's defence used to be stored. In the 16th and 17th centuries the basement cellars were used as a prison. Military commanders returning victorious from campaigns used to tide into the Kremlin either through the Troitskaya Tower Gate or through the Spasskaya Tower Gate. It was also through the Troitskaya Tower Gate that Napoleon's troops entered, and later fled from the Kremlin. It is the tallest of the Kremlin towers, and is 80 meters high to the top of its star.

Bonch-Bruyevich, chief of the office of the Council of People's Commissars, recalled that in 1918 Lenin, while looking around the Kremlin, was interested in whether they had managed to preserve the objects of value in the palaces, the *Granovitaya palata* (Faceted Hall) and *Oruzheinaya palata* (the Armoury), and the famous Patriarch's Vestry and Library with its priceless books and manuscripts.

The Kremlin at that time still bore the traces of the battles of the revolutionary soldiers and workers with the White Guard cadets. The walls were dotted with bullet-holes, and in every nook and cranny inside there were heaps of litter and rubbish of every kind: remnants of hay and straw, piled-up carriages, broken-down wagons, abandoned cannons, personal items, sacks, and matting. Lenin suggested that the warders check to make quite sure that all the relics were intact and safeguarded. A new chapter in the history of the ancient center of Moscow was opened. Let us recall some of the highlights of this history.

The construction of the Kremlin, as you already know, was begun in the 12th century during the reign of Prince Yuri Dolgoruky. This fortress was razed to the ground in 1238 during the Mongol-Tatar invasion, but Moscow continued to live and grow. In 1326-39 walls of oak were erected around the Kremlin. A cathedral built of stone, the Uspensky (Dormition) Cathedral—the predecessor of the present cathedral—rose among the wooden structures inside the Kremlin. The Kremlin became the residence of the Grand Princes and Metropolitans of Moscow. The oak walls were replaced in 1367-68 by white-stone ones and towers and Moscow began to be called the white-stone city. In 1382 the Tatar Khan Tokhtamysh and his hordes, resorting to treachery, broke into the Kremlin through undefended gates, demolished the fortress, pillaged the churches, burnt the houses inside it, and killed around half the population. Once again Moscow had to build anew.

In 1485-95, during the reign of Ivan III, the walls of white stone, which had survived many fires and sieges over a hundred years or so, were replaced by new brick walls and towers, and these, restored many times, are those still standing today. At the same time the Kremlin was extended to its present size.

In building the new Kremlin, Ivan III was concerned not only with making its walls reliable and sturdy, but with seeing to it that the Kremlin's external appearance reflected the triumph of the policy of the united centralized Russian State, which had thrown off the Mongol-Tatar yoke. Skilled craftsmen were brought from all corners of Russia, from Pskov and Vladimir, from Novgorod and Tver, to replace the old cathedrals, built over a century earlier, with new ones. By the order of Ivan III, the famous Italian architects Aristotele Fioravante, Pietro Antonio Solari, Marco Ruffo, and Alevisio Nuovi Friazine were invited to work in Moscow.

The 17th century wrote a new page in the history of the Kremlin. The consolidation of the Russian State was accompanied by a flourishing of national art and architecture, which can be seen in the new buildings that appeared then in the Kremlin. In 1712 the capital was moved from Moscow to St. Petersburg. The Kremlin became the temporary residence of the tsar's court. Russian emperors and empresses came here to be crowned, to pay their respects to their ancestors and pray at the shrines of the Kremlin.

In 1737 a great fire destroyed all the wooden structures still standing within it. The Kremlin also suffered greatly in 1812 during the period of slightly more than one month that the French troops were quartered there. When forced to retreat from Moscow they tried, on Napoleon's orders, to blow up the Kremlin. Three towers and Ivan the Great Bell-Tower were destroyed, and the Nikolskaya (St.Nicholas) Tower and other structures severely damaged.

In the 19th century the Kremlin was enriched by the Grand Palace and the new building of the Armoury.

In 1918 Lénin signed a decree on the protection of works of art and historic monuments, in keeping with which, all the monuments of the past, cultural and artistic, including the Kremlin, were placed under state protection and in the Kremlin restoration work began.

In 1937 five of the tallest towers were crowned with **ruby-red stars** designed by Academician Fyodor Fedorovsky (1883-1955), for many years the chief artistic director of the Bolshoi Theater. The span of the smallest of them, on the Vodovzvodnaya (Water-drawing) Tower, is nearly three meters and weighs a ton. The largest stars are on the Nikolskaya and Spasskaya towers with a span of 3.75 meters and weigh one and a half tons. Despite their weight, the stars rotate easily with the wind.

Restoration work was resumed in 1945, after the end of World War II. Dilapidated sections of the walls and towers were replaced. The tops of the towers were retiled and covered with sheet copper, and the walls given a damp-proof coating to protect them against the weather. The exteriors of all the

Kutafya and Troitskaya (Trinity) towers

cathedrals and the Faceted Hall were fully repaired, the old stone pavement of Cathedral Square restored, and the dome of Ivan the Great Bell-Tower regilded. Many types of work required quite specific techniques. For example, Zagorsk factory near Moscow provided the restorers with twenty different types of large-size brick varying in configuration and design to correspond with the various historical periods of the construction of the Kremlin. Thus the bricklayers were able to replace every crumbling brick. The work of painting the walls of the Kremlin's towers proved a most delicate and painstaking operation. Each brick was painted separately, by hand, making sure that the seams were left untouched. The most careful restoration work was carried out in the cathedrals and churches which are now the Kremlin's museums. Original frescoes were restituted and renovated, and in some instances brought to light; icons and priceless articles of wood, stone, and metal were restored.

Entrance to the Kremlin is unrestricted and free of charge. From morning till late evening thousands of Muscovites and visitors to the capital come here for a sightseeing tour of its remarkable monuments.

Now let us continue our excursion of the Kremlin. Inside the walls, to the right of the Troitskaya Tower is the **Palace of Congresses.** This monumental building was erected on the site of several service buildings of no historic value. The builders understood the difficulties of their task of raising a modern structure among a collection of magnificent architectural monuments of different epochs, which should become an organic part of the whole ensemble.

The builders succeeded in their task. In 1959-61 a building with expressive, yet austere lines, was erected to the design of a team of Soviet architects.

The interior of the Palace of Congresses is 40,000 cubic meters in total volume. To keep the building from towering above the other Kremlin structures, it was sunk 15 meters into the ground. It is 120 meters long, 70 meters wide, and stretches 29 meters from the ground. It contains 800 rooms and halls. Its five storeys are connected by wide staircases and 14 escalators. The main auditorium has a seating capacity of 6,000. The decorative stagedrop is a chased metal panel with a bas-relief portrait of Lenin in the center. Four thousand five hundred lighting fixtures mounted in the ceiling in combination with indirect luminescent lighting coming from behind the aluminium bands, produce a unique effect. Thanks to the excellent acoustics and a complex amplification system, the sound carries well to all corners of the huge hall, and provides ideal conditions for the performers. Powerful installations change the air in the building every 12 minutes. The stage is equipped with modern facilities which, among other things, allow for the simultaneous interpretation of speeches into 29 languages. The stage is used by the Bolshoi Theater for the presentation of its finest operatic and ballet productions. On the floor above the auditorium there is a banquet hall seating 2,500. This hall is quite unique in that it "floats", as it were, on steel springs which provide for better sound insulation. There are special buffets in the hall for the public, and from its vast windows there is a splendid view of Moscow and the ancient Kremlin cathedrals.

The Palace of Congresses is also used for People's Deputies, Communist Party and Trade Union congresses, various international conferences and mass public meetings.

The long, two-storey **building of the Arsenal** stands with its side wall opposite to the Palace of Congresses and stretches along the Kremlin wall. This building, ornamented with a carved white frieze, is over 30 meters high. The few widely spaced, deep-set pairs of windows accentuate the thickness of the walls. The Arsenal is a splendid example of early 18th-century architecture. Work on it began in 1701 on the orders of Peter the Great, and was completed in 1736.

Architects Dmitry Ivanov and Mikhail Choglokov are believed to be the principal designers. Noble and expressive, the architectural design of the Arsenal harmonizes well with the ancient Kremlin walls and towers. Lining the front of the Arsenal are 875 guns, trophies captured from Napoleon's army in 1812, as well as Russian 16th-17th-century cannons mounted on 19th-century gun-carriages. On both sides of the nearest side entrance to the Arsenal there are two memorial plaques. One commemorates the revolutionary soldiers of the Kremlin garrison who were shot on October 28, 1917 by officer cadets, while the other bears the names of the 92 soldiers, sergeants, and officers of the Kremlin garrison who died defending Moscow and the Kremlin against fascist air raids during World War II.

Beyond the small garden opposite the Arsenal stands a three-storey building with a high socle and a magnificent white-stone cornice. The long, second- and third-storey façades are divided by pilasters. Formerly the seat of the **Senate**, since March 1918 this building has housed the Soviet Government. On the wall of the building is a memorial plaque bearing Lenin's portrait in bas-relief and the inscription: "V. I. Lenin lived and worked in this building from March 1918 to May 1923." It was from here that Lenin, as Chairman of the Council of People's Commissars of the first socialist state in history, directed the defence of the Soviet state in the grim years of the Civil War and foreign intervention, guided the country's political and economic activities during the period of economic dislocation and famine. **Lenin's office and apartment** on the second floor have been made into a museum (excursions organized in advance). Everything in it is kept exactly as it was in Lenin's time. The furnishings are very modest. In the room in which Lenin lived there is a small desk with a simple desk-set and school pen. It was here that Lenin, already gravely ill, wrote his last articles and letters, which were his political testament to the Communist Party and Soviet people. On the second floor of this building is a hall where sessions of the USSR Council of Ministers are now held. The armchair once used by Lenin stands near the chairman's seat. It has been preserved as a sacred

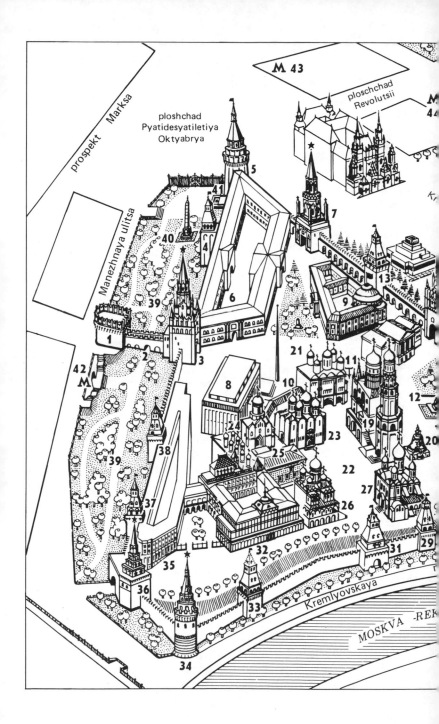

Ploshchad

4

15

17

16

18

28

zhnaya

THE KREMLIN

1. *Kutafya (Overdressed Woman) Tower. Entrance to the Kremlin*
2. *Troitsky (Trinity) Bridge*
3. *Troitskaya (Trinity) Tower*
4. *Srednyaya Arsenalnaya (Middle Arsenal) Tower*
5. *Uglovaya Arsenalnaya (Corner Arsenal) Tower*
6. *Arsenal*
7. *Nikolskaya (St. Nicholas) Tower*
8. *Kremlin Palace of Congresses*
9. *USSR Council of Ministers*
10. *Cathedral of the Twelve Apostles and the Patriarch's Palace (Museum of the 17th-Century Life and Applied Art)*
11. *Tsar Cannon*
12. *Statue of Lenin*
13. *Senatskaya (Senate) Tower*
14. *Spasskaya (Saviour) Tower*
15. *Tsarskaya (Tsar's) Tower*
16. *Konstantino-Yeleninskaya (St. Constantine and St. Helen) Tower*
17. *Nabatnaya (Alarm-Bell) Tower*
18. *Moskvoretskaya (the Moskva River), or Beklemishevskaya Tower*
19. *Ivan the Great Bell-Tower*
20. *Tsar Bell*
21. *Ivanovskaya (Ivan's) Square*
22. *Sobornaya (Cathedral) Square*
23. *Uspensky (Dormition) Cathedral*
24. *Church of the Deposition of the Robe*
25. Granovitaya palata *(Faceted Hall)*
26. *Blagoveshchensky (Annunciation) Cathedral*
27. *Arkhangelsky (Archangel Michael) Cathedral*
28. *Petrovskaya (St. Peter) Tower*
29. *Pervaya bezimyannaya (First Nameless) Tower*
30. *Vtoraya bezimyannaya (Second Nameless) Tower*
31. *Tainitskaya (Secret) Tower*
32. *Grand Kremlin Palace*
33. *Blagoveshchenskaya (Annunciation) Tower*
34. *Vodovzvodnaya (Water-drawing) Tower*
35. Oruzheinaya palata *(Armoury Chamber)*
36. *Borovitskaya (Pinewood) Tower*
37. *Oruzheinaya (Armoury) Tower*
38. *Komendantskaya (Commandant's) Tower*
39. *Aleksandrovsky (Alexander) Gardens*
40. *Monument to Great Revolutionaries and Thinkers*
41. *Tomb of the Unknown Soldier*
42. *Biblioteka imeni Lenina and Borovitskaya Metro stations*
43. *Prospekt Marksa Metro Station*
44. *Ploshchad Revolyutsii Metro Station*

Kremlin Palace of Congresses

relic, for Lenin presided over the meetings of the first Soviet Government in this hall from 1918 through 1922.

The building of the Senate was erected in 1776–87 to the design of the architect Matvei Kazakov in the Russian Classical style. The eastern façade of the building faces Red Square, and the Soviet Flag fluttering above its dome is plainly visible from there.

We proceed past 15 tall flagstaffs bearing Flags of the Union Republics and approach the small five-domed **Cathedral of the Twelve Apostles** and the **Patriarch's Palace** built in 1653–56 by the Russian architects Antip Konstantinov, David Okhlebinin, and Averki Makeyev. The former Patriarch's

Palace consists of a number of halls and rooms, with passages and stairways built inside the walls. Many of these structures preserved their original appearance to our day. Much restoration and conservation work has been carried out on them in recent years. The Patriarch's Palace and the Cathedral of the Twelve Apostles now house a **Museum of 17th-Century Life and Applied Art**, with over 700 works of art including copper, tin, and silver articles, fabrics and jewelry. There is also an interesting display of rare manuscripts and printed books, among them a collection of moral tales entitled *Spiritual Medicine* illustrated with 335 magnificent miniatures drawn in pen and water colors. Also on exhibit is *Bukvar* (a primer) hand-written in 1693. Two of the halls represent the interior of a 17th-century house.

The **Krestovaya** (Cross) **Chamber** in the Patriarch's Palace, with a stone vault unsupported by pillars, is of impressive dimensions (its area is 280 square meters). Built in 1653–55, it is the main hall of the Palace. The stove for preparing chrism, with its silver cauldrons and carved ornamental canopy, has been carefully preserved. In the Cathedral of the Twelve Apostles there is a display case with curious exhibits, among them a coffer for large wine bottles made in the shape of an evangelistary, on which the central figure of the image is not Christ but Bacchus, the god of wine and revelry. The gigantic coffer contains 28 compartments for wine bottles, and others for tobacco and pipes. Next to it is a limewood wine ladle that can hold 100 liters. These objects belonged to "The Highest and Most Jolly and Drunken Council", a society founded by Peter the Great in 1691, to poke fun at the everyday rites, rituals and customs of the past, and mainly at the religious prejudices that were impeding the implementation of his progressive reforms.

From the Cathedral of the Twelve Apostles we can see the **Tsar Cannon**, a remarkable example of 16th-century foundry work. The Tsar Cannon was cast in bronze by the Russian master craftsman Andrei Chokhov in 1586, and is 5.34 meters long, with a calibre of 890 mm and a weight of 40 tons. Experts believe it was made for stone case-shot, but this cannon was never fired. The iron cannon balls beside it, cast in the 19th century, are purely decorative.

The compositional center of the Kremlin ensemble is one of the most remarkable structures of 16th-century Russian architecture—**Ivan the Great Bell-Tower**, a three-tier white pillar consisting of elongated, octagonal sections, one on top of the other, each progressively smaller in diameter than the one below. The bells, the work of Russian masters of the 16th-19th centuries, hang in the arched bays of each section. All are richly ornamented and each one bears an inscription giving its history (the date when it was cast, its weight, and the name of the founder). The Bell-Tower has a gilded dome on a circular drum bearing an inscription in old Slavonic noting that it was completed in 1600 during the reign of Boris Godunov.

Work on the campanile, however, actually began about a century earlier. Its foundations were laid in 1508 by the Italian architect Bon Friazine (Marco Bono) on the site of an old (14th century) campanile with a church. Then in 1532-43 a four-storey *Zvonnitsa* (Belfry) was added by architect Petrok Maly, in the central embrasure of which hangs the huge Uspensky (Dormition) Bell weighing some 64 tons. About a half century later, during the reign of Boris Godunov, more tiers were added to the campanile and it was crowned with a gilded dome. In bygone days the campanile served as a church, a belfry, and the main watch-tower of the Kremlin, providing a good view of the city and its environs for a radius of up to 30 kilometers. The campanile is 81 meters high, and for many years was the tallest structure in Moscow.

Many pillar-like churches were built in old Russia on the model of Ivan the Great, which were meant to symbolize the might of the centralized Russian state. At present the Bell-Tower houses the **Exhibition Hall of the Moscow Kremlin Treasures**.

On a stone pedestal at the foot of the Bell-Tower stands the **Tsar Bell**—the largest bell in the world, which weighs 200 tons, is 6.14 meters high and 6.6 meters in diameter. Next to it is a fragment weighing 11.5 tons, that split off during a fire in 1737.

It is interesting to note that the bell was cast of brass together with 72 kilograms of gold and approximately 525 kilograms of silver—it is this combination of precious metals with the brass that imparts a special purity to its sound. The Tsar Bell is a unique example of Russian foundry work. The surface of the Bell is decorated with a delicate ornamental design and the depictions of Tsar Alexei and Tsarina Anna as well as five icons, done in relief, and two inscriptions describing the history of its casting. It was cast in 1733-35 by Ivan Motorin and his son Mikhail, and lay in its casting pit for over a hundred years. It was raised only in 1836, and placed where it now stands.

After seeing the Tsar Bell, we shall proceed to the **Tainitsky Garden** directly opposite. With its bright flowers and shady alleys, it is always a pleasant spot to relax. It was named after Tainitskaya (Secret) Tower. There was a storehouse or cache *(tainik)* here for use in sieges, hence the name of the tower. A **statue of Lenin** stands here (1967, sculptor Veniamin Pinchuk, architect Sergei Speransky).

In the Kremlin on May 1, 1920 Lenin worked side by side with the Kremlin military cadets during an all-Russia voluntary working Saturday *(subbotnik)*. Together with the others he carried rubble, logs and

planks—remnants of the barricades erected in the Kremlin during the October 1917 fighting. When persuaded by the others not to tire himself out, Lenin would answer: "I'm also a resident of the Kremlin, and this is something that concerns me too."

From this side of the garden by the statue of Lenin there is a good view of the Spasskaya Tower. Inside the Kremlin in front of the Spasskaya Tower is a three-storey building of austere Classical design. A white colonnade along its entire façade and four groups of paired columns over its entrance impart an air of splendor and majesty to its appearance. On the pediment there is a relief-work of the State Emblem of the USSR, and the Soviet Flag flutters above the building. This is the **Presidium of the Supreme Soviet of the USSR**—the highest body of state authority in the country. Here sep-

Tsar Cannon

Ivan the Great Bell-Tower

arate sessions of the two Chambers of the Supreme Soviet and of the Council of Elders are held (the joint sessions of both chambers are held in the Grand Kremlin Palace), and here, too, is the study of the Chairman of the Presidium of the Supreme Soviet of the USSR. The building was erected in 1934 to the design of architect Ivan Rerberg on the site of the old Chudov (Wonder) and Voskresensky (Resurrection) monasteries.

Just to the right of the Spasskaya Tower is the shortest of all the Kremlin towers with the impressive name of **Tsar's Tower.** This stone, tent-roofed tower was erected in 1680. The white-stone emboss- ments, a gilt weather vane, and pinnacles at the corners make it look like something out of an old Russian fairy-tale. Further to the right is another tower, called the

Nabatnaya (Alarm-Bell) **Tower.** It stands on a slope of the Kremlin Hill directly opposite Vasily the Blessed Cathedral. Named after the alarm-bell that once hung on it, it has quite an interesting history. In 1771 during a major popular upris- ing, this alarm-bell was rung to as- semble all the rebels in the Krem- lin. After the uprising was sup- pressed, the bell's tongue was removed as "punishment", and it hung "tongueless" in the tower for more than 30 years. In 1821 the bell was included into the Armoury Chamber collection. If you visit the Armoury Chamber, make sure to take note of it. It weighs more than two tons, and was cast in 1714 by Ivan Motorin, the same remarkable founder who crafted the Tsar Bell.

Further to the right and closer to the Moskva River is the **Moskvo- retskaya,** or **Beklemishevskaya Tower**, a tall, round structure 46.2 meters high, built in 1487 by

Tsar Bell

the Italian architect Marco Ruffo. This tower took the first onslaught of the Tatar hordes advancing on the Kremlin. In the 17th century it was topped with a four-storey super-structure that softened its grim appearance and gave it elegance and stateliness.

From the Kremlin Hill one also has a good view of the *Rossiya* Hotel (to the right of Vasily the Blessed Cathedral) and the tall, 173-meter-high apartment house on Kotelnicheskaya Embankment, built in 1949-52.

The part of the **Kremlin wall** extending along the Moskva River Embankment is also clearly visible from here. The walls and their 20 towers served as a strong defence line. The walls are 5 to 19 meters high and 3.5 to 6.5 meters thick and are surmounted with 1,045 *V*-shaped merlons varying in height between 2 and 2.5 meters. When the Kremlin was besieged by enemy troops, its defenders would block the openings in the merlons with wooden shields and fire at the enemy through narrow loopholes that have been preserved to this day. In the old days the walls had a protective wooden roof that sheltered the defenders in bad weather. This roof burned down in the 18th century and was never replaced.

Let us take one more look at Ivan the Great Bell-Tower. It unites all the Kremlin cathedrals into a majestic architectural ensemble, which faces *Sobornaya ploshchad* (Cathedral Square), the oldest square in Moscow. Its foundations were laid out in the early 14th century and it has been the main square of the Kremlin ever since. There the ceremonial processions were held when the tsars were invested and emperors crowned, and foreign ambassadors were received.

On the northern side of Cathedral Square stands the five-domed **Cathedral of the Dormition** *(Uspensky sobor)*, built in 1475-79 by Russian master builders under the supervision of Aristotele Fioravante, a native of Bologna invited to work in Moscow by the Grand Prince Ivan III. Fioravante carefully studied the finest examples of Russian church architecture, visiting Vladimir, Pskov, and Novgorod, and modelled his Cathedral of the Dormition on that in Vladimir (12th century)—one of the most majestic structures of old Russia. The walls of the cathedral in the Kremlin are of white stone, but the vaultings and drums are of brick. The painted portals are framed with decoratively finished white stone. The architectural proportions of the cathedral are perfect—38 meters high, 24 meters wide, and 35.5 meters long. The interior is a spacious, lofty, bright hall supported by round pillars.

In 1514 the whole interior of the cathedral—walls, vaults, and columns—was painted by Russian artists. The murals have been renovated many times since then. At the end of the 1970s Soviet experts undertook major restoration work in the cathedral, bringing to light and restoring the old, original murals and restituting the original architectural and decorative details of its interior. Fifteenth-century frescoes of exceptional artistic and historic value were uncovered at this time, and the 15th-century sanctuary partition and icons of the central and wall iconostases were cleared of later painted layers. Restoration work in the Cathedral of the Dormition is still going on. The cathedral's icons (most 14th–17th century) are outstanding examples of the creativity of Russian painters. Among the oldest of these is the 12th-century icon *St. George* and the icon *The Trinity* painted in the first half of the 14th century. The icon *Our Lady of Vladimir*, an example of 11th-century Byzantine painting, was the oldest work preserved in the cathedral; it is now on display in the Tretyakov Gallery.

The cathedral contains many fine examples of early Russian applied art. Among them is the southern door covered in copper sheets on which there are twenty scenes on biblical themes. Near this entrance stands the throne of Ivan the Terrible, the first Russian tsar, a unique monument to the craftsmanship of Russian wood carvers. It dates from 1551. A shrine of bronze openwork contains the remains of the Patriarch Hermogen, tortured to death by the Polish invaders in 1612, and later canonized (Patriarch Hermogen called on the people to rise up against the Polish invaders). The

Statue of Lenin in the Kremlin

shrine was skilfully cast in 1627 by Dmitry Sverchkov.

Daylight penetrates the cathedral through narrow windows arranged in two tiers. Twelve 17th-century chandeliers of gilded bronze (the central one, of the 19th century, of silver and bronze) provide additional illumination. When Napoleon occupied the Kremlin in 1812, he turned the cathedral into a stable. The French soldiers ransacked it and stole around 300 kilograms of gold and over five tons of silver. It is interesting that the silver used for the central chandelier was recaptured the same year from Napoleon's retreating troops.

Over the centuries the Cathedral of the Dormition was the main temple of old Russia. Its architectural forms and rich interior reflected the might and grandeur of the centralized Russian state. It was the place where tsars were invested and emperors crowned (the first Russian emperor was Peter I). In it, too, important state decrees were proclaimed and solemn ceremonies held. It was the burial place of the Moscow metropolitans and patriarchs.

To the left of the Cathedral of the Dormition stands the small, single-domed **Church of the Deposition of the Robe** (Rizopolozheniya), whose proportions lend it an exceptionally graceful appearance. Built by craftsmen from Pskov in 1484-86, it was the private chapel of the patriarchs and metropolitans. The iconostasis, the icons of which were painted by a group of artists under the supervision of Nazari Istomin (1627), is of great artistic value.

In the heart of the courtyard, by the Church of the Deposition of the Robe is the **Tsarina's Golden Chamber**, the reception hall of the 16th-century tsarinas, and the **Chapels of the Teremnoi Palace**, which we will discuss in more detail a bit later on. The chapels of the Teremnoi Palace were joined under one roof in 1681–82 and crowned with eleven gilded cupolas.

Another fine example of Russian architecture, the **Faceted Hall** *(Granovitaya palata)*, overlooks Cathedral Square facing Ivan the Great Bell-Tower.

The museums of the Moscow Kremlin are open from 10 a.m. to 6 p.m. daily, excluding Thursdays.

The **Faceted Hall** is one of the oldest civil edifices in Moscow. It was built in 1487-91 by Russian masons working under the Italian architects Marco Ruffo and Pietro Antonio Solari. As its name implies, its façade is finished in faceted white stone. The interior consists of a single spacious chamber (on the first floor) with vaults supported by a central pillar. The hall is 9 meters high and has an area of 495 square meters. In the second half of the 16th century its walls and vaults had beautiful frescoes on ecclesiastical and biblical themes. The present painting, done in replica of the old compositions, was executed in 1881 by icon-painters from the village of Palekh.

Throughout its history the Faceted Hall has been used for official ceremonies. In the 15th and 16th centuries foreign ambassadors were received in the hall. Here in 1653 the *Zemsky sobor* (the *Zemstvo* Assembly—the highest class-representative council in Russia from the mid-16th through late 17th centuries) adopted the historical decision on the reunification of the Ukraine with Russia. In May 1883 the premier performance of Tchaikovsky's cantata *Moskva* for solo, choir and orchestra took place in the Faceted Hall. Today state meetings and conferences and government receptions are held here.

On the same side of Cathedral Square, but closer to the river, stands another remarkable 15th-century edifice, the **Cathedral of the Annunciation** *(Blagoveshchensky sobor)*, with nine golden domes. It was built in 1484-89 by master builders from Pskov. After a fire in 1547 it was restored in two years' time during the reign of Ivan the Terrible. At that time a porch was added (on the southeastern side), known as the Groznensky (Ivan the Terrible's) Porch. The awesome tsar must have climbed the steps of this porch many times, for the cathedral was the private chapel of the Russian princes and tsars.

The magnificent frescoes of the Cathedral of the Annunciation were first executed in 1508. The walls, pylons and vaults were painted by the son of the famous 15th-century painter, Dionysius—Theodosus and his "brethren". The frescoes were redone many times over the centuries and covered with oil painting. For a long time it was thought that the old frescoes had been irretrievably lost, but in 1947 Soviet restorers brought them to light. The cathedral's frescoes mainly depict themes from the Apocalypse. The gilded, carved white-stone portals, brought from Rostov Veliky in the 16th century, enhance the decoration interior of the cathedral. The copper doors of the northern and western portals are engraved in gold. The iconostasis, which was taken from the 14th-century Church of the Annunciation which originally stood on this site, is of exceptional artistic and historical value. It is known that the paintings of the old cathedral were done in 1405 by the outstanding artists Andrei Rublev, Theophanes the Greek, and Prokhor of Gorodets. A portion of the icons in the Cathedral are assumed to have been executed by these same masters in the 14th and 15th centuries. On the pilasters of the cloisters of the Groznensky Porch are the portraits of Moscow princes, and philosophers of ancient Greece and Rome, including Aristotele, Plato, Homer, Virgil, and Plutarch.

Another Kremlin church, the **Archangel Michael Cathedral** *(Arkhangelsky sobor)*, faces the Cathedral of the Annunciation. Five cupolas (the central cupola is gilded and the side ones covered with silvery white iron sheets) crown this well-proportioned white-stone edifice. This cathedral combines the early Russian architectural style with that of the Italian Renaissance. Outwardly it is reminiscent of a Venetian palazzo. It was built in 1505-08 under the direction of the Italian architect Alevisio Nuovi. The walls were painted with frescoes shortly afterwards, but in 1652 they were removed together with the plaster. The present murals date from 1652-66. They were painted by Russian masters and depict scenes of Russian life at the time, vividly portraying the struggle of the Russian people for national independence. The battle scenes are painted with great skill. The more than sixty stylized portraits of Russian princes buried at

Uspensky (Dormition) Cathedral

the cathedral are of especial interest.

A gilt iconostasis, 10 meters high, separates the central part of the cathedral from the altar. It contains wonderful 15th-17th-century icons by Russian masters. The icon *Archangel Michael*, attributed to Andrei Rublev (15th century), is of outstanding beauty and perfection.

The Archangel Michael Cathedral was the burial place of the

Domes of the chapels of the Teremnoi Palace

Moscow princes and tsars. In it are 46 tombs with white tombstones bearing inscriptions in old Slavonic; they record, in particular, that Ivan the Terrible and his sons are buried in the cathedral. The oldest tomb is that of Prince Ivan Kalita, who died in 1340. Also here is the tomb of the Grand Prince of Moscow and Vladimir, Dmitry Donskoi, who led the armed struggle of the Russian people against the Mongol-Tatar invaders. During restoration work in the cathedral in 1964, it became necessary to open up several tombs. From the remains of the skeleton and skull, the Soviet anthropologist and sculptor Mikhail Gerasimov was able to make the first documentary portrait of Ivan the Terrible: the Russian tsar was portrayed as being tall and stout, with his lips compressed in disgust—very different from the way he had been portrayed by artists and sculptors earlier.

After seeing Cathedral Square, we leave it with the Cathedral of the Annunciation on our right. Immediately behind it stretches the **Grand Kremlin Palace** (1839-49; architect Konstantin Thon and others), 125 meters long. The Palace's main façade faces the Moskva River. The best view of it is obtained from the Maurice Thorez Embankment. The palace seems to have three storeys, for three rows of windows in fact decorate the façade; but it actually has only two storeys. The arched windows on the ground floor are sepa-

Blagoveshchensky (Annunciation) Cathedral

as the residence of the imperial family when in Moscow.

There are several big halls in the palace, but the **St. George Hall** deserves special mention. It is 61 meters long, 20.5 meters wide, and 17.5 meters high, and richly ornamented with stucco mouldings and 18 convoluted columns, each supporting a statue of Victory crowned with a laurel wreath. The whole decorative scheme of the hall is dedicated to the victories of Russian arms in the 15th–18th centuries. In tall niches along the walls are marble slabs engraved in gold with the names of units that distinguished themselves in battle, and of officers and men awarded the Order of St. George (awarded for outstanding military valor, this order was

rated by narrow piers. The two rows of windows on the first floor are divided by pilasters and are decorated with white-stone surrounds as was customary in 17th-century Russian architecture. The higher, central part of the building is crowned by a gilt balustrade and a flagstaff. Sessions of the Supreme Soviets of the USSR and RSFSR are held in the Grand Kremlin Palace and when they are in session the State flags of the USSR and RSFSR respectively are flown.

The Grand Kremlin Palace was erected on the site of an old ducal palace, the halls of which were incorporated into the huge rectangle of the new palace, which was built

Arkhangelsky (Archangel Michael) Cathedral

instituted in Russia in 1769). The hall is illuminated by six bronze gilt chandeliers in which burn 3,000 electric bulbs. The parquet is made of different colored woods of 20 valuable varieties. The St. George Hall is used for state receptions and official ceremonies, and it is here that the state awards are presented.

Next to the St. George Hall is the round St. Vladimir Hall, named after the Order of St. Vladimir instituted in 1782. It leads to the Teremnoi Palace, the Tsarina's Golden Chamber, and the Faceted Hall.

The Teremnoi Palace *(Teremnoi dvorets)* was built in 1635-36 by Bazhen Ogurtsov, Antip Konstantinov, and Larion Ushakov, and is a most interesting example of 17th-century Russian architecture and life. The rooms of the Teremnoi Palace have low, vaulted ceilings. Walls and ceilings are covered with colorful painting dating from 1837, and the windows are glazed with stained glass. There are tiled stoves in the corners. These royal chambers evoke pictures of a dim and distant fairyland past. The Throne Room was the tsar's cabinet in the 17th century. Its middle window was called the "petition window". A box used to be lowered from it into which anyone could put a written petition to the tsar—a *chelobitnaya gramota* or a letter of supplication or grievance, as it was called in the 15th-18th centuries, addressed to a supreme authority. Among the common people this

box was known as the "long box", since the petitions would lie in it for a long time, unread by anyone (which gave rise to a saying: "Never trust your business to the long box"; meaning, "Don't put things off").

The white-stone **Church of the Resurrection of Lazarus** is part of the architectural complex of the Grand Kremlin Palace. Dating back to 1393, it is the oldest building in Moscow and the sole architectural monument of the 14th century still surviving in the capital.

The largest hall in the Grand Palace is the Conference Hall of the Supreme Soviet of the USSR with a seating capacity of 3,000. It is adjacent to the St. George Hall. Its two tiers of windows overlook the Moskva River. A statue of Lenin by Sergei Merkurov (1881-1952) stands in a niche on the platform behind the seats of the presidium. This hall, grand and majestic, yet strikingly simple, was created in 1934 from two of the halls in the 19th-century edifice. On the ground floor of the palace, to the left of the main entrance, are a suite of rooms, the Personal Chambers that used to be the emperor's private apartments. All the rooms—the dining-room, drawing-room, empress's and emperor's studies, bedroom, and reception room—are sumptuously decorated with marble, stucco moulding, and murals, and furnished with statues, porcelain, and finely incrusted gilt furniture. The furnishings of these

Ivan the Great Bell-Tower

Arkhangelsky (Archangel Michael) Cathedral

Domes of the chapels of the Teremnoi Palace

Spasskaya (Saviour) Tower

Cathedral of Vasily the Blessed (Cathedral of the Intercession)

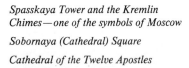

*Spasskaya Tower and the Kremlin
Chimes — one of the symbols of Moscow*

Sobornaya (Cathedral) Square

Cathedral of the Twelve Apostles

Treasures of the Oruzheinaya (Armoury) Chamber

Treasures of the Oruzheinaya (Armoury) Chamber

rooms have been preserved as monuments of the art of anonymous 19th-century Russian craftsmen.

Next to the Grand Palace is the building of the *Oruzheinaya Palata* (Armoury Chamber), which was built in 1851 by Konstantin Thon. The Armoury itself, however, was founded in the 16th century. It then consisted of workshops where armour and weapons were made and stored. Later, military trophies and royal regalia were stored there. In 1720, by decree of Peter the Great, it has been the repository of a permanent collection of weapons, silver, and precious utensils. Since 1813 the Armoury Chamber has been a public museum. On display here are unique specimens of Russian and foreign applied art, ambassadors' gifts, collections of arms and accoutrements (13th to 18th centuries), one of the world's largest and finest collections of fabrics and clothing of the 14th to 19th centuries, and some very fine articles by goldsmiths of the 12th to 19th centuries.

Among the royal regalia are the "*Shapka* of Monomach", a goldfiligree headdress adorned with precious stones and a sable trim, with which all the Russian tsars up to Peter the Great were crowned; the throne of Ivan the Terrible; the diamond-studded crowns (1682) of the brother tsars, Ivan and Pyotr; the first Russian imperial crown of Catherine I (the spouse of Peter I, who ruled after his death), made of gild silver; the wedding dress of Catherine II adorned with exquisite silver embroidery; and many other precious historical items. The museum also has a display of unique *objets d'art* in gold, silver, precious stones, ivory, and porcelain, and fabrics embroidered with pearls and adorned with precious stones. One can admire a 14th-century Byzantine sakkos, see robes made of Italian samite (type of gold brocade) of which the secret of making has long been lost, and take delight in an article sewn with 150,508 pearls. Incidentally, the average life of a pearl is considered to be 300 years, yet in the Armoury Chamber collection there is a piece of embroidery with pearls dating back almost 600 years! There is also a very big collection of ceremonial carriages, each one of which is a work of art.

There are special show-cases of ambassadors' gifts from Turkey, Austria, Poland, Denmark, Holland, Sweden, England, and other countries. The most interesting is the collection of gifts presented by Swedish ambassadors, which includes some 200 valuable items, in particular the rich gifts from Charles XII—rare work by Stockholm craftsmen, brought to Russia in 1699. The Armoury Chamber also contains the world's finest collection of old English silver, made by 16th-17th-century London silversmiths and presented for the most part by English ambassadors to the Russian tsars.

The Armoury Chamber collection is a treasury of world importance. Of the 50,000 items, approximately 4,000 are displayed at one time in the Armoury Chamber. Each exhibit is a monument of the history of Russia and the Moscow Kremlin and reflects the highest artistic achievement of the epoch to which it belongs.

Housed in two halls of the Armoury Chamber ground floor is the **USSR Diamond Fund**—a collection of precious stones and jewelry of great historical, artistic and material value. This collection was begun in the early 18th century and originally belonged to the Russian crown. Until 1914 it was kept at the Winter Palace in St. Petersburg. The collection exhibit has been open for public viewing since 1967 **(tours by advance arrangement only, through Intourist).** Among the unique precious, and in fact, priceless stones, we should mention the Orlov Diamond (189.62 carats) of the Indian rose cut with 180 facets, and the Shah Diamond (88.7 carats). Also on display are the world's largest sapphire (258.8 carats), and the Big Triangle—a gold nugget weighing 36 kilograms. Some newly found gold nuggets have recently been included in the Diamond Fund. One of them (32.7 carats) was mined from one of the deposits in Siberia, and was named "Samantha Smith" after the 11-year-old American schoolgirl who came to the Soviet Union in 1983 as a young ambassador of peace and friendship between the children of the USA and the USSR. In 1985 Samantha Smith tragically perished in an air catastrophe. For the Soviet people her name remains a symbol of the highest aspirations of mankind—peace on the Earth.

As you leave the Kremlin you will see two more towers crowned with ruby-red stars. The one on the left, by the river, is the **Vodovzvodnaya** (Water-drawing) **Tower.** It was built in 1488, but was torn down in 1805 after falling into disrepair, and built anew. After being wrecked by French troops in 1812 it was restored in 1819 to the design of architect Osip Bovet. Together with its star it is nearly 62 meters high.

Next to it is the **Borovitskaya Tower** made for vehicle passage. It takes its name from the Russian word *bor* meaning pine forest. It was erected in 1490 by Pietro Antonio Solari, and has a stepped, pyramidal form. Three graduated tetrahedrons are crowned by a tall stone tent-shaped structure.

Approximately 200 meters to the right of the **Borovitskiye Gates** is the Borovitskaya and Biblioteka imeni Lenina Metro stations with which you are already familiar. You can reach them through the Aleksandrovsky Gardens. Lev Tolstoy, the great Russian novelist, was extremely fond of the Kremlin from his childhood and used to enjoy walking here in the Aleksandrovsky Gardens along the Kremlin wall. In a school essay he once wrote: "...What a magnificent sight the Kremlin is! The dawn of Russia's liberation arose over these walls ..."

ALONG GORKY STREET

Ulitsa Gorkogo (Gorky Street) is one of Moscow's busiest thorough-fares, and leads to the Kremlin. We suggest you start this walk from either of the two entrances to the **Belorusskaya Metro Station**. If you do not go into too many shops, or get side-tracked, this walk should take about an hour and a half.

Before 1932 this street was called Tverskaya (Tver Street). From the 14th century it led from Moscow to the old Russian town of Tver (now called Kalinin), and when St. Petersburg was established, it led on to that city. For several hundred years it has been the most important thoroughfare and busiest shopping street, but before the Revolution it was not very attractive, although there were aristocratic estates upon it, as well as crowded shops and houses with furnished apartments to let. The street's appearance was greatly altered after its radical reconstruction, begun in 1937. Dozens of the old houses were demolished, while those of value were moved bodily back in the areas adjoining. The street itself was widened from 16-18 meters to 50-60 meters.

From the Metro you can see the building of the **Byelorussian Railway Station** (Belorussky vokzal), with its cupolas, towers, and intricately decorated façade. Trains arrive at this station from Berlin and Warsaw, with international through coaches from Prague, Kar-lovy Vary, Paris, Vienna, London, Oslo, Stockholm, Bern, Hamburg, and Copenhagen. The station itself is over a hundred years old, and has remained basically the same since its rebuilding at the beginning of the century (in 1909 it was rebuilt in the Classical style, with an emphasis on the sumptuous decorative elements of the Empire style). In recent years the station has undergone radical reconstruction. Is has been expanded, a basement floor added, and in 1976 a new annex was added.

This square has witnessed many warm and ceremonial public welcomes, but the one most memorable and cherished by Muscovites was the welcoming home in the spring of 1945 of the first soldiers returning from the front. Behind them was the war, and the day of June 24, 1941, when from the Byelorussian Railway Station Muscovites saw off the first soldiers departing for the front. Then, for the first time the song "Sacred War" rang out over the square, performed by the renowned Soviet Army Song and Dance Ensemble. That day the ensemble repeated its performance five times. The whole country took up this song; it was broadcast daily on the radio, and sung by soldiers as they marched towards the frontlines.

In the center of the *Byelorussian Railway Station Square*, in a small garden, is a **statue of Maxim Gorky** (1868-1936). The statue, which stands 5 meters tall, was designed by the outstanding Soviet sculptor Ivan Shadr and executed by Vera Mukhina, Nina Zelenskaya, and Zinaida Ivanova in 1951. From here to the right from Byelorussian Station runs Gorky Street. To the left begins *Leningradsky prospekt* (Leningrad Avenue), one of the most handsome avenues in Moscow, due, in part, to its broad green alleys. Before the Revolution this was a suburban region filled with unbecoming wooden houses, garden plots, and wasteland.

Before we start our walk down Gorky Street, let's briefly describe the main places of interest along *Leningrad Avenue*, since you may see them if you enter or leave the city via *Sheremetyevo* Airport, travel to Leningrad by car (696 kilometers), or make an out-of-town excursion to Arkhangelskoye. The flow of traffic is incessant over the entire 100 meter width of this transport artery.

On the right-hand side, over the Byelorussian Station viaduct, is the 2nd Moscow Watch Factory, which exports to over 60 countries. Two streets (blocks) further along is the *Sovetskaya* Hotel, in whose concert hall the *Romen* **Gipsy Theater** holds its productions. Located on both sides of the avenue are a number of major sports facilities. Running on the left, deep into the block, is an avenue which leads to the **Moscow Hippodrome.** A bit further along, still on the left-hand side, is the **Young Pioneers Stadium,** with a cycle track and an in-

door track. On the right-hand side, about a kilometer beyond the *Sovetskaya* Hotel, set in Petrovsky Park, is the **Dynamo Stadium,** with a sports arena, swimming pool, training grounds, and many other sports facilities.

Almost immediately beyond the stadium is the graceful and picturesque **Petrovsky dvorets** (Peter's Palace), built of red brick and lavishly decorated with carved white stone. It was built in 1776–96 by the renowned architect Matvei Kazakov, one of the founders of the Classic style in Russian architecture. Peter's Palace was the place where the tsars and their families rested before travelling on to Moscow from St. Petersburg. In 1812 Napoleon spent some time here following his flight from the Moscow Kremlin. This prompted Pushkin to call Peter's Palace "a witness to fallen glory". Presently the Palace is one of the buildings of the Zhukovsky Air Force Engineering Academy, where many Soviet cosmonauts have studied. **Two monuments** flank the entrance, one a bust of Nikolai Zhukovsky, the "father of Russian aviation", by Georgy Neroda, and the other of Konstantin Tsiolkovsky, the founder of the theory of astronautics, by Sergei Merkurov. On the opposite side of the avenue is the **Moscow Air Terminal,** flanked by two identical twelve-storey buildings, one of which houses the *Aeroflot* **Hotel.** A little further along the same side is the **sports complex of the Cen-**

tral **Army Sports Club**, one of the most popular sports clubs in the country. On the right side of the avenue in the garden near the **Aeroport Metro Station** is a **statue of Ernst Thälmann** (1886-1944), an activist of the German and the international Communist movement. Thälmann visited Moscow many times, and met with Lenin and addressed the workers of the city. Muscovites elected him an Honored Deputy to the Moscow Soviet of Workers' Deputies, and in 1924-33 he was a deputy to the Reichstag from the Communist Party of Germany. In 1944 Thälmann died at the hands of Hitlerites in the Buchenwald concentration camp. A 4.5-meter-high figure of the revolutionary fighter rises from a pedestal of red granite flagstone. The monument was unveiled in 1986, on the centennial anniversary of Thälmann's birth. The monument was executed by sculptors Vladimir and Valentin Artamonov and architect Veniamin Nesterov. Leningrad Avenue ends beyond the **Sokol Metro Station** (entrance pavilions on both sides of the avenue), at the glass and concrete, 100-meter-high building of the Hydroproject Institute. From here Leningrad Avenue forks into *Volokolamsk Highway* and *Leningrad Highway.* Proceeding further along Leningrad Highway (Leningradskoye shosse), you will come to the **Northern River Station**, located on the left side of the highway amidst a big park on the bank of the Khimki Reservoir. The station buildings and piers were built in 1937 to the design of architect Alexei Rukhlyadev. Dozens of tourist excursion and cruise ships depart from the Northern River Station's moorages. It's interesting to note that the star on the spire of the station building is one of the first Kremlin stars, and until 1937 crowned the Kremlin Spasskaya Tower. The *Volga* **Restaurant** is situated on the first floor of the station. On the opposite side of the highway is *Druzhba* (Friendship) **Park**, which was laid out by the young people taking part in the 6th World Youth Festival in 1957.

With every passing year the park has come to increasingly resemble a park of sculptural arts. In 1976 the sculptural composition "Bread and Fertility" by the Soviet sculptress Vera Mukhina (1889-1953) was installed here. Later the same year the erection of the **Monument of Peace and Friendship**—a gift to the city of Moscow from the residents of Budapest—was completed. This monument is a replica of the sculptural composition which stands in the Park of Soviet-Hungarian Friendship in Budapest in commemoration of the 30th anniversary of the Soviet Army's liberation of Hungary from fascist German troops on April 4, 1945. A stele almost 10 meters high with sculptural figures of two women in the center holding a banner of friendship symbolize Hungary and the USSR. The monument was executed by Hungarian sculptor Barna Búza and Hungarian archi-

Belorussky (Byelorussian) Railway Station

Peter the Great's Palace

tect István Zilahi. Still another example of friendly cultural ties between capital cities, this time between Moscow and Madrid, is the **statue of Cervantes** unveiled in 1980, and is a replica of the monument by the Spanish sculptor Antonio Sola, which was erected in Madrid back in the last century. As a reciprocal gesture, Moscow presented to Madrid a monument to Alexander Pushkin sculpted by Oleg Komov. It was installed in Madrid's Fuente del Berro Park that same year. On June 5, 1986, in one of the alleys of the Park of Friendship, a young birch sapling was planted as the **Tree of Peace**, symbolizing the aspirations of people to live in friendship and harmony. This was Moscow's response to the appeal of the leaders of the UN program on environmental conservation to plant a Tree of Peace in each country of the world in honor of World Day of Environmental Protection. On that day the Soviet Government issued a statement which said, in particular, the following: "Let the saplings strike sturdy roots everywhere, and grow into adult trees whose foliage will never be scorched by the flames of a nuclear holocaust. Let them become witnesses to our world entering the 21st century without nuclear weapons." You can explore the Park of Friendship on your way to the *Sheremetyevo* Airport, providing you check out of your hotel at least a half hour earlier.

And now let us begin our stroll down Gorky Street. There are branchy linden trees lining it on both sides, and there are scores of shops well worth visiting filled with goods to sell and crowds of buyers. At No. 46 is an antique shop with a large assortment of chrystal and porcelain ware. From the first intersection to the left runs *pereulok Aleksandra Nevskogo* (Alexander Nevsky Lane). A leisurely 10 minutes' walk along it will bring you to the original **statue of Alexander Fadeyev** (1901-56), the Soviet writer and author of works beloved by several generations, such as *The Rout* and *The Young Guard*. These novels have been translated into many languages of the world. The monument was unveiled in 1973 and was sculpted by Vladimir Fyodorov.

A little further along on the right-hand side of the street, is the **Dom detskoi knigi** (the House of Children's Books) at No. 43, where young children's interests are studied, the best children's books displayed and sold. Here meetings are arranged between children and their favorite authors. On the same side of the street, at No. 37, you might find yourself attracted to the appealing window displays of the *Podarki* (Gifts) **Store.** Here you are certain to find a souvenir to your taste and liking.

Further along we come to *ploshchad Mayakovskogo* (Mayakovsky Square), where Gorky Street crosses *Sadovoye koltso* (the Garden Ring). You may take this occasion to have a good look at the Garden Ring, whose history we have already discussed. This is a busy thoroughfare over 15 kilometers long, consisting of 16 streets and 16 squares, and passes under Gorky Street via an underpass.

In the center of the square is a **statue of Vladimir Mayakovsky**, the outstanding Soviet poet, executed by Alexander Kibalnikov and unveiled in 1958. Mayakovsky (1893-1930) was very fond of Moscow and lived here from 1906. Moscow's streets, squares, and districts are featured in one way or another in many of his works. In one of his poems he wrote: "I would like to live and die in Paris, if there were no such land as Moscow!"

As we come out onto the square, to our right we see a tall building with a spire and clock, the *Pekin* **Hotel**, opened in 1956. On the left-hand side of Gorky Street is the *Sofia* **Restaurant.** On the opposite side of the street, on the corner of the square is an imposing building with a ten-column portico—the Tchaikovsky Concert Hall, built in 1940 to the design of Dmitri Chechulin. In this hall, which seats 1,650 persons, the best Soviet orchestras, choirs, dance companies, musicians, and singers, and celebrated foreign artistes perform. Each year in July and August it is used as **Intourist's Cultural Center**, where round-table discussions and question and answer sessions are held for foreign tourists with leading Soviet journalists, specialists, scientists, statesmen, and public figures. Here in the evening, concerts are given by famous

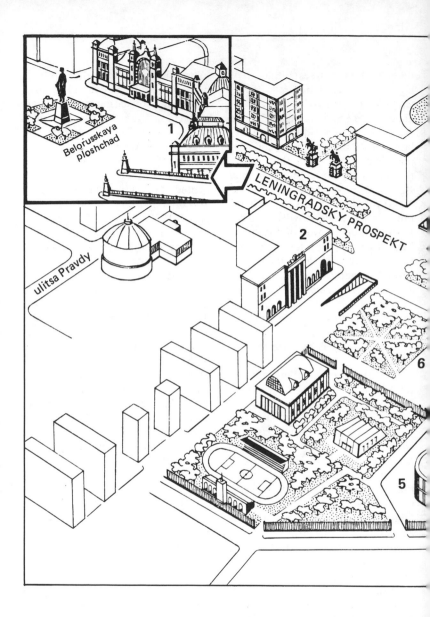

LENINGRAD AVENUE

1. *Belorussky (Byelorussian) Railway Station*
2. Sovetskaya *Hotel*
3. *Hippodrome*
4. *Young Pioneers Stadium*
5. Dynamo *Stadium*
6. *Dynamo Metro Station*
7. *Peter's Palace*
8. *Statue of Nikolai Zhukovsky*

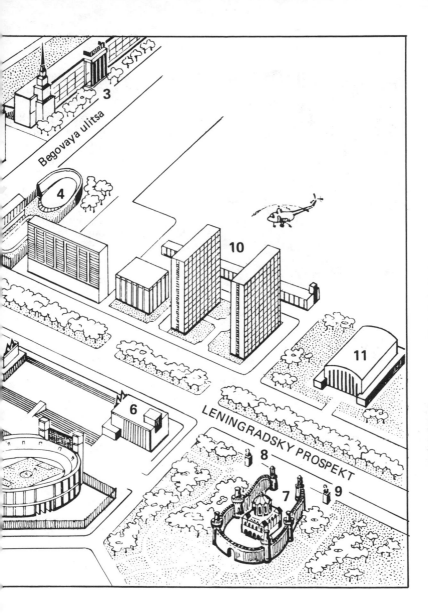

9. *Statue of Konstantin Tsiolkovsky*
10. *Air Terminal.* Aeroflot *Hotel*
11. *Sports complex of the Central Soviet Army*
    Sports Club

Statue of Cervantes

dance ensembles, choirs, and orchestras of folk music of the republics of the USSR.

Next to the Tchaikovsky Hall, on the Garden Ring, is a building crowned with a cupola whose lobby entrance is brightly lit in the evenings. This is the building of the **Satire Theater.** Behind it, in the small, cozy Aquarium Gardens, is still another, recently built theater building which houses the **Mossovet Theater.** For nearly forty of the sixty years of the theater's existence, its company was associated with the name of Yuri Zavadsky (1894–1977), a distinguished actor and one of the leading Soviet directors.

Continuing our walk along Gorky Street, to our left is the modern-looking, 10-storey *Minsk* **Hotel** (400 rooms), built in 1964. The hotel's restaurant specializes in Byelorussian cuisine. On the right-hand side of Gorky Street are big stores specializing in television and radio sets and cameras and photographic equipment and supplies. Look out for No. 25, which has a large window display of satirical posters. This is the **Exhibition Hall of the USSR Union of Artists.** When you reach *pereulok Sadovskikh* (the Sadovskiys' Lane), take note of the **Eye Hospital** behind the corner to the right. Its building, whose design is attributed to Matvei Kazakov, was erected in 1780. During the reconstruction of Gorky Street in 1939–40 it was moved back from its old site to this position and turned 90° to face this side-street. On the same side-street is the **Young Spectators' Theater** where plays for schoolchildren are presented. You will encounter one more theater on your way down Gorky Street—the **Stanislavsky Drama Theater.** Next to the theater, at No. 21, is an old mansion with a colonnade, set back from the street behind railings, with sculptured lions decorating its gates. It was built in the mid-18th century and restored after the great fire of 1812. Before the Revolution, this mansion was the English Club of the gentry and aristocracy. It has housed the **Central Museum of the Revolution** since 1924.

The museum's exhibits trace the path covered by the working people of the Soviet Union under the leadership of the Communist Party. The documents and materials displayed describe the initial period of the working-class and revolutionary movement in Russia, the history of the bourgeois-democratic revolutions of 1905 and 1917, and the victory of the Great October Socialist Revolution. An important place is given over to materials on the building of socialism in the USSR and the heroic years of the Great Patriotic War.

The museum has the status of a research institute. It houses more than a million documents, photographs, exhibits, and works of art of special scientific and artistic value. Its remarkable collection of paintings, graphics, and sculptures deserves special mention, and in-

cludes works by the greatest Russian artists of the turn of the century—Ilya Repin, Valentin Serov, Sergei Ivanov, Konstantin Savitsky, Sergei Korovin, Vladimir Mayakovsky, Boris Kustodiyev—and by leading Soviet painters and sculptors—Sergei Konenkov, Boris Ioganson, Isaac Brodsky, Igor Grabar, Konstantin Yuon, Kuzma Petrov-Vodkin, and others. We would direct your attention to an extremely interesting study by Ilya Repin, *The Tsar's Gallows. Year 1905.* The great Russian painter presented it to the museum in 1926, and it is a symbolic expression of the artist's aversion to the suffocating atmosphere of the tsar's autocracy. Also of interest is the canvas of Anatoly Pervov (1891–1943) portraying the celebration of the seventh anniversary of the October Revolution in Moscow (1925). And, of course, you should not miss *The First Demonstration* by Kuzma Petrov-Vodkin.

Exhibits include the first Soviet decrees on Peace and the Land, the Declaration of the Rights of the Peoples of Russia, adopted by the Soviet Government in November 1917. This document established legislatively the right to free development and complete equality for all the nationalities of Russia and the right of all nations to self-determination; the abolition of all national and religious privileges and restrictions. Documents are also preserved here on the Formation of the Union of Soviet Socialist Republics, which was proclaimed on

Pekin *Hotel*

December 30, 1922 at the First All-Union Congress of Soviets. Here, too, is the banner made soon after the Congress, and on which the call "Workers of All Countries, Unite!" is embroidered in six languages—Russian, Ukrainian, Byelorussian, Georgian, Armenian, and Azerbaijanian (the languages of the first republics, uniting in the Union of Soviet Socialist Republics). Here is yet another banner which was carried by workers during a manifestation in the spring of 1917. Written on it are the words: "Long Live the Democratic Republic and the 8-hour Working Day". It portrays a revolutionary soldier crushing the hydra of the counter-revolution, and a worker firmly shaking his hand. Beside them stands a young girl with the broken chains of slavery falling from her wrists. Still another historical relic are the large forged keys with which the gates of the Petropavlovsk fortress in Leningrad were opened on February 28, 1917, when the political prisoners—revolutionary fighters—were set free.

Here are unique exhibits of the period of the Great Patriotic War, including battle-orders and reports, personal belongings of the fallen heroes, and their photographs. Inscriptions on the bricks from the walls of prison chambers, where the fascist invaders tortured young partisans from the Ukrainian village of Krynka in Nikolayev Region, read: "Long Live Motherland!", and "I did not utter a word". Also on display is a thick

Gorky Street. Stanislavsky Drama Theater (on the left)

choslovakian capital of Prague which were handed over to the Soviet Army officers by the residents of these cities as a token of their gratitude for their liberation from fascist German invaders in 1944 and 1945. We shall mention two more exhibits: the first is a part of the radio unit which broadcast the first decrees of Soviet power in November 1917, and the second is the control panel of space flights, which were included in the museum's collection in 1986.

In the paved stone courtyard, in front of the museum, on big wooden wheels stands a 6-inch-calibre gun with which the revolutionary soldiers shelled the White Guards encamped in the Kremlin in October 1917. The gun was made in Paris in 1878. Also on exhibit is an old pylon for overhead tram wires which bears scars of the artillery fire during the fighting to establish Soviet power in Moscow.

volume of a Czech-Russian dictionary which was discovered in an unexploded bomb, dropped on Moscow by the Hitlerites in early March 1942. Czech anti-fascists managed to fill the bomb with sand instead of blasting charge. Another book is an account of battle engagements of the Normandie-Niémen Air Squadron. Next to it are the goggles of the squadron's first commander, Jean-Louis Tulasne, who perished in battle while covering Soviet troops advancing on Oryol in 1943. Another interesting exhibit are the keys from the Romanian city of Cluj and the Cze-

Central Museum of the Revolution

The fighting took place quite near this location, on Tverskoy Boulevard. And another historical exhibit: an armoured car with two machine-gun turrets, dating to 1916. Such armoured cars operated in the October armed uprising in Petrograd in 1917 and in battles with interventionists during the Civil War (1918-20).

Continuing our walk down Gorky Street we come to *ploshchad Pushkina* (Pushkin Square). On the left-hand side of this square, on one corner, is the building housing the editorial offices of *Izvestia* (News of the Soviet of People's Deputies of the USSR), a newspaper with a daily circulation of over 10 million copies. The entrances to the Pushkinskaya and Gorkovskaya Metro stations are located in this building.

In the center of the square is the **statue of Alexander Pushkin**, the brilliant Russian poet (1799-1837). This remarkable work by Alexander Opekushin was erected with funds raised by public subscription. The statue was unveiled in 1880. Expressed in a few words, the impression it gives is one of majestic simplicity. Inscribed on the front of the monument's pedestal are the words: "To Pushkin." On the left side are inscribed lines from one of his poems:

Rumour of me shall then my whole
*   vast country fill,*
On every tongue she owns
*   my name she'll speak*
Proud Slave's posterity, Finn,
*   and—unlettered still—*

The Tungus,
*   and the steppe-loving Kalmyk.*

Inscribed on the right side of the pedestal are lines from the same poem:

And long the people yet
*   will honor me,*
Because my lyre was tuned
*   to loving-kindness,*
And, in a cruel age, I sang
*   of Liberty,*
And mercy begged of Justice
*   in her blindness.*

Alexander Pushkin was born in Moscow, where he spent his early years, and he paid many visits to this city he loved throughout his later life.

How oft in grief, from thee
*   long parted*
Throughout my vagrant destiny,
Moscow, my thoughts have turned to
*   thee!*
Moscow ... What thoughts in each
*   true-hearted*
Russian come flooding at that
*   word!*
How deep an echo there is heard!

The monument originally stood on the opposite side of the square, on *Tverskoy Boulevard*, where the poet used to walk. In 1950 the monument was moved to a new garden, where it presently stands. There is hardly a single Muscovite who, as a youth, has not arranged a rendezvous by this monument. Regardless of weather or season, there are always fresh flowers at the foot of the pedestal.

One of the first to lay flowers at the foot of the pedestal of the statue of Pushkin was the great Russian writer Fyodor Dostoyevsky. Several days later, at a ceremony honoring Dostoyevsky himself, the Moscow literary public presented him with a laurel wreath. "Arriving at Strastnaya Square, Dostoyevsky, struggling with the enormous wreath, laid it at the foot of the pedestal of the monument of his 'great teacher' and bowed low", recalled Dostoyevsky's wife (Pushkin Square used to be called Strastnaya Square). One hundred and fifty years have passed since the time Pushkin's life ended tragically. But the unfading light of Pushkin's genius continues to kindle the hearts of millions upon millions with its generous warmth. The following lines of the poet have proven prophetic indeed:

I shall not perish entirely—
In my sacred Lyre
My soul shall outlive my dust,
And escape corruption...

Pushkin's verses and poems, some put to music, and his prose, written in crystal-pure Russian, have been translated into the languages of many nationalities of both the Soviet Union and the world. Musical and drama theaters stage plays, operas, and ballets based on his works.

As you look at the festive Pushkin Square, it's difficult to imagine that wooden houses and dilapidated structures stood here not so long ago. Behind the garden where the monument stands, at the far end of the square is the modern-looking building of the *Rossiya* **Cinema.** It was built in 1961 and has a total seating capacity of 2,870. On its vast screen, 14 meters high and 30 meters wide, films of every format, standard, or wide-screen can be shown. The cinema building was designed by a group of architects under the supervision of Yuri Sheverdyayev.

On the right-hand side of the square, opposite the *Izvestia* building, are the **offices of** *Moscow News*, which appears in different languages. This weekly newspaper is very popular among foreign tourists to the capital as it contains much useful and interesting information about Moscow and the Soviet Union.

In the same building is the **All-Russia Theatrical Society** and the **Central Actors' Club**, named after the eminent actress Alexandra Yablochkina, who performed with the Maly Theater company. Next to the club is the **Apartment-Museum of Nikolai Ostrovsky** (1904–36), the distinguished Soviet writer. Confined to his bed with a grave illness and blind, Ostrovsky both dictated and used black-lined paper to write his semi-autobiographical novel *How the Steel Was Tempered*, much loved by generations of Soviet youth. Ostrovsky's works have been printed in the USSR in more than 560 editions in 61 languages of the peoples of the Soviet Union, and in 46 other languages.

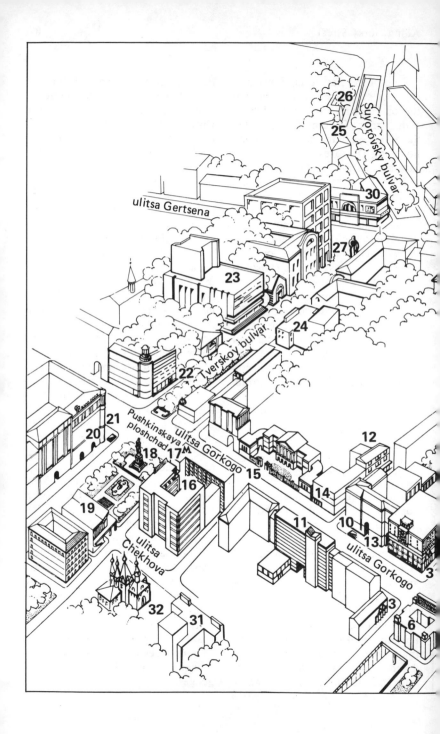

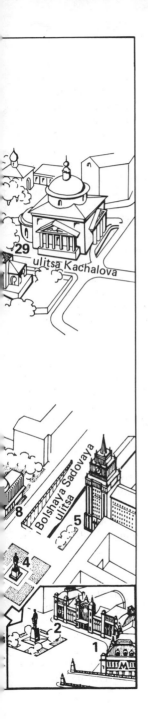

GORKY STREET

1. *Belorussky (Byelorussian) Railway Station*
2. *Belorusskaya Metro Station*
3. *Mayakovskaya Metro Station*
4. *Statue of Mayakovsky*
5. Pekin *Hotel*
6. Sofia *Restaurant*
7. *Tchaikovsky Concert Hall*
8. *Satire Theater*
9. *Mossovet Theater*
10. *Exhibition Hall of the USSR Union of Artists, 25 ulitsa Gorkogo*
11. Minsk *Hotel*
12. *Young Spectators' Theater*
13. Efir *store (television and radio sets)*
14. *Stanislavsky Drama Theater*
15. *Central Museum of the Revolution*
16. Izvestia *editorial offices*
17. *Pushkinskaya and Gorkovskaya Metro stations*
18. *Statue of Alexander Pushkin*
19. Rossiya *Cinema*
20. Moskovskiye novosti *(Moscow News) editorial offices*
21. *All-Russia Theatrical Society (VTO) and the Central Actors' Club*
22. Armenia *store. Sergei Konenkov Studio-Museum*
23. *Peoples' Friendship Theater*
24. *Pushkin Drama Theater*
25. *Museum of Oriental Art*
26. *Central House of Journalists*
27. *Statue of Kliment Timiryazev*
28. *Maxim Gorky Apartment-Museum*
29. *Church of the Ascension*
30. Povtornogo filma *(Old Films) Cinema*
31. *Lenin Komsomol Theater*
32. *Church of the Nativity of Our Lady at Putinki*

Izvestia *editorial offices (old and new premises)*

On the corner of Gorky Street and Pushkin Square, on the right-hand side of the street, is *Armenia*, a specialty store dealing in Armenian commodities. In the same house on Tverskoy Boulevard side, is the **sculptor Sergei Konenkov Studio-Museum** (1874–1971), which was opened in 1974. Everything in the studio is preserved as it was during the outstanding sculptor's life. The collection consists of 80 works, including sculptural portraits of Lenin, Mayakovsky, Gorky, and Albert Einstein, the sculptural composition "Cosmos", a self-portrait, and articles of furniture made of branches, roots and tree trunks.

But let us continue our walk. On the right-hand side of the street are various shops on the ground floors of the buildings. On the left-hand side, at No. 14, is a large store with big plate-glass windows, through which is visible a spacious, high-ceilinged hall with huge chandeliers and a sumptuous interior. This is **Gastronom** (Food Store) **No. 1**, very popular among Muscovites. Further along is the *Beriozka* **Jewellery Shop**, and next to it is the *Tsentralnaya* **Hotel.** Here, at No. 10, is a bakery which has earned a special reputation among Muscovites for the broad variety of its breads and other baked goods. A memorial plaque on the front of the building commemorates a strike staged in September 1905 by the workers of the bakery against the tsarist regime. This strike was a forerunner of the national strike in

Statue of Alexander Pushkin

October 1905 and the Moscow armed uprising in December of the same year.

Before reaching *Sovetskaya* (Soviet) *Square*, there are two bookstores—the **Moskva Bookstore** (No. 8), on the left-hand side, and the **Druzhba** (Friendship) **Bookstore** (No. 15), on the right-hand side of the street—which you might like to visit. The *Druzhba* Bookstore sells books published in other socialist countries.

Facing *Soviet Square*, on the right-hand side of the street, is the building of the **Moscow City Soviet of Working People's Deputies.** On the building's high pediment is a gilt Emblem of the Soviet Union. Above the building flutters the State Flag of the USSR. "The Moscow City Soviet is the boss of the city," Muscovites say. And this is true. "...the *people*, united by the Soviets, are the ones who should run the government," Lenin bequeathed. Deputies to the Moscow Soviet, as deputies to all Soviets in the USSR—from the Supreme So-

Rossiya *Cinema*

viet to the Soviets of People's Deputies of districts, cities, city districts, settlements and villages, are elected by the voters on the basis of universal, equal, and direct suffrage by secret ballot (Article 95 of the USSR Constitution). An important feature of the representative bodies of state authority in the USSR is the fact that the elected deputies combine their activities with active involvement in the work of the society. Since 1924 Lenin's name has been permanently on the roll of deputies of the Moscow Soviet, and after each election the first credentials are made out in his name. The banner of the city of Moscow, bearing two Orders of Lenin, the Gold Star Medal of a Hero-City, and the Order of the October Revolution, is kept inside the Moscow Soviet. The first Order of Lenin was awarded to Moscow on the occasion of its 800th anniversary in September 1947. The second Order of Lenin and the Gold Star Medal of a Hero-City were awarded to Moscow on the 20th anniversary of the victory of the Soviet people in the Great Patriotic War. In 1967 the city of Moscow was awarded the Order of the October Revolution on the occasion of the 50th anniversary of the Revolution.

The building which now houses the Moscow Soviet was originally a three-storey one, built in 1782 by Matvei Kazakov. It was the residence of the Governor-General of Moscow and one of the city's finest buildings before the Revolution.

During the reconstruction of Gorky Street in 1939, the building was moved back about 14 meters, and in 1945 it was rebuilt by Dmitry Chechulin. Two storeys were added on, and the white-stone colonnade of the portico was raised to the height of the two upper storeys. The walls were painted a deep crimson, thus providing a more effective background for the decorative gilding.

Over the entrance of the building is preserved a balcony from which Lenin spoke to mass meetings on several occasions. A plaque beside the entrance commemorates these events. Another plaque recalls that in October 1917 the building was the headquarters of the Revolutionary Military Council that led the October armed uprising in Moscow.

Opposite the Moscow Soviet, in a small garden with a fountain, is the building of the **Central Party Archives of the Institute of Marxism-Leninism.** Its archives contain more than 6,000 manuscripts of Karl Marx and Friedrich Engels, and over 30,000 documents of Lenin's. In front of the building is a red granite **statue of Lenin** by Sergei Merkurov, unveiled in 1938.

In the center of Soviet Square on a high rectangular pedestal is a **monument to Yuri Dolgoruky**, the legendary founder of Moscow. The monument was unveiled in 1954 (sculptors Sergei Orlov and others).

As you continue along Gorky Street towards the Kremlin, take note of the two granite-faced houses next to the Moscow Soviet building. In 1941 Hitler, confident of victory and the capture of Moscow, ordered that granite be brought here from Finland to erect a victory memorial in Moscow. Smashed in the battle over Moscow the retreating Hitlerite troops abandoned their wounded and dead, along with much ammunition and equipment and, of course, the granite. It was with this very granite that Moscow builders constructed the columns of the large archway spanning the buildings at No. 9 and No. 11 Gorky Street, and faced the ground floors of their façades.

Building of the Mossovet *(Moscow City Soviet)*

On the corner of Gorky Street and *Ogaryov Street* is the **Central Telegraph Office** built by civil engineer Ivan Rerberg in 1927.

On the street leading to the left from Gorky Street, *proyezd Khudozhestvennogo teatra* (Art Theater Passage), is the **Moscow Art Theater**, named after Maxim Gorky. It occupies a three-storey building which has recently undergone full reconstruction. The pediment of the building is decorated with reproductions of the Orders of Lenin and the Red Banner of Labor awarded to the company, and of a seagull, the emblem of the theater. The main stage of the Moscow Art Theater has been located here since 1902. A branch of the theater (its second stage), is located at No. 3 *ulitsa Moskvina* (Moskvin Street), not far from Pushkin Square.

The Moscow Art Theater was

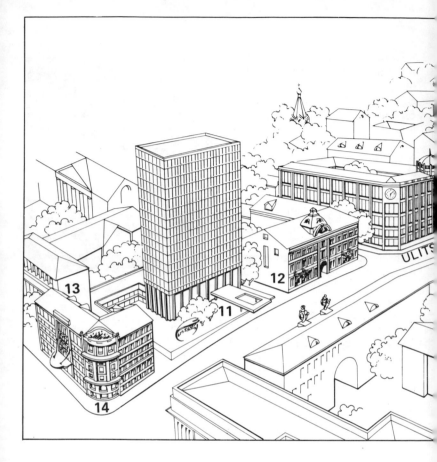

GORKY STREET

(continued)

1. *Nikolai Ostrovsky Apartment-Museum*
2. Gastronom *(Food Store) No. 1*
3. Tsentralnaya *Hotel*
4. Druzhba *(Friendship) bookstore*
5. Moskva *bookstore*
6. *Moscow City Soviet of Working People's Deputies (Mossovet)*
7. *Monument to Yuri Dolgoruky*

8. *Statue of Lenin*
9. Aragvi *Restaurant*
10. *Moscow Art Theater*
11. Intourist *Hotel*

12. *Yermolova Drama Theater*
13. *USSR State Committee for Foreign Travel*
14. National *Hotel*

Gorky Street

founded in 1898 by Konstantin Stanislavsky and Vladimir Nemirovich-Danchenko. Plays by Chekhov and Gorky are permanently in its repertoire. Among plays by Soviet playwrights are a number of remarkable ones about Lenin (*Kremlin Chimes* and *Third Pathétique* by Mikhail Pogodin and *This Way We Shall Win* by Mikhail Shatrov). In recent years the Moscow Art Theater has earned recognition as an ingenious interpreter of contemporary plays with sharp social criticism.

We will pass one more theater on our way, just before the Intourist Hotel—the **Yermolova Drama Theater.** It is housed in a small mansion and is scheduled to be

National *(on the corner) and* Intourist *hotels*

moved to new, modern premises in the future. Next to the theater is the 22-storey *Intourist* Hotel—the "glass box" as Muscovites sometimes call it—perhaps the only structure in the city's center out of keeping with the surrounding architectural pattern. It was built in 1970 by a group of architects under the supervision of Vsevolod Voskresensky. Once inside, however, you will discover that the hotel is quite comfortable, and that its interior design is quite ingenious and unique. The hotel has 458 rooms (including two-, three-, and four-room suites) and can accommodate 930 guests. Its restaurants, particularly the *Skazka* (Fairy-tale) and *Zvyozdnoye nebo* (Starry sky) with their evening entertainments, are very popular.

This completes our stroll down Gorky Street. Across the street from the *Intourist* Hotel at No. 4 is the *Podarki* (Gifts) **Store.** At the end of the street, on both sides, are the entrances to the Prospekt Marksa Metro Station from which you can transfer to the **Ploshchad Revolutsii** and **Ploshchad Sverdlova Metro stations.**

SECOND DAY

In the morning we will take a stroll along prospekt Marksa *(Marx Avenue) and make a sightseeing tour of the center of the city. Then, before lunch we will visit the State Tretyakov Gallery and the USSR State Picture Gallery, or the State Pushkin Museum of Fine Arts. In the afternoon we will get acquainted with* Leninsky prospekt *(Lenin Avenue).*

ALONG MARX AVENUE

Marx Avenue sweeps in a broad semi-arc north and west through the center from Dzerzhinsky Square to *Bolshoi Kamenny most* (Grand Stone Brigde) across two main squares, Sverdlov Square and 50th Anniversary of the October Revolution Square (near Red Square and the Kremlin). Together with the streets and areas adjoining it, it is probably one of busiest streets in the city. Located in this area are many historical and architectural monuments associated with the struggle for Soviet power and the activities of Vladimir Ilyich Lenin. Marx Avenue is approximately three kilometers long, and your walk should take about an hour and a half.

We recommend that you begin from the Ploshchad Revolutsii Metro Station.

As you come out of the Metro station you will see on your left a three-storey red brick building with a high, pitched silver roof and lavish decorative work, in imitation of Russian wooden architecture. Built by architect Dmitry Chichagov in 1892, before the Revolution it housed the City *Duma* (City Hall) of Moscow. In 1917 it became the center of Moscow's counter-revolutionary activities. In memory of the revolutionary battles fought here, the square was named *ploshchad Revolutsii* (Revolution Square).

In 1936 the **Central Lenin Museum** was transferred to this building. As the country's largest repository of Leniniana it acquaints millions of Soviet people and visitors from abroad with the life and revolutionary activity of Vladimir Ilyich Lenin (1870-1924), and his theoretical heritage. On display in the museum's 34 halls are over 12,500 of Lenin's papers and historical Party documents, photographs, Lenin's personal belongings, books and pictures. The museum also contains a replica of Lenin's study in the Kremlin. The exhibits document Lenin's titanic activity, from his membership in the first Marxist circles and the creation of the Bolshevik Party to the victory of the October Revolution and the formation of the

Central Lenin Museum

world's first socialist state.

Before entering the museum, you might take note of the relief over the entrance. This is a work by Georgi Alexeyev (1881-1951), one of the first artists to portray Lenin during his life. Alexeyev made a series of sketches of Lenin in November 1918 in the leader's study in the Kremlin. These and other portraits of Lenin drawn from life are on display in the museum. The relief over the entrance depicts a worker and a peasant both inspired by a single revolutionary ideal. It was mounted in 1918, and is one of the earliest monuments of Soviet fine arts.

In addition to the paintings, sculptures, and drawings, the museum houses a display of sculptural portraits of the revolutinary leader drawn from life by Nikolai An-

dreyev which have become part of the treasure-house of Soviet art. There is also a posthumous portrait of Lenin, on which Ivan Shadr worked non-stop for 46 hours during the days of mourning in January 1924. Also of interest are Alexander Gerasimov's painting *Lenin on the Speaker's Stand* (1930), considered one of the best works of the entire collection, and the canvases of Isaac Brodsky, one of the first artists to work on portraying Lenin.

Interest in Lenin's life and work is unfailing. In the sixty years that the museum has been open, it has been visited by over 55 million people from practically every country in the world.

Opposite the Lenin Museum is the new, twelve-storey building of the *Moskva* **Hotel**, which occupies the whole block between Sverdlov Square and 50th Anniversary of the October Revolution Square. If you head to the right, towards the *Metropole* Hotel, you will see on your right the remains of the **old**

Moskva *Hotel*

Old walls of Kitaigorod. Statue of Yakov Sverdlov

walls of Kitaigorod, erected in 1535-38. In the 16th century these walls, constructed of brick and over 6 meters high and about 6 meters thick, had 14 towers with machicolations and loop-holes. They encompassed the entire *posad*, or settlement (from the 16th century known as "Kitaigorod", presumably from the word *kita*, meaning a bundle of stakes such as those used at the time in the building of fortifications), populated with merchants and artisans. The total length of the wall was 2.6 kilometers. In 1934 during reconstruction work in the center it was almost entirely dismantled, and the remaining sections are solicitously preserved. Behind the Kitaigorod wall (with their merlons reminiscent of the Kremlin wall), at No. 15 25th October Street, is the **Historical Archives Institute**, whose windows are decorated with carved white-stone surrounds. On its site in the 16th century stood the Royal Printing House, in which Ivan Fyodorov (1510-83) on March 1, 1564 finished printing the first Russian book *The Apostle.*

As we continue our walk we come to the ***Metropole* Hotel**, built in 1899-1903. The entrance to the hotel, which is run by Intourist, is located on *ploshchad Sverdlova* (Sverdlov Square). To the right of the entrance are two other memorial plaques. The inscription on one of them recalls that in the first years after the victory of Soviet power the building housed the offices of the All-Russia Central Executive Committee of Soviets of Workers', Peasants' and Soldiers' Deputies, under the chairmanship of Yakov Sverdlov (1885-1919), outstanding organizer and builder of the Communist Party and the Soviet State and Lenin's close comrade-in-arms. In 1978 a **statue of Yakov Sverdlov** by sculptor Rafael Ambartsumyan was erected in the square near the Kitaigorod wall. The second memorial plaque is dedicated to the negotiations that took place in this building in November 1921 to establish friendly relations between the RSFSR and Mongolia in which Sukhe-Bator, the founder of the Mongolian People's Revolutionary Party and Mongolian People's Republic, took part.

The *Metropole* Hotel is a five-storey building which has been rebuilt inside several times. The upper part of the façade which faces out onto Marx Avenue is decorated with mosaic panels executed according to the drawings of the renowned Russian artist Mikhail Vrubel (1856-1910) based on the theme of the play *La Princesse Lointaine* by French playwright and poet Edmond Rostand.

In the public garden between the *Metropole* and *Moskva* hotels stands the **statue of Karl Marx**, the founder of scientific communism. Its foundation was laid in May 1920 and Lenin spoke at the ceremony, concluding his short speech with the words: "...I am certain that this monument which we have erected to our great teacher will serve as a motivation for you to devote all your attention to the necessity of working hard in order to create a society free of exploitation."

After the ceremony began the actual work of laying the foundation. One of the participants of the ceremony later recalled how one of the workers extended a shovel to Lenin. He took the shovel and began to toss the soft, damp earth into the hole. Later he laid the first bricks of the monument's foundation in cement.

The monument was unveiled during a grand ceremony in October 1961. It was sculpted according to the design of Lev Kerbel from a 160-ton granite block brought from the Ukraine. The monument is 7.7 meters tall. The figure of the great thinker, leader and teacher of the international proletariat seems to grow out of the

Statue of Karl Marx

enormous rock. Around it are granite slabs on which are engraved: "His name will endure through the ages, and so also will his work! Engels." and "Marxist doctrine is omnipotent because it is true. Lenin." On the socle is the inscription: "Workers of All Countries, Unite!" These are the concluding words of *Manifesto of the Communist Party* written by Marx and Engels in 1848.

On this same square one's attention is drawn to a decorative fountain which is probably the oldest in Moscow at present. It was built by the sculptor Ivan Vitali in 1835. At the time the fountain had highly practical significance—it provided the city with its drinking water.

Now we will cross Marx Avenue by the underpass and walk toward

CITY'S CENTER. STREETS AND
SQUARES

1. *Ploshchad Revolyutsii Metro Station*
2. *Central Lenin Museum*
3. Moskva *Hotel*
4. *Prospekt Marksa Metro Station*

5. *Old walls of Kitaigorod*
6. *Statue of Yakov Sverdlov*
7. Metropole *Hotel*
8. *Statue of Karl Marx*

ploshchad
Sverdlova

ploshchad
Revolutsii

7 5 6 1 2 3 4

the Bolshoi Theater. But if you have some time to spare, go up Marx Avenue (to the right from the *Metropole* Hotel) and look at the **statue of Ivan Fyodorov**, the first Russian printer. The statue was sculpted by Sergei Volnukhin and erected by public subscription in 1909. It stands in a small garden. The figure of the printer rises from a pedestal upon which is engraved the date April 19, 1563, the day on which Ivan Fyodorov began to print *The Apostle*. In his right hand he holds the off-print and in his left, a typesetting plate. Opposite the garden, on the left side of the street, is an enormous building with large display windows. This is the largest children's department store in the Soviet Union, ***Detsky mir*** (Children's World), built in 1957 and designed by architect Alexander Dushkin. The store has about 300,000 customers every day.

At the end of the avenue (or rather its beginning, going by the house numbers) is *ploshchad Dzerzhinskogo* (Dzerzhinsky Square) with the bronze **statue of Felix Dzerzhinsky** (1877–1926) rising from a tall, round pedestal. Dzerzhinsky was an eminent Party leader, Soviet statesman, and a close comrade of Lenin. The statue is the work of the remarkable Soviet sculptor, Yevgeny Vuchetich (1908–74). In the vicinity of this square are three museums that are well worth visiting.

The first of these is the **State Polytechnic Museum**, whose ex-

hibits trace the development of Russian engineering and the main trends in modern scientific and technical progress. The others are the **Museum of the History and Reconstruction of Moscow**, and the **Mayakovsky Museum**, housed in the building where the poet spent the last eleven years of his life.

But let us get back to Sverdlov Square. It is not fortuitous that until 1919 it was called Theater Square, for two theaters were built here at the beginning of the 19th century. One, a vast, majestic building, was intended for opera and ballet, and the other, a smaller, simpler building, for drama. Ever since these two theaters have been called the Bolshoi and the Maly (meaning the Grand and the Little theaters). Both are the national pride of the Soviet people, and everyone visiting Moscow tries to get tickets to them.

The **USSR State Academic Bolshoi Theater.** The pediment of this famous theater bears four bronze steeds racing along with Apollo, the god of the arts, at the reins of his chariot. They were sculpted over one hundred and thirty years ago. The building of the Bolshoi Theater was built at the end of 1824 according to the design of architects Andrei Mikhailov and Osip Bovet. After a fire, it was rebuilt in 1856. The Bolshoi is one of the most famous theater buildings in the world, striking in its monumentality and the beauty of its architecture. Its mighty eight-col-

Statue of Pyotr Tchaikovsky in front of Moscow Conservatoire building

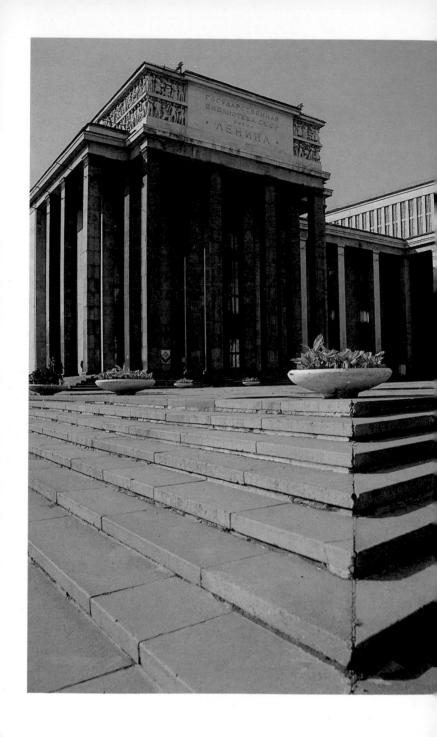

Lenin State Library

Pashkov House—one of the relics of Russian Classical architecture of the second half of the 18th century

Tomb of the Unknown Soldier and Eternal Flame

Sverdlov Square. Bolshoi Theater

Pekin *Hotel*

Building of the Gosplan *(State Planning Committee)*

State Pushkin Museum of Fine Arts

"December Evenings" in the Museum of Fine Arts

umn portico which stands 15 meters high dominates over the square, whose layout reflects a single architectural style. The theater's five-tier auditorium can accommodate over 2,000 spectators. In October 1941 the Bolshoi was damaged in a fascist air raid, but was completely restored even as the war went on, in 1943–44.

In the years since the victory of Soviet power, the Bolshoi Theater has become the premier operatic and ballet theater of the USSR, and is famed throughout the world. The outstanding works of Russian composers were given a new life on the theater's stage.

The Bolshoi Theater's total repertoire consists of forty operas and thirty ballets. Each day 8,155 spectators come to see one of the 520 performances staged either at the Bolshoi Theater proper or the Kremlin Palace of Congresses.

The company of the Bolshoi Theater numbers around 3,000, and consists of an opera troupe of 300 soloists and choral singers, a ballet troupe of the same number,

Bolshoi Theater

Politechnic Museum

and the splendid artists who make up the orchestra, the mimic ensemble, and who work as stage assistants, make-up artists, costume designers, lighting experts and props men. The Bolshoi is constantly adding talented young artists to its company. All those who aspire to join the theater's company must pass through a series of auditions. The stiffest of these are for ballet, as the Bolshoi's ballet has been acclaimed as being of world importance.

Many memorable events in the social and political life of the country have been held and continue to be held in the building of

Bolshoi Theater. Pediment, topped with the figure of Appolo in a chariot drawn by four steeds

the Bolshoi Theater. At one time Party and Soviet Congresses were held here, and Lenin frequently spoke. It was here at the 5th All-Russia Congress of Soviets in July 1918 that the first Soviet Constitution was adopted. It was also here in December 1920 that the 8th All-Russia Congress of Soviets adopted Lenin's plan on the electrification of Russia. One year later the 1st All-Union Congress of Soviets proclaimed the Formation of the Union of Soviet Socialist Republics. And it was here, on November 20, 1922, that Lenin gave his last public address. He concluded his speech with these words: "Socialism is no longer a matter of the distant future ... so that *NEP* (New Economic Policy — *Ed.*) Russia will become Socialist Russia." Memorial plaques on the façade of the Bolshoi Theater commemorate all these events.

The low building of the Maly Theatre extends from Marx Avenue to the **Central Department Store (TsUM)** on *ulitsa Petrovka* (Petrovka Street). Along Petrovka Street and the streets adjoining it is a big shopping area with a great variety of shops. In the summer of 1974 a spacious new block was added to the old *TsUM* building, which dates to 1909.

On the left-hand side of Petrovka Street, in the courtyard of building No. 15 (entrance through the first arch from the corner of Petrovka and *Stoleshnikov pereulok* (Stoleshnikov Lane) is the **USSR Company for Foreign Travel**, where one can reserve and acquire tickets on all modes of transportation from Moscow to various cities of the Soviet Union and other countries.

Running parallel to Petrovka, behind the Maly Theater and TsUM is *ulitsa Neglinnaya* (Neglinnaya Street). The street was named after the Neglinnaya River, which was piped underground in the 1820s and channeled into a new, expanded manifold in 1974. At No. 12 Neglinnaya Street is the USSR State Bank. At No. 8 are the editorial offices of the Soviet journal on travel *Puteshestviye v SSSR*. The journal is published in Russian, English, French and German, and enjoys considerable popularity abroad. Written articles, pictorial essays, articles and speeches of famous writers and travellers, cultural figures, foreign journalists and tourists, articles about places of interest and the country's tourist centers, its varied landscapes and climates, historical and cultural monuments, museums and art galleries, exhibits and art festivals, the national customs and art of the peoples of the Soviet Union—all this can be found in the journal, to which those outside the Soviet Union may subscribe through national organizations or firms which distribute Soviet periodical literature.

Between Petrovka and Neglinnaya Street runs a cross-street still known as *Kuznetsky most* (Smith's Bridge), although neither bridge nor smithy has existed for many years. On Smith's Bridge are the salons of the **Moscow House of Artists** (No. 11) and the **Union of Soviet Artists** (No. 20), the **All-Union House of Fashion** (No. 14), and the **representatives of Bulgarian, Scandinavian, West German, Yugoslavian, and Japanese airlines.**

Now let's return to Sverdlov Square and the theaters situated on it. At the entrance to the **Maly Theater** is a **statue of Alexander Ostrovsky** (1823–86), the great Russian playwright, by the Soviet sculptor Nikolai Andreyev. The statue was unveiled in 1929. The Maly Theater is often referred to as the Ostrovsky House, as 47 out of 48 of his plays were staged in it. The Maly Theater has played a prominent role in the spiritual development of Russian society, and has always been closely linked with the liberation movement in Russia. In October 1984 the whole country celebrated the theater's 160th anniversary. The plays of the Russian

Central Department Store (TsUM)

classics (Gogol, Griboyedov, Tolstoy, and Gorky) and many plays by contemporary Soviet and foreign playwrights are performed with invariable success.

After looking at the Bolshoi and Maly theaters, let us walk around the garden situated between them and come out again onto Marx Avenue. On the corner is the Ploshchad Sverdlova (Sverdlov Square) Metro Station (one of its exits). Next door is yet another theater which is quite unique, the **Central Children's Theater**, founded in 1921, and the first special theater for children in the world. The theater presents shows and stages fairy-tales for very young children, and plays for schoolchildren of various age-groups.

Let us continue our walk along Marx Avenue, leaving Sverdlov Square behind us. On the corner of *Pushkinskaya ulitsa* (Pushkin Street) you will notice a low, three-storey building with a four-column portico in the Russian Classical style. This is the *Dom Soyuzov* (the House of Trade Unions), built by

Maly Theater

Matvei Kazakov in the 1770s. Before the Revolution it was the Assembly Rooms of the Nobility, but in 1919 by decision of the Soviet Government it was handed over to the trade unions. In its Hall of Columns and October Hall important conferences and meetings are held, guests of Moscow honored, and concerts presented. And at the New Year, festive celebrations are held here for Moscow schoolchildren.

Lenin often addressed the workers of the city here. And it was here, in the January 1924, that the mourning country bid farewell to its great leader.

In 1931 the outstanding British writer George Bernard Shaw paid a visit to Moscow. "I don't want to die without having seen the USSR," he stated before his trip. A meeting was held in his honor in the Hall of Columns to mark his 75th birthday. Shaw opened his

speech with the word *"Tovarishchi"* (comrades), and the hall responded with stormy applause. Then he went on to say: "I just learned this word a week ago, but I've already come to love it."

The building of the House of Trade Unions was the only building to have been preserved during the reconstruction on this section of the city's center. Up until 1930 the whole area between Theater Square and Tverskaya Street was a maze of narrow, twisting lanes known as *Okhotny ryad* (Game Market), an enormous market, the

Statue of Alexander Ostrovsky

life-blood of the city, with butcheries and hundreds of stalls selling meat, fish, game, poultry and greengroceries. In addition, there were livestock pens, garbage dumps, and dozens of taverns and coach inns. All of this was demolished during the first reconstruction of Moscow in the 1930s, and a broad thoroughfare—Marx Avenue—was laid out where the dirty, wooden booths and shacks had been. Two large buildings dominate its central sector: on the left the *Moskva* Hotel (its first section, designed by architect Alexei Shchusev, built in 1935 and another section added in 1977), and on the right the *Gosplan* (State Planning Committee) building, built in 1936 and designed by architect Arkady Langman. After these two buildings Marx Avenue runs into *ploshchad Pyatidesyatiletiya Oktyabrya* (50th Anniversary of the October Revolution Square). Gorky Street runs off to the right. You must cross it through the pedestrian underpass, coming out at the *National* Hotel.

Lenin lived in Room 107 on the second floor of the National Hotel from March 11-19, 1918, and there is a plaque on the building commemorating this. The hotel was built in 1908 according to the design of architect Alexander Ivanov.

In 1914 the famous English writer H. G. Wells stayed at the *National* Hotel, and again in 1920 when he returned to have a look at "the country of the Bolsheviks" and to meet Lenin. In 1934 Wells

Dom Soyuzov *(House of Trade Unions)*

visited Moscow for a third time, and again stayed at the *National* Hotel. Speaking with some reporters, he recalled that in 1920 Lenin said: "Come back and see us in ten years," adding, "Fourteen years have passed, but I came back just the same." Among other things he watched the gymnasts' parade on Red Square. "He was stunned, deafened by the loud bands and singing, blinded by the pageantry of colors," wrote the *Literaturnaya gazeta* (Literary Gazette) at the time, "stirred by the thousands upon thousands of smiling young faces..." Thus he stood, the writer with an international name, absorbing with keen-sighted and curious eyes this new, enigmatic, incomprehensible world. Turning at one point to his Soviet companion, Wells, the author of the once highly sensational *Russia in the Shadows*, said that he had come expressly to see these new people of the Soviet Land, and that they impressed him most, more even than the amazing modern industrial achievements of the country...

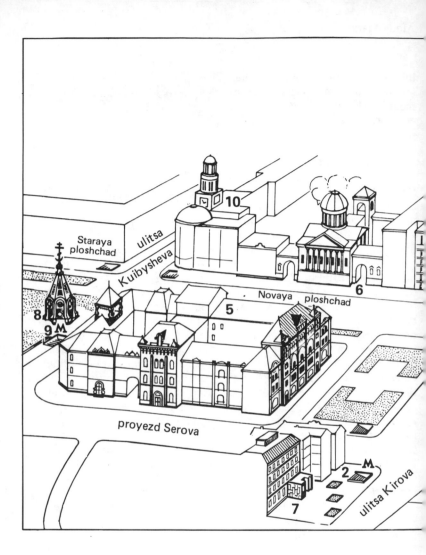

CITY'S CENTER. STREETS AND
SQUARES

(continued)

1. Slavyansky bazar *Restaurant*
2. *Dzerzhinskaya Metro Station*
3. Detsky mir *(Children's World) Department Store*

4. *Statue of Felix Dzerzhinsky*
5. *Polytechnic Museum*
6. *Museum of the History and Reconstruction of Moscow*
7. *Vladimir Mayakovsky Apartment-Musuem*

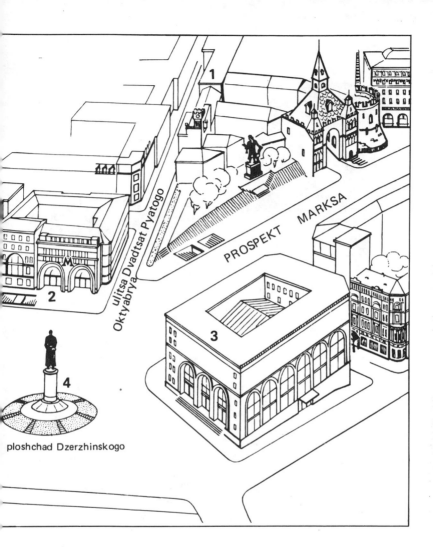

ulitsa Dvadtsat Pyatogo Oktyabrya

PROSPEKT MARKSA

ploshchad Dzerzhinskogo

Building of the Gosplan *(State Planning Committee)*

The building next to the *National* Hotel on Marx Avenue is the Intourist house. This seven-storey building, with architectural motifs from the Renaissance period, was built in 1934 by the eminent Soviet architect Ivan Zholtovsky (1867–1959), and houses the **USSR State Committee for Foreign Travel** (the Intourist), and the **Intourist Travel Bureau** which arranges travel for foreign tourists to the USSR and for Soviet tourists going abroad. One of the world's biggest travel agencies, Intourist cooperates with over 700 travel firms and transport organizations in almost every country of the world. Through *Intourist*, visitors can see all fifteen republics of the USSR. In Moscow, staffed by 1,300 guide-interpreters versed in every major language of the world, Intourist offers a great variety of interesting tours. These tours have been set up to help acquaint the tourist with as many diverse aspects of the city as possible, including its age-old history, cultural monuments of various epochs, and contemporary life. In addition to general tours of the city, there are optional, thematic tours, such as "Literary Moscow", with visits to memorial museums of the great Russian writers Lev Tolstoy, Dostoyevsky and Chekhov; "Moscow and Sport", with a look at the unique sports buildings and complexes built for the 1980 Olympic Games; "The Moscow Metro", with a tour through the underground halls whose architecture delights and amazes everyone, and in summer there is "Moscow From Aboard a Motor Ship", a tour along the city's "blue thoroughfare". Specialized tourism has greatly expanded in Moscow over recent years. In addition to acquainting the tourist with the major sights and places of interest, the special tours program includes visits to various businesses and factories, scientific establishments, higher educational institutions, hospitals and schools.

The traditional festivals of Soviet art, the **Moscow Stars festivals** (May 5–13), and the **Russian Winter festival** (December 25–January 5) are events which enjoy great popularity each year. Special Intourist tours provide visitors from abroad with a unique opportunity to become participants in a great event—a parade of stars of Soviet arts. Moscow theaters stage their finest productions, and for each festival there are premier performances at which talented new actors and actresses demonstrate their art alongside renowned masters and artists of world-wide fame. The festivals' programs encompass every facet of the arts, including opera, drama, ballet, circus performances and variety shows. The "Russian Winter" festival coincides with the celebration of the New Year, with outdoor festivities in Moscow's gardens and parks, *troika* rides, traditional folk games and entertainments on the snow-covered grounds of *VDNKh* (the USSR Economic Achievements Exhibition), and dances around the decorated green firs—Muscovites celebrate the New Year with great cheer.

Also included in the programs are visits to Intourist's cultural centers and the sampling of Russian cuisine in the best restaurants of the city. The visitor can also sample a wide variety of dishes from Ukrainian, Byelorussian, Uzbek, and Georgian cuisine.

Marx Avenue merges here with an enormous square, *ploshchad Pyatidesyatiletiya Oktyabrya* (50th Anniversary of the October Revolution Square). The 2-meter-high granite slab in the center of the square was laid out on the eve of the 50th anniversary of the Revolution, as the site of a future monument.

From Intourist House there is a splendid view of the Kremlin. Just beyond it, on the other side of a forecourt, is one of the **old buildings of the Lomonosov Moscow University**, with two wings overlooking Marx Avenue. A gently curved dome rises up above its Doric colonnade. The smooth surface of its walls and portico, and its precise geometric proportions are all characteristic of Russian Classicism. Built in 1786-93 by architect Matvei Kazakov, the building was destroyed in the great fire of 1812, and was restored and partially altered in 1819 by architect Domenico Gigliardi (1788-1845). Gigliardi contributed much to the rebuilding of Moscow after the fire, and left behind a number of architectural masterpieces.

In the forecourt are **statues of Alexander Herzen and Nikolai Ogaryov**, Russian revolutionary thinkers and former students of the University, both sculpted by Nikolai Andreyev. Moscow University was always a powerful source of knowledge and enlightenment in Russia. It was here that progressive democratic culture and science evolved in the persistent and difficult struggle against the tsarist government. Moscow University was the *alma mater* of many of the young aristocrats who attempted a coup d'état against the tsar, the Decembrist revolt of 1825. Some of these are: Ivan Yakushkin, Nikolai Turgenev, Alexander and Nikita Muravyov; literary critic and philosopher Vissarion Belinsky, writers Mikhail Lermontov, Alexander Griboyedov, Alexander Goncharov, Alexander Ostrovsky, Ivan Turgenev, Anton Chekhov; men of the theater, Vladimir Nemirovich-Danchenko and Yevgeny Vakhtan-

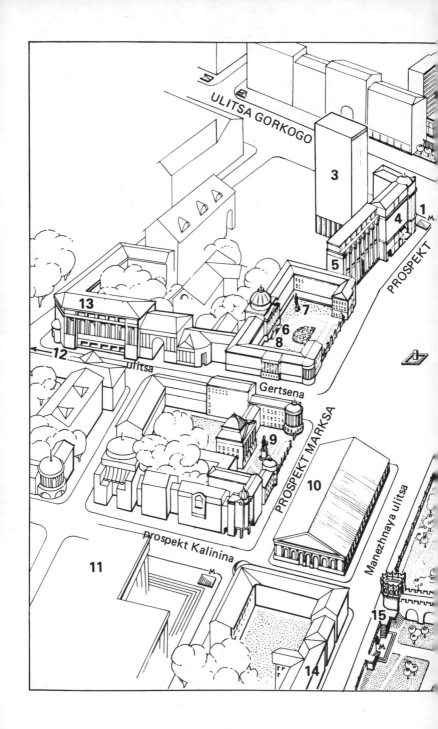

ULITSA GORKOGO

3

1
M

4

5

PROSPEKT

13

7

6

8

12

ulitsa

Gertsena

9

PROSPEKT MARKSA

10

Manezhnaya ulitsa

prospekt Kalinina

11

M

15

M

14

MARX AVENUE

*The Lomonosov University (old premises).
Architectural details (bottom left)*

Two old university buildings, one on each corner, mark the beginning of the street, which bears a curious mixture of structures representing 18th- and 19th-century architectural styles. There are monuments of architecture and history at each step of the way along this street, now under state protection which bears the name of the great Russian revolutionary, philosopher and writer, Alexander Herzen (1812–70), who was born in Moscow and lived here for half of his life. On the right, at No. 6, is the **Zoological Museum**, one of the largest scientific research and educational institutions in the world. Located on the left at Nos. 11 and 13 Herzen Street are the buildings of the **Tchaikovsky State Conservatoire.** Founded in 1866, the conservatoire has always played a leading role in the musical life of Moscow and the country as a whole. Its school for composers and the performing arts has received world-wide acclaim. Pyotr Tchaikovsky taught at the conservatoire for twelve years. The great composer's name is closely linked to Moscow, and it was here that premier performances of most of his works were staged. The conservartoire prepares composers, conductors, musical performers, singers, and music historians and theorists.

The conservatoire building was originally a part of the mansion of Princess Ekaterina Dashkova (1743–1810), the first woman director of the St. Petersburg

gov; and revolutionary Leninists Nikolai Semashko, Sergei Mitskevich, Ivan Rusakov, and Dmitry Ulyanov.

When the new university complex on the Lenin Hills was built in 1953 most of the departments were transferred there.

And now a few words about *ulitsa Gertsena* (Herzen Street).

Academy of Sciences and President of the Russian Academy — a scholarly center for the study of the Russian language and philology, founded at her insistence in 1783. It was rebuilt in the 1880s by architect Vasily Zagorsky, and now boasts two concert halls, the Bolshoi and Maly. Outside the main entrance stands a **statue of Pyotr Tchaikovsky**, which was unveiled in 1954. A set of railings behind the statue is modelled in the form of notes of six musical phrases from the composer's works, and bear his monogram and the date of his birth and death (1840-93). One line is taken from his most popular opera, *Eugene Onegin*, a second from *Swan Lake*, the composer's

Tchaikovsky Conservatoire

most famous ballet, a third from his last symphony, the Sixth, or *Pathétique*, a fourth, from the first quartet, based on themes from a folk song, a fifth, from a concert for violin and orchestra, and a sixth, from a romance.

Each year in early May a Song festival is held which traditionally starts off at the statue of Tchaikovsky with a large choir and brass band composed of professionals and amateurs.

On the corner of the next block is the **Mayakovsky Theater.** Herzen Street runs into *ploshchad Nikitskikh vorot* (Nikitskiye Gates Square). Although the gates have long been dismantled, the square still bears their name. To the left of the square runs *Suvorovsky bulvar* (Suvorov Boulevard), and to the right — *Tverskoy bulvar* (Tver Boulevard), on which two theaters are located: the **Peoples' Friendship Theater**, and the **Pushkin Drama Theater.** Tverskoy Boulevard leads out onto Pushkin Square and Gorky Street. On the corner of

Statue of Alexander Herzen

Statue of Pyotr Tchaikovsky

Herzen Street and Tverskoy Boulevard is the **building of the Telegraph Agency of the Soviet Union (TASS).** At the beginning of the boulevard is a **statue of Kliment Timiryazev** (1843–1920), one of the founders of the Russian school of plant physiology, and one of the first advocates of Darwinism and scientific materialism in Russia. The work of sculptor Sergei Merkurov, the monument was erected in 1923. Across from Nikitskiye Gates Square is the **Church of the Ascension** (1827–40), attributed to architect Afanasy Grigoryev. Alexander Pushkin was wed here on February 18, 1831. It is said that Pushkin entered the church in good spirits, but during the ring ceremony, one of the rings fell to the floor. Pushkin turned pale and while leaving the church said: *"Tous les mauvais augurs."* The wedding crowns which were held over the heads of the poet and his bride in the Church of the Ascen-

sion have been preserved, and are on display in the Kremlin Armoury Chamber.

Opposite the church to the right (No. 6/2 *ulitsa Kachalova*) is the two-storey **Gorky Museum.** It was here that the writer spent the last five years of his life, from 1931–36. The mansion was built in 1902 in the Moderne style by the famous architect Fyodor Shekhtel, who designed a great number of noteworthy structures at the turn of the century in Moscow.

If you continue along Herzen Street, you will come out onto a large square, *ploshchad Vosstaniya* (Uprising Square). Looming above

*Set of railings behind
the statue of Tchaikovsky. Detail*

Mayakovsky Drama Theater

the **Central Institute of Advanced Medical Training.**

Uprising Square is one of many squares along the Garden Ring. If you turn off Herzen Street to the right and walk a distance of about 150 meters, you will have the pleasant opportunity of visiting the place where the world renowned Russian writer Anton Chekhov (1860-1904) lived. Today this two-storey house seems a bit whimsical and out of place on this busy Moscow street. Chekhov lived here with his parents from 1886-90, the period during which some of his best works were written. Over one hundred short stories, the novella *The Steppe*, the drama *Ivanov*, the first of his works to be staged, and the one-act farces *The Bear, The Propos-*

the square is a twenty-two-storey building, one of Moscow's so called high-rise buildings, which was built in 1950-54 by architects Mikhail Posokhin and Ashot Mndoyants. This is a residential building. To the right of the small garden in front of the high-rise is a yellow, two-storey-building which is quite imposing in appearance. Built in 1775 by architect Ivan Gigliardi it was rebuilt repeatedly over the years. In 1823 Gigliardi's son, architect Dementy Gigliardi added details of the Empire style to the architecture, and thus it has remained to the present day. This splendid relic of Russian architecture is known as the **Vdovy dom** (Widows' Home), and now houses

Building of TASS (Telegraph Agency of the Soviet Union)

al and *The Wedding*, were all written in the ground-flour study of the mansion. The **Chekhov House-Museum** was opened here in 1954.

If you enter the study you will see the writer's desk, which stands far from the windows since Chekhov always wrote by candlelight. On the desk are a marble inkwell with a bronze horse, candleholders in the shape of dragons, a sheet of manuscript and photographs bearing the autographs of close friends. Other furnishings include a couch, bookshelves, and a small cupboard with medical supplies. Every now and then Doctor Chekhov would set aside his literary pursuits and receive patients in this study...

Two large rooms have been set aside for a literary exposition presenting the first editions of Chekhov's works. Evenings of music and literature and meetings with admirers of the famous writer are held in the museum's concert hall.

Chekhov loved Moscow, and in one of his letters wrote: "...I miss Moscow. I miss the people, and the Moscow newspapers, and the ringing of bells, which I love so much."

Let us return now to Marx Avenue. Crossing Herzen Street you will see another old building of **Moscow University**, built in 1836 by architect Yevgraf Tyurin. In front of the building is a **statue of Mikhail Lomonosov**, the University's founder and the incarnation of the Russian folk genius. "Combining unusual will-power and an unusual power of perception," Pushkin wrote of him, "Lomonosov

embraced all the branches of enlightenment. Thirst for science was the strongest passion of this ardent soul. Historian, rhetorician, mechanic, chemist, mineralogist, artist and poet, he tried everything and penetrated everything." The statue, executed by sculptor Ivan Kozlovsky in 1957, replaces one destroyed by a fascist bomb in 1941.

Opposite the University buildings, on the left of Marx Avenue, is a massive building decorated with plaster friezes and eighty half-columns which fills one entire block. This superb monument of Russian architecture reflecting the Empire style of the first third of the 19th century is the **Manège.**

The Manège was built in 1817 to the design and under the supervision of Augustin de Bethencourt (1758-1824). Of Spanish descent, Bethencourt helped to design many important works in Russia during the 16 years he was employed there. Its unique suspension roof supported by wooden girders nearly 45 meters across was considered at the time an example of great engineering and construction skills. The Manège is 166 meters long. The architect Osip Bovet (1784-1834) was responsible for the building's decorative work. Bovet played a major role in the architectural layout of the center of Moscow.

Originally the Manège was used for military parades and exercises. It was spacious enough to accommodate an infantry regiment of two

High-rise building. Uprising Square

thousand soldiers. Beginning in 1831 the Manège began to be used for exhibitions and various festive occasions. In 1867 a concert for choir and orchestra (about 700 persons) conducted by French composer Hector Berlioz drew a crowd of 12,000 spectators. In 1957 after major reconstruction (in 1940 the wooden rafters were replaced by metal ones), the **Central Exhibition Hall** was opened here, which houses major Soviet and international art exhibitions.

The next street, leading off to the right from Marx Avenue, is *prospekt Kalinina* (Kalinin Avenue). In the building to the right on the corner of the two avenues are the reception rooms of the presidiums of the Supreme Soviets of the USSR and RSFSR. For twenty-seven years the prominent Soviet statesman and Communist Party worker Mikhail Kalinin (1875–1946) worked in this building.

Now we suggest that you slow your pace and take time to enjoy the truly impressive view from this corner of the Troitskaya Tower and Kremlin walls, the Kutafya Tower, and the Palace of Congresses.

The whole of the next block, to the end of Marx Avenue, is taken up by the **Lenin State Library.** The new library building on the corner was built by Vladimir Shchuko and Vladimir Gelfreikh in 1940. A portico of tall pylons joins the library's two side wings and serves as a monumental frame for the main entrance. In front of the building is a broad terrace and flights of steps. On the Marx Avenue side the façade is adorned with busts of great scientists and writers and sculptures of a male and female worker,

Building of the former Manège

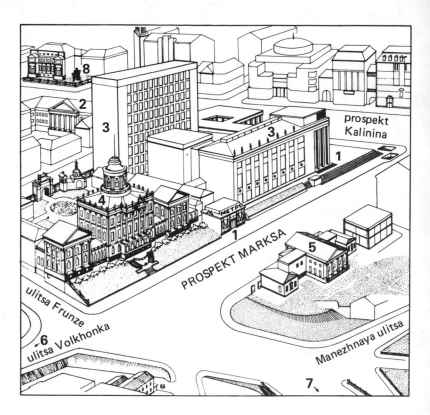

MARX AVENUE

(continued)

1. *Biblioteka imeni Lenina and Borovitskaya Metro stations. Kalininskaya Metro Station*
2. *Shchusev Museum of Architecture*
3. *Lenin State Library*
4. *Pashkov House*
5. *Mikhail Kalinin Museum*
6. *To Pushkin Museum of Fine Arts*
7. *To Tretyakov Gallery*
8. *Statue of Mikhail Kalinin*

a peasant, a scholar, and a student. Visible behind the main library complex is a 19-storey book repository. Adjoining the new complex is the library's old building, the **Pashkov House** (named after its original owner), one of the finest examples of Russian Classical architecture of the second half of the 18th century. It was built from 1784–86 by the great Russian architect Vasily Bazhenov (1737/8–99), one of Moscow's leading architects and city-planners. Together with his close assistant, Matvei Kazakov, Bazhenov was the creator of the Moscow Classical style of architecture of the 18th and first quarter of the 19th centuries. Unfortunately, there are only a small number of Bazhenov's authentic works in Moscow. The Pashkov House is the finest of these. It is a typical example of a private noble house of that period. It is situated on the top of a high hill facing the Kremlin. Two four-column side wings emphasize the central block, with its formal flight of steps, high portico, and belvedere. During the 1970s the structures situated between the Pashkov House and the Kremlin were torn down, thus opening up a beautiful panorama: high on a green hillside rises a gracious, white-stone palace, a masterpiece of Russian architecture.

The Lenin Library is the central library of the country and one of the world's largest. It is a bibliographical institution covering all fields of knowledge, and a research institute in the fields of bibliography and librarianship. When the library was founded in 1862 it held over 100,000 volumes, and was then located in the old Pashkov House. In 1915 its one reading room had a seating capacity of only 170. Lenin worked in this room in 1893 and 1897. After the Revolution the library became a major cultural and educational institution. It now has 22 reading rooms with a seating capacity of 2,500, and a book fund of 31 million volumes in 247 of the world's languages. Every day the library responds to 12,000 book search requests.

In a small house on the left side of Marx Avenue is the **Kalinin Museum.** Its exhibits tell of the life and work of Mikhail Kalinin, Lenin's devoted pupil and comrade-in-arms. The son of a peasant, for almost 30 years he held the post of Chairman of the All-Russia Central Executive Committee, and later was appointed Chairman of the Presidium of the Supreme Soviet of the USSR.

When you reach the corner of *ulitsa Frunze* (Frunze Street) you will have covered the entire length of Marx Avenue. We suggest that you now cross over to the Borovitskaya Tower of the Kremlin and walk back through the Aleksandrovsky Gardens to the Ploshchad Revolutsii Metro Station. But if you are tired, you can return to your hotel by Metro from the Biblioteka imeni Lenina or Borovitskaya Metro stations.

Alternatively, if you have time,

Mikhail Kalinin Museum

it would be better to continue your excursion and visit either the Tretyakov Gallery or the Pushkin Museum of Fine Arts (which is not far from where you finished your walk along Marx Avenue). You can get to the Tretyakov Gallery (No. 10 *Lavrushinsky pereulok*) by taking a "K" bus, which stops near the intersection of Marx and Kalinin avenues. You must get off at the third stop, which is called "Lavrushinsky pereulok". For the Pushkin Museum (No. 12 *ulitsa Volkhonka*) it is better to walk, as it is only ten minutes further along on Volkhonka Street.

The **State Tretyakov Gallery** *(Tretyakovskaya Galereya)* is situated in a quiet side-street on the other side of the river and the bypass canal, opposite the Kremlin.

The Tretyakov Gallery is famous throughout the entire Soviet Union. It was founded as a city museum in 1892. Its founder, Pavel Tretyakov (1832-98), a Moscow merchant, began collecting the finest works of Russian artists in 1856. Thirthy-six years later, when he had collected 1,200 paintings and several hundred sculptures and works of graphic art, he presented the whole collection to the city of Moscow. Today the Tretyakov Gallery has over 6,000 canvases, more than 3,000 icons and works of early Russian art, over 1,000 sculptures, and 30,000 drawings, watercolours, and engravings.

The gallery building—Tretyakov's former home—was rebuilt in the traditional Russian style, and resembles a Russian terem. The building's façade was refaced in 1902 to the design of Victor Vasnetsov, and gives it an intricate, bright, rather fairyland appearance. Moscow's old coat of arms **St. George Slaying the Dragon**, occupies a prominent position on the upper central section of the façade. In recent years the gallery has undergone major renovation and reconstruction work which is scheduled to be completed in 1990. It has received additional space for new exhibits, and a special depository has been built which is equipped with the most modern lighting and temperature and humidity regulating devices.

The Tretyakov Gallery is country's treasure-house of the fine arts, and its collection reflects the whole history of Russian and Soviet art, from 11th century mosaics and icons to the most important works of contemporary Soviet artists. The collection of early Russian art includes icons by the brilliant artist

Andrei Rublev (*circa* 1360-1430), the outstanding masters Theophanes the Greek (*circa* 1340-after 1405) and Dionysius (*circa* 1440-after 1502/3), and Simon Ushakov (1626-86).

The gallery has many interesting 18th-century works by such artists as Alexei Antropov, Fyodor Rokotov, Dmitry Levitsky, and Vladimir Borovikovsky. Russian art of the first half of the 19th century is also well represented, and includes among other things Orest Kiprensky's portrait of Pushkin, Vasily Tropinin's *Lace-maker*, Karl Bryullov's *Horsewoman*, and Alexander Ivanov's *The Appearance of Christ Before the People*, to which the artist dedicated over 20 years of his life.

The works of the second half of the 19th century occupy the central position in the gallery. Fully represented is the rich legacy of works of the *peredvizhniki* (Itinerants), a democratic union of artists called the "Society of travelling art exhibitions" which was formed in 1870. Practically every leading realist painter in the country belonged to the society, which set itself the task of creating highly progressive art for the people. The works of these artists enjoyed wide popularity and fame due to the broad exposure they received as the exhibitions moved from town to town.

Among the more notable of these works are Vasily Perov's *Tea-drinking in Mytishchi*, Grigory Myasoyedov's *Zemstvo at Dinner*, Nikolai Yaroshenko's *Life All Around*,

Vladimir Makovsky's *On the Boulevard*, and Vasily Polenov's *A Moscow Backyard*. All these works are a unique pictorial encyclopedia of Russian life during that period. We also recommend that you devote your attention to the canvases of Ivan Kramskoy *(Portrait of Lev Tolstoy)*, Alexei Savrasov *(The Rooks Return)*, Ivan Aivazovsky *(Black Sea)*, Konstantin Savitsky *(Repair Work on the Railroad)*, Ivan Shishkin *(Rye)*, Arkhip Kuindzhi *(Birch Grove)*, and Vasily Vereshchagin *(General Skobelev at Shipka Pass)*.

Special rooms are devoted to the workes of such outstanding artists as Ilya Repin *(Procession in the Kursk Province, Barge Haulers on the Volga, They Did not Expect Him, Ivan the Terrible and His Son Ivan*, and *Self-portrait)*, and Vasily Surikov *(Morning of the Streltsy Execution, Boyarina Morozova,* and *Menshikov in Beriozovo)*. Among works by artists of the beginning of the century are Valentin Serov's *Girl with Peaches,* Mikhail Vrubel's *Pan*, and Nikolai Kasatkin's *The Woman Miner.*

In 1986 the gallery's collection of Soviet art was transferred to the USSR State Picture Gallery on *Krymskaya naberezhnaya* (Crimean Embankment), where it was provided with spacious new quarters capable of accommodating the entire collection. The new exposition is located at No. 10 Crimean Embankment, and is near both the Oktyabrskaya and Park Kultury Metro stations. We will describe it in greater detail during our excursion along Lenin Avenue.

As the gallery is visited by around 4,000 people daily, you would be well advised to book a group excursion in advance, through the Service Bureau of your hotel. This will enable you to get in without a long wait in line. The Metro station nearest to the gallery is **Tretyakovskaya.**

The **State Pushkin Museum of Fine Arts** is at No. 12 *ulitsa Volkhonka* (Volkhonka Street), one of Moscow's old streets, about a ten minutes' walk from either Biblioteka imeni Lenina or Kropotkinskaya Metro stations. The museum has a marvellous collection which attracts both Soviet visitors to the capital and those from abroad. Many come to Moscow expressly to visit this museum.

Beyond low wrought-iron railings and a line of blue spruces rises the imposing building of the museum with its high portico and glass roof. Twenty-four columns of light grey granite adorn the façade. This is one of the country's finest museum buildings. It was built in the neo-Classical style, much like an ancient Greek temple, by Roman Klein in 1912 to house a museum of fine arts which was founded on the initiative of Professor Ivan Tsvetayev, the father of the famous Russian poetess Marina Tsvetayeva. Since 1937 it has been known as the Pushkin Museum of Fine Arts. It has one of the world's largest collections (second in the USSR only to the Hermitage in Leningrad) of the ancient orien-

tal, Classical and Western European arts.

The collection has been considerably extended in Soviet times. The additions include many valuable works acquired from other Soviet museums and private collections, and interesting new finds discovered during archaeological expeditions sponsored by the museum.

The museum's Egyptian department has one of the world's largest collections of ancient papyruses, *objets d'art*, bas-reliefs, painted sarcophagi, Fayum portraits and Coptic fabrics.

In addition to replicas of all the most famous sculptures of ancient Greece and Rome, there are also original Greek and Etruscan terracottas and vases, and Classical sculptures.

The pride of the museum is its rich collection of Byzantine, Italo-Cretan, and Italian icons.

The picture gallery has over 2,000 works of various schools of painting. Among the masterpieces exhibited are pictures by Italian masters of the Renaissance (Botticelli, Perugino and Veronese, among others) and the 17th-18th centuries; fine pictures by artists of the Netherlands school (15th-16th centuries), the German, English and Spanish schools (15th-19th centuries), and by 17th-century Dutch and Flemish masters.

There is a particularly comprehensive collection of French paintings of the 17th-20th centuries, including works by Poussin, Chardin,

State Pushkin Museum of Fine Arts

Delacroix, Corot, Courbet, Sézanne, Matisse, Van Gogh, and Picasso, and an outstanding collection of French Impressionists (Monet, Pissarro, Renoir, and Degas).

The museum's collection of modern works includes paintings by the American artists Rockwell Kent, the Italian artist Renato Guttuso, the German Expressionist Hans Grundig, and the Czech and Slovak masters Antonin Prochazka and Josef Čapek.

The Pushkin Museum periodically holds exhibitions of the art of various countries and of individual outstanding artists of past and present. Among these there have been special exhibitions of the Tutankhamun treasures from Egypt, and of Leonardo da Vinci's world-famous *Mona Lisa*. In the past

several years alone masterpieces from the Louvre, the Prado, the Dresden Picture Gallery, and the leading museums of Austria, the United States, and other countries have been displayed in the museum. The museum also carries out extensive research into the world's heritage of art, and maintains contacts with the biggest museums and galleries of the world.

Since the early 1980s the museum has become widely known among devotees of music for its musical concerts held every December. The organizers of these "December Evenings" are Irina Antonova, Director of the Pushkin Museum of Fine Arts, and the outstanding Soviet pianist Svyatoslav Richter, one of the world's most famous contemporary musicians. Exhibitions based on themes corresponding to the musical programs are held at the same time as the concerts. This synthesis of the arts creates a unique atmosphere which fosters a better appreciation of both realms of art, and a new and

"December Evenings" in the Museum of Fine Arts

better understanding of the cultures of various periods and various peoples. These musical concerts last the entire month, and are made accessible through radio and television to an audience of many million people.

The "December Evenings" have acquired an international character. Assistance in setting up the art exhibitions has been provided by museums of England, the GDR, France, and Poland, and performers from Switzerland, the United States, England, Hungary, Yugoslavia, Ecuador and other countries have participated in the musical programs. One of the programs presented a premier performance of the opera *Albert Herring* by the contemporary English composer Benjamin Britten. The musical impressions were augmented by an exhibition of portrait paintings of 16th–19th century English artists, organized with the cooperation of various London museums. Performances by famous musicians from abroad has already become a traditional part of the "December Evenings".

To the right of the museum building on a quiet, narrow side-street (No. 4 *ulitsa Marshala Shaposhnikova*), is a modest relic of Moscow Classicism, a two-storey 19th-century house with an attic and a balcony with an openwork railing. The **museum's collections of graphic art and engravings** are housed here. A few steps further along is another architectural monument—the **Church of St. Antipy**

built in the first half of the 16th century. The bell-tower and refectory adjoining it and the side-chapel were all added on in the 18th century. The church underwent restoration work in 1984 and the whole complex was passed over to the Pushkin Museum.

Behind the Pushkin Museum at No. 5 *ulitsa Marksa i Engelsa* (Marx and Engels Street) is another museum which is visited frequently by guests from abroad. This is the **Marx and Engels Museum**, located on the first floor of the main house of a typical 18th-century town estate with a garden. The museum was opened in May 1962 and its materials (in its archives are over 100,000 separate items) illustrate the revolutionary activity of Marx and Engels against the broad backdrop of the international workers' and Communist movement. Around 4,000 exhibits are on display in the museum's 9 rooms, including original manuscripts of Marx and Engels, first editions of their works printed in their lifetime, the world's largest collection of photographs of Marx and Engels and their associates, a unique collection of their personal belongings, and works of art devoted to their life and activity.

At the entrance to the museum is a sculptural composition by the Ukrainian sculptors Evgeny Belostotsky and Yuri Fridman. Carved in a large block of granite are the images of the great thinkers and revolutionaries, Marx and Lenin.

On display in the first room of

the museum are models of the house in Trier in which Karl Marx (1818–83) was born, and the house in Barmen in which Friedrich Engels (1820–95) was born. Also of interest is a model of Marx's study in London, at No. 1 Maitland Park Road, where he lived from March 1864 through March 1875.

In glass show-cases in the fifth room are personal objects which belonged to Marx and Engels, family members and close friends. Among the relics donated to the museum by Marx's relatives in 1939 are a locket with a portrait of Marx and a lock of his wife's hair preserved by Marx's daughter, Jenny Longuet. Also on display is the armchair in which Karl Marx spent the last minutes of his life.

In the seventh room is an extensive collection of documents dealing with the activities of Marx and Engels as leaders of the International Workingmen's Association — the first mass international proletarian organization (the First International), as well as manuscripts in which Marx draws general conclusions from the heroic struggle of the Paris Commune of 1871. Two red banners once belonging to the Paris Commune are also displayed here. One is a banner of the Basel section of the First International which was presented to the CPSU by the Swiss Labor Party on the centenary of its founding. The other, a banner of the 67th Battalion of the Paris Commune, was a gift to the CPSU from French Communists. On the wall

Karl Marx and Friedrich Engels Museum

of this room are Marx's famous words: "...in contrast to old society, with its economical miseries and its political delirium, a new society is springing up, whose international rule will be Peace, because its national rules will be everywhere the same—Labor!"

On display in the eighth room are highly interesting documents which show how deeply interested Marx and Engels were in the history, economy, and culture of Russia.

Before leaving the museum, we would direct your attention to the plaster model of the monument to Karl Marx at the Highgate Cemetery in London. Sculpted by Lawrence Bradshaw and erected with funds provided by workers of various countries, the monument was unveiled on March 14, 1956.

A little further along Volkhonka Street from the Pushkin Museum, on the left-hand side, is the heated open-air *Moskva* **Swimming Pool.** Constructed in 1960, the pool is a circular basin 130 meters in diameter. It is equipped to accommodate

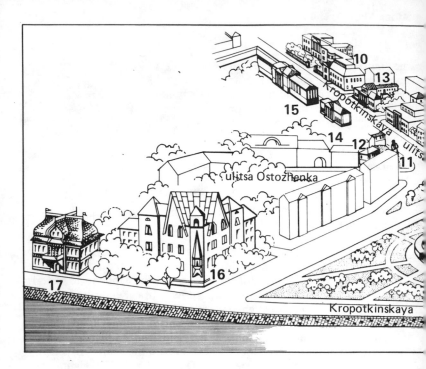

VOLKHONKA AND KROPOTKINSKAYA STREETS

1. *Pushkin Museum of Fine Arts*
2. *Fine Arts Museum. Graphic Art Section*
3. *Church of St. Antipy*
4. *Marx and Engels Museum*
5. Moskva *swimming pool*
6. *Kropotkinskaya Metro Station*
7. *Exhibition Hall of the USSR Union of Artists*
8. *Central Chess Club of the USSR*
9. *Soviet War Veterans' Committee*
10. *Scientists' House*
11. *Statue of Friedrich Engels*

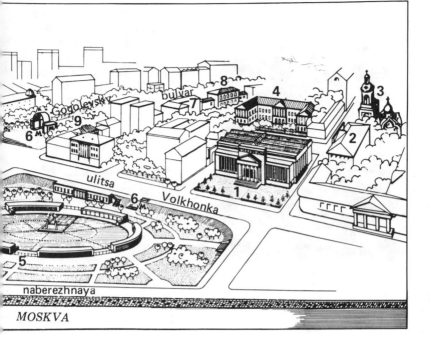

ulitsa

bulvar

Gogolevsky

Volkhonka

naberezhnaya

MOSKVA

House No. 29 Kropotkinskaya Embankment

bankments. At No. 29 *Kropotkinskaya naberezhnaya* (Kropotkin Embankment), about a 10 minutes' walk from your present location, is a memorable spot much revered by Muscovites. This is a two-storey building which stands out among its surroundings with its high roof, large balcony, and decorative details in the spirit of old Russian architecture. During World War II it housed the French Military Mission. There is a memorial plaque on the building with an inscription. Inscribed on yet another plaque are the names of 42 pilots fallen in battle, members of the "Normandie-Niémen" Squadron of the fighter group "Fighting France". In 1943–45 this group fought at the Soviet-German front, and its pilots took part in 869 air battles, and shot down around 300 German aircraft. For their distinguished services in battle, courage and heroism, 80 French officer pilots were decorated with Soviet orders and medals, and four of them awarded the title of Hero of the Soviet Union. You can reach this **building-monument of the Soviet-French military alliance** in the fight against fascism by taking *Soimonovky proeyzd* (Soimonov Passage), which connects *Kropotkinskaya naberezhnaya* (Kropotkin Embankment) with *Kropotkinskaya ploshchad* (Kropotkin Square).

both those who just wish to relax or exercise for an hour or two, and serious sportsmen who come there to train. There is a high diving board and a special 50-meter section marked with 8 swimming courses. In the sports training section the pool reaches a depth of 6 meters. For small children there are five shallow wading pools with running water. These pools are only 40 centimeters deep. The *Moskva* Swimming Pool is open the year round, and the water temperature is never lower than 27 °C, regardless of the temperature outside. The water is changed three times daily.

We suggest that you pause for a few minutes on the observation area overlooking the swimming pool to take in the panoramic view of the Moskva River and its em-

Volkhonka Street ends at the junction with *Gogolevsky bulvar* (Gogol Boulevard). At the beginning of boulevard is the **Kropotkinskaya Metro Station.** Gogol

Boulevard is the first of a series of boulevards forming the horse-shoe shaped Boulevard Ring which encompasses the center of the city. This is a favorite relaxation spot for Muscovites, who come here from all corners of the city to enjoy the shade of the lindens, poplars, and maples, and the beautifully tended flower gardens which line the quiet, peaceful avenues. Here pensioners often gather to reminisce about the past, exchange news, and to play dominos, checkers and chess. Many children also gather here to play. The boulevard connects Kropotkin Square with Arbat Square. At the end of the boulevard is a statue of the famous writer, Nikolai Gogol, which we will discuss in greater detail in the next chapter.

A walk along Gogol Boulevard offers many fascinating things to see. You will notice that the right side of the boulevard is considerably higher than the left. This is the remains of an earthen rampart built at the end of the 14th century on the edge of a deep ravine. The boulevard (formerly Prechistensky Boulevard) was laid out approximately 180 years ago on the site of ancient defence works which formed a mighty brick wall with gate-way towers. Along the left-hand side of the boulevard are primarily 5-6-storey apartment buildings constructed in the late 19th and early 20th centuries. The houses lining the right-hand side were built one century earlier, in the late 18th and early 19th centuries.

On the corner of Volkhonka Street and Gogol Boulevard is a three-storey building which presently houses the **Russian Language Institute of the USSR Academy of Sciences.** Before the Revolution this building housed a grammar school where, during the 1830s, the future playwright, Alexander Ostrovsky, studied (a statue of Ostrovsky, you may remember, stands at the entrance to the Maly Theater). At No. 4 Gogol Boulevard is the **Soviet War Veterans' Committee.** Meetings and various activities are held here for World War II veterans, fighters of the anti-fascist Resistance, former prisoners of Nazi concentration camps, representatives of anti-war organizations and veterans' associations from all over the world. The Soviet War Veterans' Committee devotes its activities to the strengthening of peace, total and universal disarmament, and the prevention of a nuclear war. The Committee maintains close ties with national veterans' organizations of other countries.

A bit further along Gogol Boulevard, at No. 8, is a noteworthy building which houses the **Exhibition Hall of the USSR Journalists' Union.** In addition to the permanent exposition on the history of Russian and Soviet photojournalism housed here, the Exhibition Hall regularly conducts international photographic exhibitions ("Interpress Photo"). Next to the Exhibition Hall, at No. 10, is a house with a six-column portico built at the end of the 18th century. On the building's façade are two memorial plaques. The first bears a symbolic representation of chains and a laurel wreath, and the inscription: "In this house in the early 1820s gathered members of the secret society of Decembrists". The owner of the house at that time was Colonel Mikhail Naryshkin (1798-1863), who was sentenced to eight years of hard labor for his participation in the conspiracy against the tsar. The second plaque commemorates the fact that the Russian writer Ivan Turgenev (1818-83) was a frequent guest of this house. At present this building houses the **governing body of the Union of Artists of the USSR.**

Another monument of the past is the building at No. 14 Gogol Boulevard, which presently houses the **Central Chess Club of the USSR.** Here chess fans, both young and old, gather to match wits with renowned Soviet masters with world-famous reputations. This house was built in 1822-26, and changed owners many times up until the Revolution. For a period of time it belonged to patroness of the arts, Nadezhda von Meck (1831-94), who exchanged correspondence with composer Pyotr Tchaikovsky for many years. The house was totally restored in 1980.

This brings us to the end of Gogol Boulevard. If you like, you may return to your hotel by Metro from the Arbatskaya Metro Station (entrance on Kalinin Avenue).

Kropotkin Square marks the end of Volkhonka Street and the beginning of Ostozhenka and Kropotkin streets. A **statue of Friedrich Engels,** by Ivan Kozlovsky, stands at the spot where they diverge. Unveiled in 1976, the 6-meter-high bronze sculpture is mounted upon a red granite pedestal. We would also note that Marx Avenue and Volkhonka Street unite the monuments to the two great thinkers— Karl Marx (statue on Sverdlov Square) and Friedrich Engels (statue on Kropotkin Square).

We will continue our walk along *Kropotkinskaya ulitsa* (Kropotkin Street), on which there is much worthy of attention. In the 16th century Kropotkin Street was known as Prechistenka, and was the road which led from the Kremlin to the Novodevichy Convent.

This is the region of old Moscow in which the Moscow nobility built its palaces, estates and mansions after the fire of 1812. Many of these buildings have been preserved, and nowhere else in the city are there so many wonderful monuments of architecture in the Russian Empire style. If you were to drive along Kropotkin Street, you would be struck by the great number of white colonnades dating back to the late 18th and early 19th centuries. But in order to truly enjoy the marvelous buildings, small picturesque blocks with green courtyards, you must make the excursion on foot. A walk along this street, one of the city's nine preserved zones mentioned earlier, is more than an excursion into the past. In addition to seeing interesting 18th- and 19th-century architectural works, you will discover much here that is connected with the lives of many famous Russian people. This is the Moscow of Pushkin and Griboyedov, the nest of the gentry, above which hovered the freedom-loving spirit of the Decembrists, many of whom lived on this street.

We will begin our walk at the **statue of Engels.** From here you must walk uphill, but after that the street will level out. At the beginning of the street on the right-hand side is an **ancient 17th-century palace** with thick brick walls, and narrow arched windows with grillework and fanciful white-stone surrounds. Recently completed restoration work has returned this palace to its original appearance. For long years their architectural originality lay hidden beneath layers of alterations. At No. 10, at the top of the hill on the right, is a twostorey mansion which houses the headquarters of a number of public organizations, including the **Soviet Peace Fund**, the **Soviet Afro-Asian Solidarity Committee**, and others.

Built in the 1830s, this mansion belonged to the Decembrist Major-General Mikhail Orlov (1788-1842), and later on was one of the centers of the city's artistic life. Many talented Russian artists who would later become famous attended painting classes held in this mansion. This mansion is a splendid example of the Moscow Empire style. Its one-and-a-half-meter-thick outer walls, preserved brick and white-stone vaults, iron braces and large brick attest to the fact that 17th-century palace once formed part of it. Thus this mansion combines three centuries of history and two epochs of Russian architecture.

Just past this mansion is an old estate (No. 12) with a garden, a former manor-house, which is protected by the state as an interesting monument of 19th-century Russian architecture. It was built in 1814 by the noted Moscow architect Afanasy Grigoryev (1782-1868). A façade adorned with six columns faces out upon Kropotkin Street, while four pairs of elegant columns decorate the façade which faces on a side-street. The house is wooden, and stands on a high stone base, much like the old Russian structures. Built upon such an imposing foundation, the upper part of the two-storey house with its attic appears especially light and graceful. The balcony with the flight of stairs adjoining the garden is especially characteristic of estates in the outskirts of Moscow, particularly of the period. The interior of the house is strictly planned out. The wall panels, elegant ceiling paintings, and the symmetry of fire-places and mirrors all create the impression of solemnity and comfort. This house is strikingly characteristic of the epoch during which Pushkin lived.

Alexander Pushkin Museum

It is quite fitting then, that at this mansion which embodies the finest features of Russian architecture of the first third of the 19th century, is housed the **Alexander Pushkin Museum.** The museum was opened in 1961 and tells of Pushkin's life and literary career through exhibits which include manuscripts, household articles, works of art, and the poet's personal belongings. In the museum's recital hall you can hear Pushkin's works performed by famous readers, singers and musicians, and see films about the poet's life or based upon his works.

Opposite the museum, at No. 7 Kropotkin Street, is a large three-storey building with a memorial plaque. A bas-relief on the plaque depicts Red Guard soldiers firing upon the enemy. In October 1917 fierce battles were fought on the corner of Kropotkin Street. Revolutionary soldiers and Red Guard workers attacked and seized the White Guard Headquarters of the Moscow military district, which were housed in this building at the time.

Further along, at No. 16, set back in a courtyard behind the gates with two stone lions, is the *Dom uchenykh* (Scientists' House). This is a club of Moscow scientists, with a membership of over 5,000. The concert hall here is quite popular among Muscovites. This mansion was built at the end of the 18th century and underwent subsequent rebuilding, assuming its present appearance in 1910.

Across the street at No. 11 is a single-storey house with a six-column portico on a white-stone base. Built in 1822 by Afanasy Grigoryev, the architect who designed the mansion which houses the Alexander Pushkin Museum, the house is wooden with an imitation stone finish and decorative bas-reliefs. It is of especial value in that it has undergone very little alteration over the years, and both exterior and interior have been well preserved. Today it houses the **Lev**

Scientists' House

Tolstoy Museum, which began as a small exhibition organized in 1911 on the first anniversary of the great writer's death (1828-1910). In 1939 the Soviet Government decided to turn the museum into a repository of all the materials connected with the life and literary career of Lev Tolstoy. Today the museum's archives contain over 160,000 pages of the author's handwritten manuscripts, including literary works, diaries, notebooks and other documents. For each of several of his works there are as many as 10,000 pages of different edited versions, which testifies to the highly industrious and exacting nature of the great master. Works of art on display in the museum include portraits of Tolstoy drawn from life by such artists as Ilya Repin, Ivan Kramskoy, Nikolai Ghe, and others. There are also old phonographic records of Tolstoy's voice, and a rich collection of photographs and film reels preserving the image of the writer.

Continuing along Kropotkin Street, you will come to a house with a small front garden set back from the street (No. 17, on the left-hand side). Here lived the poet and hero of the Patriotic War of 1812, Denis Davydov (1784-1839). He served Tolstoy as the prototype of Denisov in *War and Peace*. A bit further along, at No. 19, is a large two-storey palatial building—the former residence of the Dolgoruky Princes, which was built in the 1780s and restored in 1837 after the great fire of 1812. Adjoining it,

Entrance to Lev Tolstoy Museum

at No. 21, is the building which houses **the USSR Academy of Arts**, built in the early 19th century. Here personal, commemorative **exhibitions** are held of the works of Soviet painters, sculptors and graphic artists.

On the right-hand side of the street, just beyond the Scientists' House is a green two-storey house (No. 20) with a rich sculptural decoration. In the 1920s it served as the studio of the famous American dancer Isadora Duncan (1878-1927), who lived here with her husband, the Russian poet Sergei Yesenin (1895-1925). Isadora Duncan came to Moscow in the summer of 1921 at the invitation of the Soviet Government. "Duncan was called 'the goddess of ges-

Lev Tolstoy Mansion-Museum

tures'", wrote Anatoly Luna-charsky, "but of all her gestures this last—her trip to revolutionary Russia despite all her fears and misgivings—is the most beautiful and deserves the loudest applause." Duncan remained in the USSR until 1924.

The building at No. 22 is also of historical interest. Before the Revolution it was a police-station, and in 1834 Alexander Herzen was held here under arrest.

Now that we have covered the entire length of Kropotkin Street (just over one kilometer), you will have noticed that somewhere midway along, many-storey buildings dating back to before the Revolution began to appear with increasing frequency. These housed furnished apartments which were rented out by their owners.

Kropotkin Street's quiet, peaceful charm is also something which you have probably not failed to notice; here there are no noisy crowds, and no large stores. There is, however, a certain store, quite

unique, which we recommend that you visit. This is the *Beriozka* **store** at No. 31, which sells books in Russian and other languages, photograph albums, picture postcards, guide-books, journals, and stamps. The *Beriozka* accepts only hard currency.

Kropotkin Street ends at the Garden Ring. Before continuing on, we would like to add that the street bears the name of Pyotr Kropotkin, (1842–1921), prince, Russian revolutionary, geographer, and traveller, who was born at No. 26 Kropotkin Lane. The nearest **Metro Station, Park kultury**, is a fifteen minutes' walk to your left, and you can reach the **Smolenskaya Metro Station** to your right by going two stops on any trolleybus.

Kropotkin Street continues on as *Bolshaya Pirogovskaya ulitsa* (Big Pirogov Street) towards the Lenin Central Stadium at Luzhniki. It begins at *Zubovskaya ploshchad* (Zubovskaya Square). To the right at the beginning of the thoroughfare stands a **statue of Lev Tolstoy**, unveiled in 1972. The work of sculp-

tor Alexei Portyanko, it is one of the city's finest sculptural monuments. Lenin's exclamation to Gorky about Tolstoy, "What a titan! What a colossal human being!" served as the sculptor's creative inspiration. Imprinted in the austere granite block and the sparing plastic forms is the majestic figure of the brilliant writer and sage. A few blocks away on the left, No. 21 *ulitsa Lva Tolstogo* (Lev Tolstoy Street), is the **Tolstoy Mansion-Museum**, where the great Russian writer lived and worked practically every winter from 1882 to 1901.

The plain, two-storey wooden mansion has a high, carved gate, and a small courtyard with outbuildings and an orchard which Tolstoy particularly enjoyed. The interior recreates the period of 1893-95, and consists of the dining-room where the writer's large family often gathered, the drawing-room, where prominent figures of Russian culture met and conversed, the children's rooms, and Tolstoy's study. Here many of his works were written, including the novel *Resurrection*, the novellas *Kreutzer's Sonata, Father Sergius*, and *The Death of Ivan Ilyich*, the dramas *The Living Corpse* and *The Power of Darkness*, the comedy *The Fruits of Enlightenment*, and many other literary and publicistic works. Tolstoy's final visit to this house was in September 1909, one year before his death. In the autumn of 1921 the Soviet government opened up the mansion as a museum. We can justifiably say that every educated person considers it his moral duty to visit the home of the great Tolstoy, of whom Maxim Gorky said: "The whole world, the whole earth looks at him ... His spirit is for all, and forever."

Big Pirogov Street ends at **Novodevichy Monastyr** (New Maiden's Convent), a monument of 16th-17th-century Russian culture. A bit further, beyond the Moscow Circular Railway is the Lenin Central Stadium, a huge sports complex which we will discuss in greater detail in the next chapter. Today we will continue with an excursion along Lenin Avenue.

ALONG LENIN AVENUE

Since Lenin Avenue *(Leninsky prospekt)* is 14 kilometers in length, we recommend that you make the excursion by taxi or by car, which you can arrange through the Intourist Service Bureau. Lenin Avenue begins at *Oktyabrskaya plosh-* *chad* (October Square), which is located to the south-west of the center of the city on the Garden Ring. It is from this square that we will begin our acquaintance with the highly interesting south-west section of the city. You can also

Oktyabrskaya (October) Square. General view

reach the square by taking the Metro to the **Oktyabrskaya Metro Station** via either the circular or radial lines.

The October Square ensemble is an example of the work being carried out in the city according to the General Plan for the Development of Moscow which was adopted in 1971. Now it is difficult to imagine the way this square looked ten

Igumnov House

years ago. It was taken up for the most part by 2- and 3-storey houses built before the Revolution without much regard to their external appearance. Back then this was the outskirts of the city, and old Kaluga Road ran from here through working-class districts, garden plots, and small country orchards. The history of the square actually dates back to the end of the 16th century. Up until 1922 it was known as Kaluzhskaya Square. It was renamed in honor of the October Revolution. It was one of the centers of the workers' battles for Soviet power during the revolutionary period.

Looking down on October Square from the height of one of the top floor balconies of one of the buildings surrounding the square, you are able to see all its beauty, spaciousness and breadth, and the harmony of all its architectural elements. The square has a Classical square form, considered the most monumental and strict. In the square's center is a **monument to Lenin.** The residential and administrative buildings surrounding the square are finished with natural white stone. This is consistent with the image of Moscow as a city of white stone which has its roots in ancient Russian folklore. Sculpted of polished red granite with a dark pink pedestal, the monument to Lenin stands out vividly at the center of the architectural ensemble. Around the monument there is a small platform of paved stone, green grass plots criss-

Statue of Vladimir Mayakovsky

Arbat. High-rise buildings on Kalinin Avenue (in the background)

Bolshoi Theater. Restoration work in progress

Obvodnoy (Bypass) canal

The Lomonosov University, one of the old buildings on Marx Avenue

Building of TASS (Telegraph Agency of the Soviet Union) and Church of the Ascension (in the foreground)

*Pushkinskaya Square. Statue of
Alexander Pushkin*

Gogolevsky Boulevard

Central House of Artists

Folklore festival at Kolomenskoye

Church of the Ascension at Kolomenskoye

crossed with straight alleys, and a public garden with birch and spruce trees.

The monument was unveiled on November 5, 1985, on the eve of the 68th anniversary of the October Revolution. The sculptors Lev Kerbel and Vladimir Fyodorov and architects Gleb Makarevich and Andrei Samsonov strove to portray Lenin as the leader of the October Revolution in this majestic monument which stands 22 meters tall. Lenin's figure is elevated upon a massive column and a bronze grouping at the base of the monument depicts a woman personifying Liberty and the figures of a worker, soldier and sailor against the backdrop of the revolutionary banner. The monument is especially impressive in the evening, when it is illuminated by spotlights and lamps.

In order to get a close look at the monument, you must take one of the underpasses from the Oktyabrskaya-Circular Metro Station. The Metro station is built into the massive building of the *Varshava* (Warsaw) **Hotel.** In a recently constructed building to the right of the monument to Lenin is the Children's Library. In the building next to it are the permanent offices of the airlines of Algeria, France, India, Cuba, and Angola.

Lenin Avenue begins to the right of October Square. To the left is *ulitsa Dimitrova* (Dimitrov Street), a continuation of Lenin Avenue which runs towards the Kremlin. As a result of radical reconstruc-

tion work in 1978-85, this street now harmonizes well with Lenin Avenue. It has been transformed from a narrow, crooked street to a broad, modern four-lane thoroughfare with three pedestrian underpasses. In addition, attractive new buildings were constructed, including a multi-storey hotel, apartment buildings with wide loggias, and various stores. Next to October Square on the right-hand side of Dimitrov Street is another entrance to the **Oktyabrskaya Metro Station** (the radial line).

You will find a walk along Dimitrov Street quite interesting and pleasant. Directly beyond the Metro station at No. 43 is a red brick building known as the **Igumnov House** which now houses the French Embassy. This is one of the most interesting relics of Russian 19th-century architecture. Built in 1893 according to the neo-Classical design of Nikolai Pozdeyev, it borrows from motifs of 17th-century Russian stone architecture. The new Embassy building adjoining it, designed by French architects and built in the early 1980s, contrasts sharply with the old building. The Igumnov House affords a splendid view of another architectural monument, the **Church of St. John the Warrior**, which was built in 1709-13 in the Baroque style and is attributed to architect Ivan Zarudny. It is interesting that the forged grille fence was transported by rail a distance of 35 meters closer to the church when Dimitrov Street was widened. On the

Krymsky (Crimean) Bridge

left-hand side of the street is the **salon** *Khudozhnik* **(Artist) of the RSFSR**, where you can find interesting paintings, prints, and articles crafted by masters of decorative applied arts.

The **House of Toys** (No. 28) can attract your attention. It occupies the ground and the first floors of a new residential house, near October Square (one stop on a trolleybus).

Dimitrov Street was named in 1975 after Georgi Dimitrov (1882–1949), one of the outstanding figures in the Bulgarian and international workers' and Communist movement. A **statue of Dimitrov** stands at the spot where Dimitrov Street merges with *ulitsa Bolshaya Polyanka* (Big Polyanka Street). Sculpted by Konstantin and Merab Merabishvili and unveiled in 1972, the monument depicts Dimitrov as a champion of the people appealing to his audience with an impassioned revolutionary speech.

If you continue a bit further along Big Polyanka Street and cross the **Maly Kamenny most** (Small Stone Bridge) over the Ob-

vodnoy (Bypass) Canal, you will see the *Udarnik* **Cinema** on your left, and a large square with a garden on your right. In the garden facing Lavrushinsky Lane is a **statue of** the great Russian artist **Ilya Repin** (1844–1930). The work of sculptor Matvei Manizer, the monument was erected in 1958. This square, once known as Bolotnaya (Swamp) Square, is famous as the place where the leader of the peasant uprising, Yemelyan Pugachov, was executed in 1775.

Up ahead is the **Bolshoy Kamenny most** (Big Stone Bridge) which spans the Moskva River. From here there is a wonderful view of the Kremlin, the Grand Kremlin Palace, and the Kremlin's cathedrals and towers. You will surely agree that the walk along Dimitrov Street was worthwhile, if only for this reason! (You may also use this route across Big Stone Bridge returning towards the center from the Tretyakov Gallery.)

Returning to October Square, we would like to point out the tunnel which cuts beneath the square and helps to relieve the area of much congested traffic. From here the traffic flows on towards **Krymsky most** (Crimean Bridge), which is perhaps the most beautiful of all Moscow's bridges. The bridge is suspended on chains which stretch across powerful steel columns 27 meters in height. It was built in 1938 to the design of engineer Boris Konstantinov and architect Alexander Vlasov.

On the left-hand side of *Krymsky*

val (Crimean Rampart), the road which runs from October Square to Crimean Bridge, is the main entrance to the **Gorky Central Recreation Park** *(Park kultury i otdykha)*. Past the main entrance arch on a spacious square is a music-and-light fountain. In the evenings the beams of 400 powerful spotlights and 2,000 colored lamps illuminate the water firework display. Water, light and music are the three "dramatis personae" in the program which lasts for one hour. The fountain's basin is approximately 4,000 sq. m. And surrounding the fountain and stretching beyond are a profusion of bright flowers, whimsical flowerbeds, rose-gardens, shady alleys, and green grass plots. There are over 300 varieties of trees and shrubs in the park, which occupies a territory of nearly 300 acres. These include oaks and birch, elms and lindens, Siberian blue spruces, southern chestnuts, Ukrainian poplars, taiga larches, and apple, pear, and other fruit-bearing trees. The park was laid out in an area where there was once garden plots and vacant land. In 1923 the First Agricultural and Cottage-Industry Exhibition was opened in the park. Later the territory of the exhibition was re-planned, and in 1928 it was opened as a recreation park. From the Fountain Square, which lies directly beyond the terrace of the main entrance, begins a broad central avenue with decorative sculptures. It leads to Golitsynsky pond where one can take a ride on a

Central House of Artists and State Picture Gallery of the USSR

swift pleasure-boat. On the banks of the pond there is a café called "Kafe vstrech" (*Rendezvous* café). To the right of the central avenue is an amusement area with all kinds of attractions and rides, the most popular among which is an enormous Ferris Wheel.

If you follow along the embankment of the Moskva River (which stretches for 3 kilometers along the park) from the main entrance, it will take you to the other side of Golitsynsky pond, and to the beginning of Neskuchny Garden—a large green expanse with age-old trees and picturesque sloping hills. Here in the summer it is always cool und quiet, and one can relax and enjoy nature. A bit further is the Green Theater, an open-air theater which seats 12,000 persons. It is situated on the embankment,

LENIN AVENUE

1. *Church of St. John the Warrior*
2. *Igumnov House*
3. *Oktyabrskaya Metro Station*
4. Khudozhnik *RSFSR salon-shop*
5. *State Picture Gallery of the USSR and the Exhibition Hall of the House of Artists*
6. *Gorky Recreation Park*
7. Varshava *Hotel*
8. *Statue of Lenin*
9. *Central Children's Library*
10. Podarki *(Gifts) shop*
11. *Former Golitsyn Hospital premises*
12. *Neskuchny Palace*

MOSKVA

6

7

5

3

Oktyabrskaya

9

ploshchaa

8

3

4

ulitsa

1

2

Dimitrova

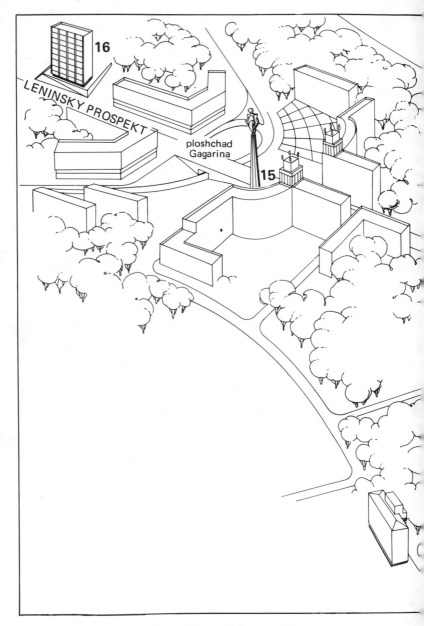

LENINSKY PROSPEKT

16

ploshchad
Gagarina

15

13. *Alexander Fersman Museum of Mineralogy*
14. *Donskoy Monastery, (Branch of the
    Museum of Architecture)*

15. *Statue of Yuri Gagarin*
16. Sputnik *Hotel*

MOSKVA

LENINSKY PROSPEKT

Donskaya ulitsa

13

14

not far from the wharf where the motor ships come in to dock. In winter the avenues of the park are flooded with ice, rendering 100,000 square meters available to Moscow's many ice-skating fans.

Opposite the entrance to Gorky Park set back in a large open square with grass plots and park sculpture is a large building girded by a row of columns which extends along the Moskva River. This is the building of the **State Picture Gallery of the USSR** and the **Central House of Artists of the Artists' Union of the USSR.** It was built in the 1970s to the design of architects Nikolai Sukoyan, Yuri She-

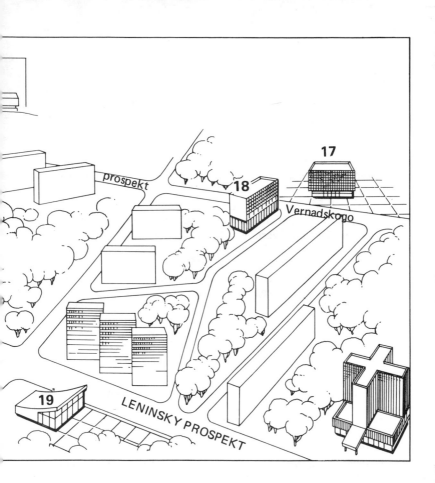

23. *Trinity Church at Troparyovo*
24. Salyut *Hotel*
25. *To Vnukovo Airport*

verdyaev, and others. Its exhibition rooms exceed 17,000 square meters in area, and to see every collection would require covering a distance of 6 kilometers.

We have already mentioned that a permanent exhibition of Soviet art was opened here in 1986. Its basis was the collection of Soviet art which was built up over a period of many years at the Tretyakov Gallery. Presented here fully and systematically is the history of the multinational art of the country from October 1917 to the present.

As you approach the building from Crimean Embankment, you will see the main entrance to the

Central House of Artists, where temporary exhibits of Soviet artists and artists from abroad are organized. The entrance to the Picture Gallery is located on the right side of the building. In front of the entrance is a copy of Yevgeny Vuchetich's (1908-74) famous sculpture *Beating Swords into Ploughshares.* The original was given to the United Nations Organization in 1957 by the Soviet Government, and stands in front of the Headquarters building in New York.

A white marble staircase leads from the lobby to the spacious, high-ceilinged exhibition rooms. The collections, representing the finest works of Soviet art, have been arranged in an historical-chronological order. Also on display are monographs about a number of outstanding artists, including Boris Kustodiev (1878-1927), Kuzma Petrov-Vodkin (1878-1939), Pyotr Konchalovsky (1876-1956), Alexander Deineka (1899-1969), Arkady Plastov (1893-1972), and others.

Among those canvases to which we would like to draw your attention are the sunny, vivid paintings of Konstantin Yuon (1875-1958) *Cupolas and Swallows* (1921) and *Students* (1923); the works of Petrov-Vodkin, including *Petrograd. 1918* (1920), *Death of the Commissar* (1927), and *Portrait of D. Mstislavsky* (1929); and the paintings of Abram Arkhipov (1862-1930), which glow with the colors of red calico and depict the figures of Russian peasant women full of life

and *joie-de-vivre*, such as *Girl with a Pitcher* (1927). Among the works of Boris Kustodiev we would draw your attention to the small but very striking painting *Bolshevik* (1920). The work of Pyotr Konchalovsky is well represented by *Family Portrait* (1926) and *Portrait of Vsevolod Meyerhold* (1938). The finest among Alexander Deineka's works are on display: *Defence of Petrograd* (1928), *Ball Game* (1932), *Mother* (1932), and *Defence of Sevastopol* (1942).

Other artists whose works constitute an important part of the collection are Isaak Brodsky, Boris Ioganson, Sergei Gerasimov, Pavel Korin, and many others. The art of other Soviet republics is represented by the works of, among others, Ukrainian artist Tatyana Yablonskaya, Azerbaijanian Tair Salakhov, Turkman Izzat Klychev, Latvian Indulis Zarinš, Jānis Pauluks, and Armenian Martiros Saryan.

The gallery takes great pride in its large collection of nearly 2,000 works of contemporary Soviet sculpture. Some of these are arranged in the Park of Sculpture and Applied Art outside the main entrance to the Gallery. Inside they have been skilfully arranged to utilize space, light, and foreshortening to the best possible effect, and serve as a refreshing counterpoint to the paintings. Among the many outstanding works of sculpture we would like to mention Vera Mukhina's (1889-1953) *Peasant Woman* (1927), Ivan Shadr's

(1887–1941) *Sower* (1922), Leonid Sherwood's (1871–1954) *Sentinel* (1933), and Sergei Bulakovsky's (1880–1937) *Woman Bearing a Stone* (1933).

Now let us return to Lenin Avenue. The portion from October Square to Gagarin Square acquired its present aspect for the most part during the first post-war years, with the exception of such architectural monuments as the old Moscow hospital buildings situated at the beginning of the avenue on the right-hand side. The former Golitsyn Hospital at No. 8 was built in 1801 by the outstanding master of Russian Classicism, Matvei Kazakov, and is considered one of his finest works. It is a simple, massive building adorned with a six-column portico surmounted by a triangular pediment. Visible above the portico is the cupola of the hospital chapel with a high, elegant rotunda. Beside the hospital is a three-storey building with an eight-column portico which is also an architectural monument. The work of Osip Bovet, it is more austere in style than the other building. Opposite these buildings is a 17-storey administrative building which provides a contrast to the somewhat uniform buildings on this side of the avenue. Built by Moscow architects in 1970, the building is composed of three interconnected prismatic glass towers.

Set back from the street on the right-hand side (at Nos. 14–20) is another monument of architecture. This is the **Neskuchny** *(sans souci)*

Lenin Avenue. Neskuchny Garden (on the left)

Palace, built in 1756 and rebuilt for Emperor Nicholas I in the 1830s by Yevgraf Tyurin. A broad avenue leads from the entrance gates decorated with sculptural compositions to the palace grounds. The fountain in the forecourt, the work of Ivan Vitali (1835), is a sculptural grouping consisting of youths supporting a bronze bowl, and is a twin of the one on Sverdlov Square. The palace itself is a building of modest proportions adorned with elegant colonnades. One, with double columns, forms a portico, while two others support open terraces. Before the Revolution the Neskuchny Palace was an imperial estate, and had two side wings, a kitchen building, a riding school, summerhouse and hunting lodge, and a guard-house. Since 1935 the palace has housed the Presidium of the Academy of Sciences of the USSR, which will soon be relocated to a modern building nearby on the banks of the Moskva River.

Located in the former riding

Lenin Avenue. Gagarin Square

school building is the **Alexander Fersman** (1883-1945) **Museum of Mineralogy.** Fersman was a Soviet geochemist and mineralogist, and one of the founders of geochemistry. The museum was founded in 1716, and is associated with Peter the Great.

The museum has a rich collection of gems, rare groups of crystals, and other treasures of the earth as well as "messengers from space"—meteorites. There are 130,000 items in the museum's stock, some of which are one of a kind. The museum takes especial pride in its exposition "New Minerals", which displays specimens of minerals discovered since 1976. Although newly discovered minerals are traditionally named after the place where they were found, there are exceptions to the rule. In 1961 Soviet scientists discovered a deposit of a previously unknown mineral in Eastern Kazakhstan. It was named Gagarinite, in honor of Yuri Gagarin, and its large, light yellow crystals are on display in the museum. The collection of meteorites includes 337 specimens, among which is the largest "drop" of the Sikhote-Alin meteorite rain,

which weighs 1,745 kilograms.

The Neskuchny Garden, a large, lovely garden which extends right up to the Palace itself, provides a charming complement to the palace's elegant beauty. Neskuchny Garden, as we mentioned earlier, is now a part of Gorky Park. As we walk along Lenin Avenue towards Gagarin Square, Neskuchny Garden will remain on our right, behind a chain of buildings.

In addition to the Presidium of the Academy of Sciences of the USSR many scientific research and educational institutions are located along Lenin Avenue. It was on this avenue that tens of thousands of Muscovites greeted cosmonaut Yuri Gagarin on his triumphal return to the capital from Vnukovo Airport.

The **statue of Yuri Gagarin** was erected in 1980 on the square which bears his name. There is a splendid view of the monument from Lenin Avenue, especially from the vantage of the large "Shoe House" and "Fabric House" stores. The 13-meter-tall statue of the space hero stands on a gigantic 30-meter-high fluted column. It seems fitting that the figure of the cosmonaut be elevated to such a lofty height, as if vaulting into flight. At the foot of the pedestal is a model of a spaceship which bears the date April 12, 1961, the historical day on which Yuri Gagarin made the first manned orbital flight around the Earth on the spaceship *Vostok*. The statue was executed by Yakov Belopolsky,

Pavel Bondarenko, and Fyodor Gazhevsky.

Ploshchad Gagarina (Gagarin Square) is an interesting architectural ensemble. Two semi-circular 8-storey buildings with towers on the corners mark the entrance to the portion of Lenin Avenue which leads to the center of the city and to October Square. At one time the square was situated on the boundary of the city. In recent years many multi-storey apartment buildings have been built around the square. Many specialized stores are housed in the ground floors of these buildings, such as "A Thousand Odds and Ends", the "Shoe House" and "Fabric House" mentioned earlier, and a large *Gastronom* (Grocery). Just behind the building which houses the grocery you can see the new building under construction for the Presidium of the Academy of Sciences of the USSR. Near the square, in the direction of "A Thousand Odds and Ends", is the **Leninsky Prospekt Metro Station.**

Ulitsa Kosygina (Kosygin Street) runs from the right of the square towards the Lenin Hills. Situated on it are the **Orlyonok** (Eaglet) **Hotel** and the **International Youth Travel Bureau**, *Sputnik.* To the left, *Profsoyuznaya ulitsa* (Trade Union Street) runs towards the city's large newly developed residential areas. Stretching straight ahead is a continuation of Lenin Avenue, a broad thoroughfare flanked on both sides by rows of trees and shrubs. You may be in-

Central Tourists House

terested to learn that it was along old Kaluga Road which at one time ran across Gagarin Square, that Napoleon's troops passed during their retreat from Moscow in 1812.

From this point to the Moscow Circular Motor Road Lenin Avenue connects regions which have been built since the 1950s. Blocks of handsome, modern buildings now stand on the site where there were once small villages, fields and ravines. These are apartment and public buildings and annexes of scientific institutes and laboratories, with children's play areas and sports complexes.

Lenin Avenue is a busy shopping street, with a lot of different stores including one of Moscow's largest department stores, the *Moskva* Department Store at

Salyut *Hotel*

No. 54. Other stores are the "Porcelain House" near Gagarin Square and the "Furniture House" near the end of the avenue. Also on the avenue are the **Sputnik and Sport hotels**, the **Gavana Restaurant**, and the **Central Tourists House** built in 1980 by architect Vsevolod Kuzmin and others, with a movie and concert hall, a swimming pool, restaurant, and a year-round **exhibit "Tourism in the USSR"**. Set back from the street at No. 42 on the right-hand side are the buildings of the **All-Union Central Council of Trade Unions** (ACCTU), constructed in 1939–58.

Soviet trade unions (31 professional unions) are the country's largest mass public organization, with over 136 million total members. The trade unions are involved with the growth of the national economy, and take part in the management of state and public affairs. One of the main concerns of the professional unions and the ACCTU has been protecting the rights and interests of the workers and improving the conditions of

their work and daily life. The trade unions have a large chain of rest homes and sanatoriums, tourist bases and boarding houses, as well as summer and winter youth camps. Each year the number of trade union palaces of culture, clubs and sports complexes grows. Soviet trade unions actively participate in the anti-war movement and stand up for the defence of peace, for disarmament, and for the promotion of international cooperation. The ACCTU is a member of the International Labor Organization. Soviet labor unions have friendly working contacts with the labor unions of 145 countries.

If you turn to the right at the intersection of Lenin Avenue and *Lomonosovsky prospekt* (Lomonosov Avenue) a ten to fifteen minutes' walk will bring you to the **Universitet Metro Station.** At the very end of Lenin Avenue is the 26-storey *Salyut* **Hotel**, which was built for the opening of the 1980 Olympic Games held in Moscow. This building is the architectural center of a large, new block at the entrance to the city from Vnukovo airport. Another large housing unit was built in the early 1980s on the left-hand side of the avenue.

From the *Salyut* Hotel it is a fifteen minutes' walk to the nearest **Metro Station**, **Yugo-Zapadnaya** on *prospekt Vernadskogo* (Vernadsky Avenue). If you were to retrace our route along Lenin Avenue to October Square, it would take over two hours.

THIRD DAY

In the morning we suggest you walk along prospekt Kalinina (Kalinin Avenue) and Kutuzovsky prospekt (Kutuzov Avenue) or get acquainted with prospekt Mira (Peace Avenue) and the USSR Economic Achievements Exhibition (VDNKh). In the afternoon you may wish to go for a stroll on the Lenin Hills.

ALONG KALININ AVENUE AND KUTUZOV AVENUE

It would be best to begin your walk at the spot where *Kalinin Avenue* joins Marx Avenue. Exiting from the Biblioteka imeni Lenina (Lenin Library) Metro Station we come out onto Kalinin Avenue and turn to the left. On the corner of Kalinin Avenue and Marx and Engels Street, just behind the Lenin Library stands an old, three-storey mansion. From here begins the narrowest part of the avenue, which is scheduled to undergo reconstruction in the future. The first project will be to move this massive mansion back further from the street. Built to the design of the famed architect Matvei Kazakov in the late 18th century, the mansion is under state protection as a monument of Russian architecture. It houses the **Shchusev Museum of Architecture**, organized in 1964, which contains materials and documents on the history of Russian and Soviet architecture.

Beyond the large department store on the right-hand side of the street stands a **statue of Mikhail Kalinin**, unveiled in 1978 (sculptor Boris Dyuzhev, architect Yevgeny Kutyrev).

On the left-hand side of the avenue is an enormous administrative building which occupies the entire block. An exit from the **Arbatskaya Metro Station** is located here in the building. In front of the building behind a lattice-work fence is a public garden. Here at one time stood an apartment building which was destroyed during a Nazi air raid in 1941. On the right-hand side of the avenue is a building of strikingly original architecture — it was built in 1899 according to the whim of its former owner, the wealthy textile manufacturer Morosov, in the style of a Spanish-Moorish castle (architect Victor Mazyrin). For many years now it has been the **Dom druzhby** (House of Friendship with Peoples of Foreign Countries). Fifty million Soviet citizens are involved in the activities of the Union of Friendship Societies with Peoples of Foreign Countries — an organization which unites nearly 100 different societies and associations.

House of Friendship with Peoples of Foreign Countries

In Moscow a total of 1,600 primary organizations belong to these societies and associations as affiliated members. The Union actively promotes exchanges of delegations and tourist groups with related organizations in different countries. Its societies and associations have working contacts with over 7,000 analogous social unions and organizations in 135 countries. The Union naturally has the most wide-scale and varied ties with corresponding organizations in fraternal socialist countries. In the Friendship House, meetings are held between foreign tourists and delegations and Soviet factory and office workers, and people in the art and cultural fields. These are meetings of people with the same professional and other interests. Debates, talks, press-conferences, exhibitions, and concerts are organized here with the aim of helping Soviet people and guests from abroad to gain a better understanding of one another.

We come out onto *Arbatskaya ploshchad* (Arbat Square)—one of the city's oldest squares. Its appearance changed completely as the result of radical reconstruction carried out during the post-war years.

On your left is the building of the **Khudozhestvenny** (Art) **Cinema.** Opened in 1909, this cinema has an outstanding history. In 1931 it presented the first Soviet sound film, and in 1936, the first Soviet colored film premiered here. A decision has already been made to move the cinema building to a new site at the beginning of Arbat Street, opposite the *Praga* (Prague) Restaurant. Another architectural landmark is the star-shaped pavilion of the **Arbatskaya Metro Station** (1935), one of the original stations on Moscow's first Metro lines.

Two boulevards which form part of the city's Boulevard Ring have been connected by a vehicle underpass: on your left is Gogol Boulevard, with which you are already familiar, and *Suvorovsky bulvar* (Suvorov Boulevard) begins on the right. At No. 7 Suvorov Boulevard stands the house where Nikolai

Gogol (1809–52), the author of the immortal works *Dead Souls, Inspector-General*, and *Taras Bulba*, lived and died. A **memorial exposition devoted to Nikolai Gogol** is now open here. In the courtyard of the building is a highly interesting statue of Gogol sculpted by Nikolai Andreyev (1909), which portrays the writer deep in thought and wearily looking down, his head bowed as if beneath the weight of an invisible burden. Portrayed in bas-relief on the monument's pedestal are heroes from Gogol's works. Another **statue of Gogol** stands at the beginning of Gogol Boulevard near Arbat Square. The monument was unveiled on the centenary of Gogol's death (sculptor Nikolai Tomsky). On Suvorov Boulevard also are the **Central House of Journalists** at No. 8 and

Arbat scenes

the **Museum of Oriental Art** at No. 12. *Praga* **Restaurant** with its second-storey open terrace and elegant corner tower is one of the dominant elements in the architectural ensemble of Arbat Square. One of the finest restaurants in the city, it is famous for its Czechoslovakian specialties. The *Praga* Restaurant building connects, as it were, the Old Arbat with the New Arbat, i. e., Arbat Street with that portion of Kalinin Avenue which Muscovites call *Novy* (New) *Arbat.*

Ulitsa Arbat (Arbat Street) is one of Moscow's oldest streets, first mentioned in the chronicles of the late 15th century. Muscovites are very fond of this narrow, winding street with its houses of different

Statue of Gogol (sculptor Nikolai Andreyev)

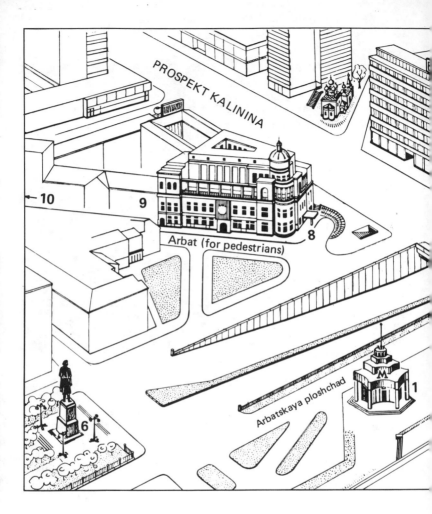

KALININ AVENUE

1. *Arbatskaya Metro Station*
   Arbatskaya Metro Station
2. Khudozhestvenny *Cinema*
3. *House of Friendship with Peoples of Foreign
   Countries*
4. *Union of Societies of Friendship with
   Peoples of Foreign Countries*
5. *Statue of Nikolai Gogol (sculptor Nikolai
   Andreyev)*

6. *Statue of Nikolai Gogol (sculptor Nikolai
   Tomsky)*
7. *Central House of Journalists*
8. Praga *Restaurant*
9. Iskusstvo *bookstore*
10. *Alexander Pushkin Apartment-Museum*

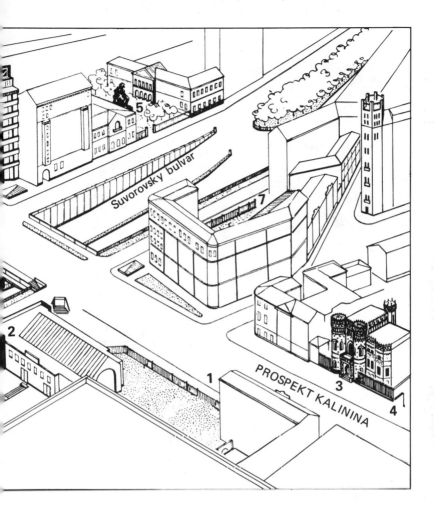

Arbat scenes

lived at No. 53 on the Arbat itself. This two-storey building with an elegant balcony is one of the pearls of the Arbat "collection". On its first floor was the poet's first and only Moscow apartment. Pushkin rented it in 1831, and supervised the interior finishing work himself as he made preparations for married life. On February 18 of the same year he brought his beautiful young bride Natalya Goncharova

heights and styles and its variety of small shops. Much local color has been preserved in this picturesque street, along which Muscovites enjoy taking leisurely strolls. Quiet and charming side-streets run off from the Arbat in both directions, where you can find old houses and mansions, many of which are associated with the names of famous figures in Russian culture. Pushkin

here following their wedding ceremony in the Church of the Ascension near Nikitskiye Gates. For three months this building was filled with happiness, radiant hopes, and love. On May 15, 1831 the young couple moved from Moscow to St. Petersburg. One hundred and fifty years later Pushkin's spirit made itself at home here once again when the **Apartment-Museum of Alexander Pushkin on Arbat** was opened.

In the rooms on the top floor,

basically devoid of furniture, there are only two objects which indicate that the Pushkins once lived here: one is the desk at which the poet wrote, with his pen and a page of manuscript; the other is a small table for needlework which belonged to the young poet's wife. Among the portraits on display is a watercolor by Pyotr Sokolov (1791–1848) which portrays Pushkin in his favorite pose: reclining in an armchair with his arms folded across his chest. The museum has made every effort to recreate the atmosphere which surrounded the great poet.

Pushkin Apartment-Museum on Arbat

Located on Arbat Street is one of the capital's most popular drama theaters, the **Vakhtangov Theater**, named after its founder, the actor and director Yevgeny Vakhtangov (1883–1922).

Arbat Street is one of the city's most important landmarks. It is a monument of the history of Moscow architecture and a witness to the city's history. The Arbat has changed its appearance many times. In the 18th century it was a fashionable aristocratic area, and the majority of its mansions and houses then belonged to the nobility. As a result of the great fire of 1812 and subsequent rebuilding, the street's appearance was totally altered. Luxurious mansions were built up once again in the then fashionable Empire style. At the end of the 19th century multi-storey buildings where furnished rooms and apartments were let, merchants' stalls, and shops began

to appear on the Arbat and adjacent areas. The Arbat gradually became one of the city's main trade streets.

The contemporary life of the Arbat began in the early 1980s when a plan was adopted to create a pedestrian mall in the Arbat state-protected district. A decision was made to preserve this unique and historically valuable street and to return its buildings to their 19th-century appearance, to the period when the street's architectural ensemble was definitively formed. Much of this work has already

Kalinin Avenue

been completed. The Arbat was closed to traffic, allowing people to stroll leisurely along the street. The sidewalks were removed, and the entire street paved with colored tile slabs reminiscent of those which covered old Russian roads. The buildings have been repainted in various hues: blues, yellows, whites and pinks, and with their diversity, have made the Arbat even more attractive. The goal of this work, which is still being continued, is to preserve the Arbat not only as a remarkable architectural ensemble, but as the trade and cultural center of the city, still alive with the inimitable atmosphere of old Moscow. As Anton Chekhov wrote, "may the Arbat and its adjoining side-streets be the most pleasant and prosperous place on Earth."

The *Novy Arbat* (New Arbat) is the popular name for the broad new section of Kalinin Avenue between the Boulevard and the Garden rings. Work on it began in the spring of 1962, though it had long before been envisaged in the General Plan for the Development of the city, since the Old Arbat was unable to cope with the growing stream of west-bound traffic. The city needed a new thoroughfare which would provide the shortest route between the center and Kutuzov Avenue and *Minskoye shosse* (Minsk Highway). The avenue was built on the site of old one- and two-storey, mostly wooden houses. One of them was a single-storey house with columns which stood on former *Kompositorskaya ulitsa* (Composers' Street) where Maria

KALININ AVENUE
(continued)

1. *Arbatskaya Metro Station*
2. *Church of St. Simon the Stylite*
3. *Mikhail Lermontov Apartment-Museum*
4. Malakhitovaya shkatulka *(Malachite Casket) jewellery shop*
5. *Moscow Book House*
6. Valdai *Café*
7. Novoarbatsky *supermarket*
8. *Transport Agency*
9. Moskvichka *(Miss Moscow) fashion shop*
10. Charodeika *(Sorceress) hairdressing salon*
11. Jupiter *shop (cameras, film and photographic supplies)*
12. Melodia *shop (records)*
13. Oktyabr *Cinema*
14. Vesna *shop*
15. Metelitsa *Ice-Cream Parlour*
16. Podarki *(Gifts) shop*
17. Arbat *Restaurant*
18. *Council for Mutual Economic Assistance.* Mir *Hotel*
19. *Kalinin Bridge*
20. *To* Belgrad *Hotel*

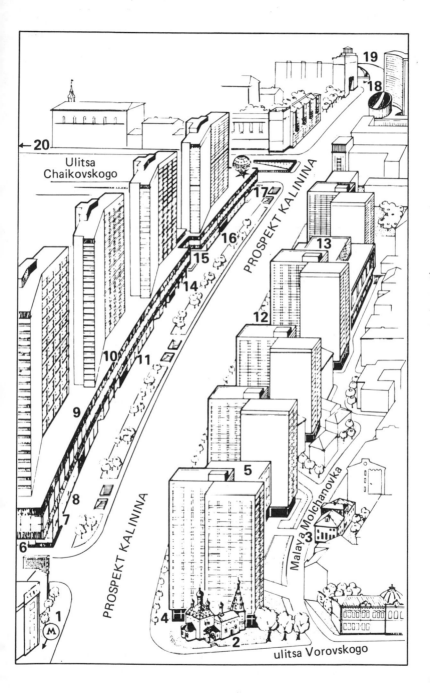

Ulitsa Chaikovskogo

← 20

PROSPEKT KALININA

19
18
17
16
15
14
13
12
11
10
9
8
7
6
5
4
3
2
1

Malaya Molchanovka

PROSPEKT KALININA

ulitsa Vorovskogo

M

Ulyanova, Lenin's mother, lived from 1897–99. In February 1897 Lenin stayed there on his way to exile in Siberia, and walked along the Arbat and its side-streets and visited the reading-hall of the library in the Pashkov House.

The Plan for the new thoroughfare contained a number of original architectural ideas. The architects, Mikhail Posokhin, Ashot Mndoyants, Boris Thor and others were awarded the Grand Prix of the Paris Architectural Research Center in 1966 for their modernization of architectural forms and successful contribution to urban planning. Stretching from the Kremlin to *Novoarbatsky most* (New Arbat Bridge), the new thoroughfare also solved the transport problem of connecting the center with the city's west area. Upon completion in 1963, the whole thoroughfare was renamed Kalinin Avenue and the New Arbat became a part of this avenue.

Let us continue our walk. Across the avenue from the *Praga* Restaurant is **Dom svyazi** (Communications House), built in 1968. A bit further on the right is the **Church of St. Simon the Stylite**, a monument of 17th-century architecture, which now houses the **Exhibition Hall of the All-Russia Society for the Preservation of Nature.** Not far from the church, on *Malaya Molchanovka*, a small side-street which runs parallel to Kalinin Avenue, is a single-storey, wooden building with a mezzanine floor (No. 2) where the great Russian

poet Mikhail Lermontov lived in 1829–32. In this house he wrote over one hundred lyrical verses and worked on the early editions of his poem *The Demon.* In one of his letters, reminiscing about the period of his life spent in Moscow, the poet wrote: "Moscow is my home and will always remain so. There I was born, there I suffered, and there I also experienced great happiness." The house has been opened as the **Lermontov Apartment-Museum.**

The old white-stone Church of St. Simon the Stylite sets off the austere form and laconic architecture of the modern 24-storey apartment building nearby. There are five high-rises on the right-hand side. They were built in 1964–68 and each contains 280 comfortable apartments.

On the left-hand side are four huge administrative blocks whose façades line the avenue. These blocks house a number of ministries, and are connected by a two-storey glass-fronted gallery 850 meters long, with shops, cafés, and restaurants. In order to provide the shops and restaurants with the essential goods, a special underground transportation tunnel was built which is 1000 meters long and 9 meters wide. Kalinin Avenue has become one of the capital's busiest shopping districts.

Further on, near the apartment building whose ground and first floors are taken up by the **Malakhitovaya shkatulka** (Malachite Casket) jewellery shop, is the **Dom** knigi (Moscow Book House), the city's largest bookstore. Situated in the next building is the cozy *Ivushka* (Willow-tree) **Café**, a favorite spot of Moscow's young people.

On the opposite side of the avenue is the huge **New Arbat Supermarket**, which occupies two floors of the gallery. Next to the supermarket is the *Valdai* **Café**, with a beer bar (entrance from sidestreet). In the next building is the **Moscow Transport Agency** with a small shop where newspapers and journals, including those published in the USSR in foreign languages, and postcards and stamps are sold.

Just beyond a **florist shop** is the *Pechora* **Café** where young jazz musicians perform in the evenings. The next shop is *Moskvichka* (Miss Moscow) **fashion shop**, and right beside it is the best hairdressing salon in the city (women and men), called *Charodeika* (the Sorceress). Next door to it is an establishment of special interest to women—the **Institute of Beauty**—where, it is said, the cosmeticians work wonders.

Beyond a small **photographic studio** where you can have movie and camera film developed is the *Jupiter* **store** dealing in cameras, film, and photographic supplies. Above the store on the first floor of the gallery is the *Angara* **Café**. Across the avenue from the café on the right-hand side (No. 40) is the two-storey *Melodia* **record shop.**

Next to it, stretching nearly 100 meters along the avenue is the building of one of the city's finest cinemas, the *Oktyabr* **Cinema.** The whole of the façade above the ground floor is covered by a mosaic panel executed by Nikolai Andronov, Andrei Vasnetsov, and Victor Elkonin. The *Oktyabr* Café is also situated in this building.

Next to the cinema, on the ground and first floors of the apartment building at No. 44, is *Siren* (Lilacs), **a shop that sells perfumes.**

Trubnikovsky pereulok (Trubnikovsky Lane) runs off to the right from the avenue. An exposition of the **Literature Museum** is located in the building at No. 17, a small mansion in the Empire style with a mezzanine floor. The exhibition here should interest those who would like to learn about the history and development of Soviet literature.

On the left-hand side of the avenue opposite the *Oktyabr* Cinema and set back somewhat from the esplanade is the **Ice-Cream Parlour** *Metelitsa* (Snowstorm), very popular with young Muscovites. To the left and right of the parlour are two large stores: *Vesna* (Spring) and *Podarki* (Gifts). To the left on the corner of Kalinin Avenue and the Garden Ring is the *Arbat* **Restaurant**, with a bar and the *Labirint* (Labyrinth) Hall in the basement. The restaurant offers fine cuisine, as well as an evening floor-show "The Evening Arbat" which is changed quite frequently.

From this same intersection there is a good view of the tall

Building of the Council for Mutual Economic Assistance (CMEA)

building on *Smolenskaya ploshchad* (Smolensk Square) that houses the USSR Ministries of Foreign Affairs and Foreign Economic Affairs. It was built in 1951 (architects Vladimir Gelfreikh and Mikhail Minkus) and is 172 meters high. We would like to note that there are only seven among Moscow's many tall buildings that are actually called **high-rises**: these were built in 1948–54 according to a single urban-construction plan of 1947. These are: the main building of Moscow State University on the Lenin Hills, the administrative building on Smolensk Square, the

administrative-apartment building on Lermontov Square, the apartment buildings on Uprising Square and Kotelnicheskaya Embankment, the *Leningrad* Hotel on Komsomol Square and the *Ukraina* Hotel at the beginning of Kutuzov Avenue. These buildings are visible from a great distance and add a picturesque element to the city's silhouette, emphasizing the unique, historically formed radial-circular structure of its layout. Opposite the high-rise building on Smolensk Square are the two high blocks of the **Belgrad** Hotel (each has 850 suites).

Kalinin Avenue continues to the Moskva River. At No. 50, on the right-hand side, is the **Central Research Institute of Spa Treatment and Physiotherapy**, and at the very end the tall 31-storey **building of the Council for Mutual Economic Assistance** (architects Mikhail Posokhin, Ashot Mndoyants, and Vladimir Svirsky). Headquartered here are the Executive Committee, Secretariat, and various administrative bodies of this international organization.

The Council (CMEA) was founded in 1949 as an economic organization of socialist countries, which are Bulgaria, Hungary, Vietnam, the GDR, Cuba, Mongolia, Poland, Romania, the USSR, and Czechoslovakia. Yugoslavia takes part in the work of some of the Council's bodies (in areas of mutual interest). The People's Republic of Korea, Laos, Angola, Afghanistan, Ethiopia, the People's

Democratic Republic of Yemen, and Mozambique participate as observers in the work of some of the Council's bodies. CMEA has agreements on cooperation with Finland, Iraq, Mexico, and Nicaragua, maintains contacts with other international economic organizations, and has possessed the status of observer in the UN since 1974.

In December 1985 the CMEA member countries collectively created and adopted a Comprehensive Program for Scientific and Technological Development Until the Year 2000. The member countries put forward the conception of the acceleration of socio-economic progress in all the countries on the basis of further broadening and strengthening of comprehensive mutual cooperation and socialist integration. They agreed on the coordination of activities relating to the creation and application of new kinds of materials and technologies by uniting their efforts and promoting close and versatile cooperation within the CMEA in five main directions: the development of atomic energetics, the creation of new materials and manufacturing technologies, the computerization of the national economy, multifaceted automatization, and the development of biotechnology.

The main, 105-meter-tall block of the CMEA building is connected to a circular conference hall seating 1,000 and the 13-storey *Mir* (Peace) **Hotel** (entrance at *Bolshoi Devyatinsky pereulok*— Big Devyatinsky Lane). Together, the Coun-

Gorbaty Bridge

cil's buildings form one of Moscow's most original and impressive architectural ensembles of the 1960s. Specialists and workers from the GDR, Poland, Bulgaria, Hungary, Czechoslovakia, Romania, and Mongolia took part in the construction of the CMEA complex. You can get a fine view of it from the *Ukraina* Hotel on the other side of the river. We shall proceed towards it along Kalinin Bridge.

Before continuing, however, you can have a look at an interesting monument of the mid-18th century—**Gorbaty most** (Hunchback Bridge), which is situated to the right of Kalinin Avenue at the end of Big Devyatinsky Lane. *Gorbaty most* is a historical monument to the revolutionary events of 1905. At the outset of the December armed uprising, the workers set up a round-the-clock watch over it in order to prevent the tsarist punitive detachments from crossing over it to Presnya, the rebellious workers' district. In time this bridge was for-

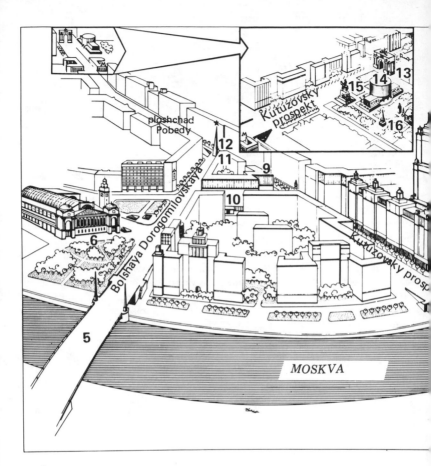

KUTUZOV AVENUE

1. *Kalinin Bridge*
2. *World Trade Center*
3. *Gorbaty (Hunchback) Bridge*
4. *Block of the CMEA buildings*
5. *Borodino Bridge*
6. *Kievsky (Kiev) Railway Station*
7. *Ukraina Hotel*
8. *Statue of Taras Shevchenko*

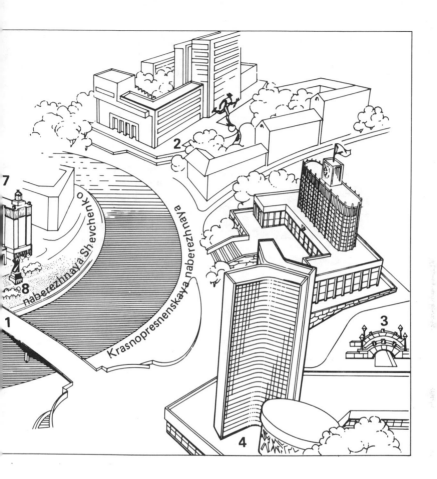

9. Russky suvenir *shop*
10. *Central Salon of the USSR Art Fund*
11. Khrustalnoye *Café*
12. *Obelisk "Moscow — Hero-City"*
13. *Arch of Triumph*

14. *Panorama Museum of the Battle of Borodino*
15. *Statue of Mikhail Kutuzov*
16. *Kutuzova* izba *(hut)*

Building of the Council of Ministers of the RSFSR

gotten, and was later covered over with earth together with the pond which it had spanned. In 1979 the bridge was unearthed and restored. On the spot behind the bridge — renamed 1905 Bridge — stands a bronze sculptural composition on a high pedestal, by Dmitry Ryabichev. Three figures symbolize the three generations of fighters who participated in the December uprising.

Now let us turn to **Kalininsky most** (Kalinin Bridge), which we will cross to the other bank of the Moskva River. This is a unique structure in that its metal pier is an all-welded construction. It is 43 meters wide and with its ramps, around 500 meters long. The bridge was built in 1957 to the design of engineer M. Rudenko. From the middle of the bridge we can see the beginning of *Kutuzovsky prospekt* (Kutuzov Avenue) up ahead, and on the left bank of the Moskva

River the already familiar CMEA building and the majestic whitestone **Building of the RSFSR Council of Ministers** with a clocktower and the State Flag of the Russian Federation on its top.

From here there is also a good view of the dark grey building of the **World Trade Center** (WTC). In actuality it is not just one building, but a whole complex of structures built in the late 1970s. The Center was designed by Soviet and American organizations within the framework of an agreement signed by the President of *Occidental Petroleum Corporation*, Armand Hammer, a staunch supporter of Soviet-American cooperation in the interests of peace and the preservation of life on the Earth. The Center began its operation in 1980. More than 500 varied events in the socio-political, trade, economic, scientific and technical spheres, have been held in the Center during the last five years, ranging from small symposiums and seminars to large international forums.

The Center's buildings provide all the necessary conditions for effective work and relaxation. Several hundred representatives of foreign firms and organizations have accommodations here. For business people coming to Moscow there is the *Mezhdunarodnaya* (International) **Hotel** with high-class accommodations for 1,100 and a block with apartments for long-term lease by representatives of foreign firms and their families. In addition there are exhibition halls, a conference hall seating 2,000 and a cinema-concert hall seating 500.

The *Ukraina* Hotel is one of Moscow's high-rise buildings. It is ornamented with unusual corner turrets, and has a high, imposing portico and a tall spire crowned with a star. It stands 172 meters high. A 36-storey tower forms its central section which is flanked by 12-storey blocks. The hotel has over 1,000 rooms. The hotel's interior décor and its façade reflect a certain pomposity and ostentatiousness of ornamentation characteristic of all Moscow's high-rise buildings. The hotel was designed by architect Arkady Mordvinov and was opened in 1957. In the garden in front of the hotel there is a statue of the Ukrainian national poet and revolutionary democrat **Taras Shevchenko** (1814–61), unveiled in 1964. The 6-meter-tall bronze statue of Shevchenko stands on a pedestal of Ukrainian granite (sculptors Mikhail Gritsyuk, Yuli Sinkevich and Anatoly Fuzhenko).

If we proceed further along Kutuzov Avenue, we can get acquainted with another of Moscow's interesting new regions. Before the revolution it was one of the crowded outlying working-class districts of Moscow, with narrow, dirty side-streets and blind alleys, cobblestone streets, and wooden huts which testified eloquently to the desperate poverty of their inhabitants. "Moscow," wrote the French publicist Pierre Courtade after a visit in 1957, "is a workers'

city, the capital of fraternal nationalities. And that is the first thing that strikes you. That is why, in Moscow, there is no East End for the poor and West End for the rich, as in London, no Harlem for the Negroes as in New York and Fifth Avenue for the people who have absolutely nothing to complain about in the American way of life."

There are a number of stores of interest to the tourist on both sides of Kutuzov Avenue: on the right-hand side is *Malysh* (Tiny Tot) selling baby clothes, and opposite it are the **Russian Souvenir** and *Beriozka*, where you will find an assortment of hand-made goods by national craftsmen of Russia. We recommend that you visit the **Central Salon of the USSR Art Fund** at No. 6 *Ukrainsky bulvar* (Ukrainian Boulevard), about a hundred meters to the left of Kutuzov Avenue. There you can find works by Soviet artists and hand-crafted, one-of-a-kind articles.

You can continue along Ukrainian Boulevard to **Kievsky vokzal** (Kiev Railway Station) and the **Kievskaya Metro Station.** The Kiev Railway Station was built in 1913–17 to the design of engineer Ivan Rerberg. High above the platforms is a hangar-like glass ceiling. The façade of the station, which faces the Moskva River, is decorated with a tall clock-tower. From this station, which was totally reconstructed and enlarged in the early 1980s, trains depart for the south of the country: Kiev, Odessa, Kishinyov and other cities of the

Kievsky (Kiev) Railway Station

Ukraine and Moldavia, as well as Prague, Budapest, Bucharest, and Sofia, with through coaches to Belgrade, Rome and Athens. In the large garden in the square in front of the station a monument will be erected in commemoration of the reunification of the Ukraine with Russia in the mid-17th century. There is a small pier on the bank of the Moskva River from where motor ships embark on their voyage towards the Kremlin. You can get a good view of **Borodinsky most** (Borodino Bridge) spanning the Moskva River (over 150 meters wide in this spot) from *ploshchad Kievskogo vokzala* (Kiev Railway Station Square). The bridge was built to the design of architect

Borodinsky (Borodino) Bridge. Granite colonnade

Roman Klein and engineer Nikolai Oskolkov in 1912 to mark the centenary of the victorious end of the Patriotic War against Napoleon's Grande Armée. Engraved on obelisks which flank the beginning of the bridge are the names of the Russian military leaders Mikhail Kutuzov, Pyotr Bagration, and Mikhail Barklay-de-Tolly and other distinguished generals and heroes of the War of 1812. In 1954 the bridge underwent reconstruction and its width was doubled. At the other end of the bridge are semicurcular granite colonnades crowned with bronze laurel wreaths. From Borodino Bridge you can get a wonderful view of the Lenin Hills, with the contours of the new building of Moscow State University standing out distinctly against the horizon. Borodino Bridge leads to *Smolenskaya ploshchad* (Smolensk Square), which you have already seen from the Garden Ring.

The *Khrustalnoye* (Crystal) **Café** is situated near the junction of Kutuzov Avenue and *Bolshaya Dorogomilovskaya ulitsa* (Big Dorogomilovskaya Street). Before the Revolution this was *Dorogomilovskaya zastava* (or checkpoint) located at the city limits. Beyond it stretched the old Smolensk Road, lined with low, wooden cottages. In Soviet times the city's borderline has changed considerably. Kutuzov Avenue extends for several more kilometers from here.

At the junction of Kutuzov Avenue and Big Dorogomilovskaya

Street, surrounded by trees, rises the "Moscow—Hero-City" Obelisk, which was unveiled in 1977. Sculptor Alexander Shcherbakov and architect Zinaida Chernysheva created an impressive monument in commemoration of the heroic defence of Moscow and the defeat of Nazi troops in the Moscow suburbs in the winter of 1941-42.

Here we shall end our walk. You can return to the Arbatskaya Metro Station and the city center by trolleybus No. 2 or bus No. 89. However, you may wish to continue you ride along Kutuzov Avenue to the Panorama-Museum of the Battle of Borodino and the Triumphal Arch.

At the very end of Kutuzov Avenue (named in honor of the Russian Field Marshal Mikhail Kutuzov, 1745-1813) are several remarkable monuments commemorating the heroic Patriotic War of 1812. The quickest and most convenient way of reaching it is by Metro to **Kutuzovskaya Station** and then either by bus or trolleybus (three stops) or on foot (10 minutes) to the Triumphal Arch and *ploshchad Pobedy* (Victory Square). The square was named in honor of the 30th anniversary of the Victory of the Soviet people in the Great Patriotic War of 1941-45.

The **Triumphal Arch** was erected in 1829-34 to the design of architect Osip Bovet and sculptors Ivan Vitali and Ivan Timofeyev. The first Triumphal Arch (known as the Triumphal Gates) was erected on August 17, 1829 at *Tverskaya zastava* (Tver Check-

point), which marked the beginning of old Tver Street, Moscow's main thoroughfare at the time (you may remember that Tver Street is now Gorky Street, and Tver Checkpoint is the Byelorussian Railway Station Square in front of the Byelorussian Railway Station). The Triumphal Gates stood on the square of the Tver Checkpoint for more than one hundred years. In the summer of 1936, during the reconstruction of Gorky Street and the square of the Byelorussian Railway Station the Triumphal Gates were dismantled and the statuary carefully preserved. Many of the gates' large architectural elements and statuary were exhibited in the branch of the Museum of Architecture in the Donskoy Monastery (No. 1 Donskaya Square). In 1968 the monument was re-erected in its original form.

We would recommend that you take a closer look at the arch by taking the underpass which leads to the observation platform. The restored monument is a monumental 28-meter-high structure with a broad span, decorated in all four sides with pairs of Corinthian columns. Between the columns are the statues of warriors in ancient armour and Roman mantles—a tribute to Classical style which was dominant in the early 19th century. Above the warriors' figures are bas-reliefs entitled "Expulsion of the French" and "Liberated Moscow". The colonnades are crowned by allegorical female figures representing Victory. The goddesses on the main façades hold the laurel wreath of victory in one hand and a myrtle branch, the symbol of peace, in the other. On the side façades the goddesses of Victory are holding broken swords. The arch is topped with the winged figure of Glory in a chariot drawn by six steeds, shielding the victors with a wreath of Glory. The arch bears 44 emblems of Russian cities whose inhabitants participated in the struggle against Napoleon's army and its expulsion from Russia.

Near the Triumphal Arch is another monument to the Patriotic War of 1812, **the Panorama Museum of the Battle of Borodino.** It is a large cylindrical building of glass and aluminium, over 40 meters in diameter, designed by a group of architects headed by Alexander Korabelnikov, and erected in 1962. Along the stone parapet in front of the museum are 68 cannons captured from Napoleon's army during the Battle of Borodino. The façades of the wings are decorated with colored mosaics. In front on a high pedestal is a bronze equestrian statue of Mikhail Kutuzov by the Soviet sculptor Nikolai Tomsky, unveiled in 1973. On three sides of the pedestal are images of the commanders, soldiers, and partisans who rose in defence of the country. The surname of each of the sculptured figures is given, which lends the whole composition a documentary character. In the museum there is a remarkable panoramic painting of the Battle of Borodino by the Russian artist Franz Roubot (1856–1928), 115 meters long and 15 meters high. Roubot completed his work in 1912 for the centenary of the battle. For more than forty years the painting was kept rolled around a wooden shaft, and was later restored by a group of Soviet artists headed by Igor Grabar and Pavel Korin.

Visitors see the panorama from an observation platform 6 meters high. Between them and the painting is a relief reconstruction of the battlefield 12 meters wide, which gives them the impression that they are in the midst of the raging battle that took place on August 26, 1812. Napoleon later wrote that, of the 50 battles he had fought, in the one near Moscow the greatest valor was displayed and the smallest victory won, and that the Russians had won the right to claim themselves undefeated.

In the courtyard of the museum there is an obelisk marking the common grave of 300 officers and men of the Russian army, heroes of the War of 1812. A few yards away is a wooden hut, an exact copy of the one at Fili where the historic Council of War was held on September 1, 1812, when Kutuzov made his bold decision to abandon Moscow but save the army. The hut became known as *Izba* **Kutuzova**; the original one was burned down in 1868.

Now let us return to Victory Square. Here begins *prospekt Marshala Grechko* (Marshal Grechko

Avenue) which leads towards the Moscow Circular Motor Road.

To the left of the Avenue is *Poklonnaya Hill*, which for long centuries has provided a splendid view of Moscow. On September 2, 1812 Napoleon, surrounded by his magnificent retinue, waited vainly here for a deputation of "boyars" with the keys to the city (Napoleon was not very well versed in Russian history: *boyars* were members of the highest feudal class during the 9th-17th centuries).

In 1941 Soviet soldiers left Poklannaya Hill behind as they headed west to defend Moscow from the German fascist armies. Victory park has been laid on Poklonnaya Hill in commemoration of the great feats of the Soviet people in the Great Patriotic War of 1941-45.

You can return to the city center by Metro from the Kutuzovskaya Station or by bus or trolleybus.

ALONG PEACE AVENUE

Prospekt Mira (Peace Avenue) begins at *Kolkhoznaya ploshchad* (Collective Farm Square), situated on the Garden Ring to the north of the city's center. You can start your walk along Peace Avenue at the exit of the **Kolkhoznaya Metro Station.** Before 1957 this was one of the city's most important thoroughfares, and was called *Pervaya meshchanskaya ulitsa.* In the summer of 1957 columns of participants and guests of the 6th World Youth Festival marched along this street. Muscovites and the envoys of youth from many countries were united in their common aim—to struggle for peace. It was decided then to rename the street Peace Avenue in commemoration of the important events connected with the World Youth Festival.

Since ancient times this road has led out of Moscow towards the famous Troitse-Sergiyev (the Trinity and St. Sergius) Monastery (now in Zagorsk) and the old Russian towns of Rostov Veliky and Yaroslavl, and later to Arkhangelsk—the White Sea port-city. There are very few structures still remaining here from Russia's ancient past.

In 1939 the two corner buildings which still frame the entrance to the avenue from Kolkhoznaya Square were crowned with flagstaffs and monograms of the All-Union Agricultural Exhibition, which opened the same year. In 1958 it was decided to make this exhibition a part of the USSR Economic Achievements Exhibition, towards which we are heading.

Reconstruction work during the postwar years was concentrated mainly on the section beyond the Riga Railway Station, and 800 poplar trees were planted there. Multi-storey apartment buildings of original architectural design appeared on both sides of the avenue.

Kolkhoznaya Square is the junction of two of the city's most important transport arteries: the Garden Ring, which encircles the whole city, and Peace Avenue with *ulitsa Sretenka* (Sretenka Street) which runs contiguous to it and connects it with the city's center. Sretenka is an extremely interesting old street which had not yet undergone significant reconstruction. Sretenka is a lively and very busy street, with a row of small grocery stores with a great variety of goods. The building of the **Church of the Dormition** (a monument of architecture built in 1695) now houses **The USSR Navy** exhibition.

To the right of Peace Avenue near Kolkhoznaya Square is one of the masterpieces of Russian Classical architecture—the former Count Sheremetev Hospital. The bow-shaped façade of the monumental building faces the Garden Ring. In the center is a semi-circle of two rows of columns and the building is crowned with a cupola. Sheremetev established an asylum in this building for the poor and ill in memory of his wife Praskovya Zhemchugova, the former serf actress, who died young. The building was constructed in 1792–1807 by the serf architect Yelizvoy Nazarov together with the Italian architect Giacomo Quarenghi who worked in Russia at the time. Today the building and the new blocks behind it house the **Sklifosofsky Institute of Emergency Medical Aid.**

Now let us begin our acquaintance with Peace Avenue itself. At its beginning are historical monuments which are under state protection. On the right-hand side at No. 26 is the entrance to the **branch of the Botanical Gardens** of Moscow University. It was founded in 1706 as a medicinal herbs garden by decree of Peter the Great. Today the garden has a dendrological collection of about 300 varieties of trees and shrubs, as well as an alpinary and plantations of decorative perennial plants. At No. 21 on the left-hand side of the avenue is *Dom mody* (House of Fashion), which you might find interesting to visit. New fashions are regularly demonstrated here. On the right-hand side of the avenue there is a two-storey mansion with two different-sized attics (No. 30). The poet and literary critic Valery Bryussov (1873–1924) lived here for many years. One of the founders of Symbolism in Russian poetry, Bryussov took an active part in the development of Soviet culture after the Great October Revolution and did much public-educational work.

Located at No. 36 is the **Soviet Peace Committee**, which coordinates the activities of peace committees in all the Soviet republics, takes an active part in the actions of the World Peace Council, and cooperates with foreign organizations of peace-loving forces in 120 countries. The Soviet Peace Committee, expressing the will of the Soviet people to live in peace and friendship with other peoples, supports the peaceful initiatives of

Space Obelisk

ДОСТИЖЕНИЯ В ОСВОЕНИИ КОСМИЧЕ

Statue of Yuri Gagarin
World Trade Center (WTC)

Muscovites are very fond of Arbat, one of Moscow oldest streets

VDNKh. *Pavilion "Consumer Goods and Services"*

Church of St. Nicholas at Khamovniki

*Statue of Mikhail Kutuzov in front of the
Battle of Borodino Panorama Museum*

Arch of Triumph

Praga *Restaurant*

Moscow industrial architecture

the Soviet Government and the CPSU, and peace-loving forces in the world aimed at preserving peace on Earth, eliminating the threat of nuclear war, improving the international situation, returning to a course of détente, and building relations among nations on the basis of the Helsinki Agreement. In 1974, in commemoration of the 25th anniversary of the peace movement in the USSR, the Soviet Peace Committee was awarded the Order of Friendship of Peoples.

After you pass the next two buildings you will come to the **Prospekt Mira Metro Station** (Circular Line). If you are tired, you may wish to continue your trip to VDNKh by Metro, by crossing over to the left-hand side of the avenue, to the Prospekt Mira (Radial Line) Station. As you walk along, take notice of the **Olympic Sports Complex** to the left of the avenue, the capital's largest sports complex. Midway along on an open square, stands the **Church of the Metropolitan Philipp**, a monument of 18th-century Classical architecture. Above its rotunda is an elegant colonnade supporting the church's lesser dome. The church was built by Matvei Kazakov, the Moscow architect, whose other creations we have already encountered in previous walks through the city.

The **Olympic Sports Complex** was built for the 1980 Summer Olympics in Moscow. Plans for its construction, however, were made

Former Count Sheremetev Hospital (asylum for the poor and ill). At present the building houses the Sklifosovsky Institute of Emergency Medical Aid

long before as part of the General Plan for the Development of the capital. Its indoor stadium is the largest in the city, and was planned for various kinds of sporting events as well as theater performances, concerts and meetings. During the Olympics, boxing and basketball competitions were held here simultaneously, thanks to a sliding acoustic partition which makes it possible to divide the stadium into two separate halls. The basketball competition hall had stands for 16,000 spectators and the hall for boxing matches—18,000. The sports arena, 120×86 meters in size, was covered with wooden flooring during the games, and can be converted to other types of flooring such as artificial turf, an athletic track, and artificial ice. The arena can accommodate stands for 12,000 spectators and a movable stage. The building is elliptical in shape with a diameter of

Soviet Peace Committee

224 and 183 meters and a height of 40 meters. The gigantic ceiling above the arena and stands is over 30,000 square meters in area and has no intermediate supports. Special lighting equipment provides the necessary illumination for the entire arena and the stands and powerful conditioners maintain normal temperature and humidity levels. There is also equipment for simultaneous translation into 6 languages. There are buffets, cafés, bars and restaurants on every floor of the stadium. Covered passages of the elegant podium connect the stadium with the swimming pool, which has stands for 13,000 spectators. The swimming pool has an original design: it resembles a giant open scallop shell with two large sections—two pools at its bottom. Swimming competitions were held in these pools during the Olympics. The first pool is 50 meters long, 25 meters wide, and 2.2 meters deep, with ten swimming tracks and a regulated depth which provides equal conditions for all the swimmers and identical speed qualities along the whole length of the track. The second pool, separated from the first by a glass partition, is 33.3×25 meters, with a depth of 6 meters, and can be used for diving and water polo competitions, which were held here during the Goodwill Games in 1986. There are four more training halls here and three special pools where the water temperature can be regulated up to 30 °C for warming up the muscles. The water is changed five times daily and modern methods of water purification are employed. The pools are surrounded by a gallery with glass observation holes from which television, photo, and film reporters can observe the sportsmen under the water and carry out their reporting and filming.

The sports complex was erected on a site where there were once old, dried-up ponds and a number of narrow side-streets lined with old buildings of little historic value. This once unattractive region has become one of the capital's most sightworthy spots. The covered stadium and swimming pool were built to the design of a group of architects headed by Boris Thor.

If you decide to forgo the Metro and continue on foot, a 10 minutes' walk will bring you out to *ploshchad Rizhskogo vokzala* (Riga Railway Station Square). Here Peace Avenue intersects the city's third ring—a superhighway whose northern and north-eastern sections are already in operation. When the highway is completed, it will be 35 kilometers long and will relieve the Garden Ring of a considerable traffic load. To cite one example, at present 2,000 cars an hour pass through Kolkhoznaya Square.

On the left-hand side of Riga Railway Station Square is the main building of the **Riga Railway Station**, a low building stretching along the square which resembles a row of old Russian *terems*. It was built in the late 19th century in neo-Russian style and is the most low-keyed of the capital's railway stations. It receives and dispatches only 116 local and long-distance trains each day. From here trains depart for Riga—the capital of the Latvian Socialist Republic, and for a number of other cities in the north-west.

The **Rizhskaya Metro Station** is on the right-hand side of the avenue. We recommend that you take the Metro from here in order to complete your acquaintance with Peace Avenue in the vicinity of the VDNKh Metro Station, as a walk on foot would take you close to one hour. Take notice of the **sculpture "Sputnik"** in front of the Rizhskaya Metro Station, one of the first creative responses to the world's first flight of an artificial earth satellite on October 4, 1957. The unpretentious but impressive monument is the work of sculptor Semyon Kovner.

The **VDNKh Metro Station** is situated amidst green alleys and flower gardens near the entrance to the exhibition. When you come out of the station, turn left and you will see the **Space Obelisk**, a silvery shaft soaring in a curve to a height of nearly 100 meters. It was unveiled in 1964, and was designed by sculptor Andrei Faidysh-Krandiyevsky and architect Mikhail Barshch. The main shaft consists of a steel frame faced with sheets of polished titanium, a durable metal not affected by atmospheric precipitation. On both sides of its granite base are sculptures depicting the people who made the first manned space flight possible and those who today are boldly continuing exploration of outer space.

... By efforts hard and
                 unremitting
that outmatched ignorance and
                         crime,
We hammered wings of fire
befitting our souls, our country
                 and our time!

These lines written by Soviet poet Nikolai Gribachev are inscribed on the face of the obelisk.

Situated within the base of the obelisk is the **Memorial Museum of Cosmonautics**, with an exposition demonstrating the development of space exploration and the major achievements in this field— from the world's first artificial earth satellite and manned orbital stations to the methods of planetary exploration and the solution of economical problems through the use of space technology, and provides information about tests of the new carrier rockets, designed to launch shuttle-type orbital spaceships and other large space apparatus of scientific and utilitarian significance into orbits around the Earth. On display are various articles used by cosmonauts during space flights, as well as instruments from Soviet spaceships and personal belongings of the cosmonauts. All these things create an atmosphere of authenticity and give the visitor a feeling of immediate involvement in these momentous events. Visitors can also see a film which transports them into a world of galactic nebulae and takes them on a flight around the Earth.

In front of the obelisk is a **statue of Konstantin Tsiolkovsky** (1857–1935), the Soviet scientist and inventor who not only predicted interplanetary flight within the solar system, but also created the theory of modern rocketry and astronautics. Between the obelisk and Peace Avenue is the *Alley of Cosmonauts*, a walk lined with bronze busts of Soviet cosmonauts **Yuri Gagarin, Valentina Tereshkova, Alexei Leonov, Pavel Belyayev,** and **Vladimir Komarov.** At the end of the alley are two **monuments**, one **to Sergei Korolyov** (1906–66), the outstanding scientist and designer of the first Soviet rockets and spaceships, and the other **to Academician Mstislav Keldysh** (1911–78), mathematician and mechanical engineer, and the head of many Soviet space programs.

From the square in front of the Space Obelisk you can get a good view of the *Kosmos* cinema, the Ostankino TV Tower, the main entrance to the Exhibition grounds, the "Montreal" pavilion (the original USSR Pavilion at the Montreal World Fair, which was dismantled and returned to Moscow), and the *Kosmos* **Hotel**, which deserves special mention. It was built in 1979 according to a project jointly designed by Soviet and French architects. The 28-storey hotel has 1,777 rooms; a conference hall seating 1,000; several restaurants; and a sports complex with a swimming pool.

From the observation platform you will not be able to get a full view of the **monument *Worker and Collective-Farm Woman*** sculpted by Vera Mukhina (1889–1953), but it is worthy of a closer look. It is a unique work of monumental art and has become a symbol of the Soviet Union for people throughout the world. Called "A Hymn to the New World", the sculptural composition was created fifty years ago, and was first seen by Parisians who attended the opening ceremony of the Soviet Pavilion at the 1937 Paris World Fair. The stainless steel sculpture is 25 meters high and weighs 75 tons and depicts a worker and collective-farm woman raising aloft a hammer and sickle as they step forward in unison. Their figures express strength and confidence. The sculptural masterpiece has stood in front of the Exhibition's North Entrance since 1939.

Now some facts about the exhibition itself. The **USSR Economic Achievements Exhibition** (the Russian abbreviation is *VDNKh*) can be called the country's biggest "museum". It was opened in 1959, and today is an actively functioning exhibition with 100,000 annually renewed exhibits which show the state-of-the-art developments in industry, agriculture, building, transport, science and culture in the USSR. The exhibition's main purpose is to reflect the way of life and the achievements of the world's first socialist state, and to acquaint the public with the latest methods and technologies so that they might be incorporated on a broad scale to raise the standards and productivity of labor. The exhibition grounds cover an area of 578 acres and there are 80 pavilions with open-air displays. More than half the exhibition's territory is occupied by parks, gardens, and flowergardens. Please note that the **Building Section** is on the other side of Moscow, at No. 30 *Frunzenskaya naberezhnaya* (Frunze Embankment), not far from the **Frunzenskaya Metro Station.** Its exhibits and displays trace the development of construction in the USSR (including housing construction), its methods, the machinery used, and future plans.

The exhibition is always bustling with life and activity. Visitors from various parts of the country come here, many of them by the special invitation of *VDNKh.* Specialized programs acquaint them with that

Statue of Konstantin Tsiolkovsky

branch of industry which corresponds to their professional interests. Meetings with the leading people in industry, scientists, writers, journalists, and artists are organized in the pavilions. Scientific symposiums and seminars, lectures, and meetings of people working in the same branches of industry are held. Working demonstrations are given for the majority of the machines, machine tools, mechanisms, and instruments on display. You can acquire informational material about the exhibits at any of the exhibition's 32 information centers.

Let us continue our walk. A monumental portico with an imposing colonnade and sculptural figures of a collective-farm man and woman raising aloft ears of wheat marks the Main Entrance to the exhibition.

A broad walk with fountains, a rose garden 1,200 square meters in area, and a double row of lamp standards in the shape of ears of wheat leads to the Central Pavilion,

Monument Worker and Collective-Farm Woman *(sculptor Vera Mukhina)*

where the exhibition proper begins. With its 35-meter-tall spire crowned with a star, the pavilion is visible from every corner of the exhibition. In front of the pavilion there is a statue of Lenin (1954, sculptor Pyotr Yatsyno), and above the entrance are the state emblems of the 15 Union Republics and of the USSR.

A huge illuminated map of the Soviet Union in the main hall reflects the development of key industries. The figures are impressive: today the USSR produces one-fifth of the world industrial output. Along with various exhibits there are two dioramas in the pavilion, one of which presents the Sayano-Shushenskaya Hydroelectric Power Station, the largest in the world, which produces 24 billion kilowatt-hours of electricity after its third unit has been put into operation. The other diorama shows the city of Ulyanovsk, where Lenin was born. One of the most beautiful cities on the Volga, Ulyanovsk

today is a rapidly developing city with a highly organized industry and blocks of new apartment buildings. The small house where Lenin was born is preserved as a relic sacred to all mankind.

All the excursion routes through the exhibition begin at the Central Pavilion. A thorough acquaintance with the exhibition would require more than just one or even two days. However, you could board one of the sightseeing trains at the Main Entrance to make a comfortable 45 minutes' tour of the exhibition grounds.

As you leave the Central Pavilion you will see side alleys along both sides of the lawn with rose beds. The alleys are lined with chestnut trees planted at various times by Soviet cosmonauts and their colleagues, astronauts from other countries who took part in joint space flights.

Beyond the Central Pavilion is the vast expanse of Friendship of

VDNKh *of the USSR*

the Peoples Square, with pavilions on either side and two fountains. The first, with bronze sculptures of young girls symbolizing the Union Republics, is situated at the beginning of the square and bears the same name. Built in 1954 by architect Konstantin Topuridze and others, the fountain is one of Moscow's most noteworthy sights. Its basin is 3,700 square meters in area, and it has 800 jets which spray water to a height of 24 meters. Five hundred and twenty five lamps and projectors are used to illuminate the fountain at night.

At the end of the square is the *Stone Flower* fountain. Its jets spray water to a height of 20 meters. The fountain is particularly attractive at night when its lit-up stones sparkle in a fairy-like emerald cascade of water.

The first pavilion on the right is the Atomic Energy Pavilion, with scale models of all the existing atomic reactors in the country. The exposition "The USSR—Country of the Atom for Peaceful Purposes" is dedicated to the 1984 celebration of the 30th anniversary of the first operation of the world's first atomic power plant in the town of Obninsk. Another exposition—"Atomic Energy in the National Economy"—demonstrates how atomic energy is used in the Soviet Union to desalinate sea water, in the chemical industry and metallurgy, for heating and the introduction of heating systems, for equipping ice-breakers, and in various other spheres.

To the left of the Central Pavilion is the Education Pavilion, followed by three pavilions of the USSR Academy of Sciences—"Biology", "Chemistry", and "Physics"—devoted to the work of outstanding Soviet biologists, chemists, and physicists, particularly in the fields of solid state physics, semi-conductors, quantum radio-electronics, cybernetics, radiation chemistry, and the biology of the living cell. In 1984 the Soviet people marked the 260th anniversary of the foundation of the USSR Academy of Sciences.

The next pavilion on the same side is "Standards". An electronic tableau with changing figures on its glass façade indicates the exact time and air temperature. In this pavilion you can see the latest achievements in Soviet industry, which are displayed according to State standards and bear the USSR State Mark of Quality. Consumer goods and industrial and technical products are given this mark after passing state quality control.

Developments in the Soviet iron and steel industry are broadly demonstrated in the Metallurgy Pavilion. On display, for instance, is a scale model of the Krivoi Rog blast furnace that produces four million tons of pig iron a year, an amount equal to the total volume of the country's iron output in 1929.

The Health Pavilion has an interesting exposition which illustrates the social foundations and directions in the development of Soviet public health care. The visitor may be interested to learn that the cost of hospital treatment, which averages some 240 roubles a month per person, is borne totally by the state. On display in the exposition are the latest achievements in medical technology, particularly diagnostic apparatus.

Opposite the Health Pavilion across the square is the Soviet Culture Pavilion, with an exhibition hall in which works by artists of the 15 Soviet republics, and material about the Soviet theater, circus, and cinematography are displayed.

Beyond the *Stone Flower* fountain is a pavilion the color of wheat. This is the Agriculture Pavilion, one of several pavilions demonstrating achievements in Soviet agriculture.

On the left-hand side of the walk are the Computers, Radio-Electronics and Communication and Electrical Engineering pavilions. We recommend a visit to the latter. The models of the latest refrigerators, electric and immersion heaters, and electric kitchens in the exposition of consumer goods are a good illustration of the Soviet standard of living.

We have come to Industry Square. Directly in front of us is the Space Pavilion, the largest of the exhibition, with a dome which is visible from the Main Entrance and every point of the grounds. On display beneath its arches are space rockets, artificial satellites, and a great variety of flight equipment, instruments, and personal gear worn by the cosmonauts. The exhibits provide information about the most recent achievements in space technology, the application of space technology in various branches of the national economy, and international cooperation in space exploration for peaceful purposes. A sign above the entrance bears the highly appropriate words of Konstantin Tsiolkovsky: "Mankind will not remain forever on the Earth, but in its pursuit of light and space it will first make tentative probes beyond the atmosphere and then conquer all of outer space."

To the right of the Space Pavilion is the Electrification of the USSR Pavilion and to the left, the Transport Pavilion. Further along on Industry Square are two modern-looking glass buildings of interest to visitors. These are the pavilions housing both international and domestic industrial exhibitions.

On the right near the North Entrance is one of the largest pavilions of the exhibition — the Consumer Goods and Services Pavilion, which occupies an area of 48,000 square meters. Its two exhibition buildings are connected by a high arch and a glass-enclosed hall. Its distinctive architectural design sets it apart from the other pavilions of the exhibition. Visitors are drawn to the section "Dwelling and Comfort", which presents the interiors of apartments equipped with all the necessary conveniences: modern, low-priced furniture, household and kitchen appliances, and radio and electric devices. The country's top Fashion Houses display their creations in the "Apparel" section. Also interesting are the "Private Farm", "Private Orchard", and "Private Garden" expositions.

If you proceed to the right from Industry Square you will come to the Livestock Center and its show ring. If you walk to the left you will come to the Michurin Orchard, so called because it is mainly planted with the best varieties of hard and soft fruits developed by the renowned plant breeder Ivan Michurin (1855–1935). There is a **statue of Michurin** in the orchard.

On the exhibition grounds there are 24,000 trees, 100,000 decorative shrubs, and several million flowers. There are birches, oaks, pines, maples, poplars, lindens, and firs characteristic of the wealth of Russian forests.

The exhibition is also a recreation park with various entertainments. There is an open-air theater seating 3,400, where the best professional and amateur companies perform (dance ensembles, choirs, and symphony orchestras). There is also a variety theater, the Fun Fair (with carrousels, Russian swings, rockets, and bumper cars, etc.), a small zoo, and a Cyclorama, a cinema with no seats, where you stand in the middle of a round hall with a great screen all around you. Shows last 20 minutes. The Cyclorama and the Fun Fair are both near the Main Entrance. At the exhibition you can sample the national dishes of many of the peoples of the USSR. We would recommend you start, with the *Zolotoi kolos* (Golden Sheaf) Restaurant situated on the bank of a pond. There is a fountain in front of the restaurant which bears the same name. A pleasant stroll along the exhibition's walks will bring you to the restaurant, which is only about 3,000 meters from the Main Entrance.

The exhibition is open all year round. In winter many of its walks and squares are flooded and converted into skating rinks. And during the annual Russian Winter festival (December 25 to January 5) there are folk games and festive winter entertainments on open-air stages and snow-covered glades. You can hear songs in Russian and other languages of the peoples of the USSR, watch song and dance competitions, or take part in traditional round dances to the lively tunes of an accordion. You can also enjoy a ride in sleigh drawn by a team of three horses—the famous Russian *troika*. The horses' harness is festively decorated, with bells beneath the shaft-bow. Every year at this time a national *troika* competition is held. Every detail is important: the condition of the animals' coats, their compatibility, temperament, the decoration of the sleigh and harness, and the skill of the driver himself. And after a ride in the frost it's pleasant to relax in the warmth of *Zolotoi kolos* Restaurant, to listen to Russian music while drinking tea from a *samovar*

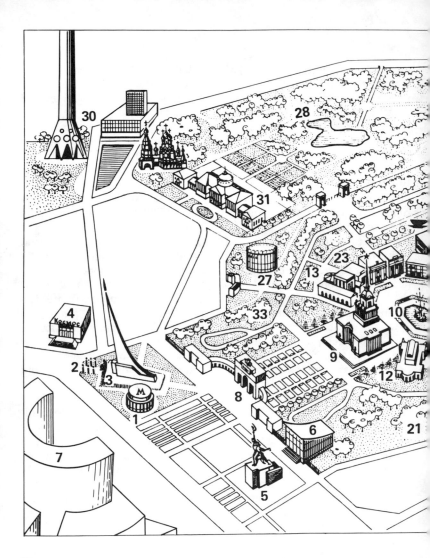

VDNKh

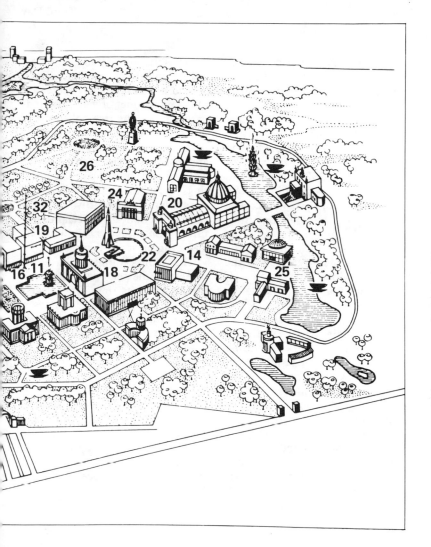

and eating pies with jam and honey, and to enjoy the company of Grandfather Frost and the Snow Maiden.

The grounds of the USSR Economic Achievements Exhibition adjoin two other interesting open spaces—the Main Botanical Gardens of the USSR Academy of Sciences and the Dzerzhinsky Recreation Park in Ostankino. The best way to get to the Botanical Gardens is to go through the grounds of the Exhibition to the Khovansky Gate, to the left of the Central Pavilion.

The **Botanical Gardens** cover an area of 890 acres. Their shady oak woods, birch groves, rose gardens (which contain 16,000 different varieties of roses) and other flower gardens attract many visitors.

Dzerzhinsky Park borders on the grounds of the Ostankino Palace, a remarkable monument of Russian architecture and decorative art. It once belonged to the family of Counts Sheremetev, and was built in 1791-98 at the time of Nikolai Sheremetev by serf architect Pavel Argunov (1768-1806) and other serf architects. It is a summer palace built completely of wood in the Russian Classical style. The façade facing the entrance to its grounds has a high portico with six columns. The façade facing the garden has a portico with ten columns and is less austere in style, as if emphasizing the intimate atmosphere of the garden.

The interior of the palace— foyer, state rooms, and galleries—

is lavishly decorated. The exquisite gilt wood carving of the furniture, doors, and walls, the skilfully laid parquet of valuable kinds of wood, and the rich collection of the cut-glass and bronze chandeliers, carved gilt standard lamps and *pot pourri* vases were all the work of serf craftsmen. The paintings, especially those by the Argunovs, who were serf artists, and the rich collection of porcelain, pictures, prints, and sculptures are also of interest.

The whole central section of the palace is a theater, one of the finest in Russia of its time. The players were all serf actors and actresses, among whom the talented singer Praskovya Kovalyova-Zhemchugova (1768-1803) and the dancer Tatyana Shlikova-Granatova (1773-1863) were particularly renowned. In 1917 the Ostankino estate was nationalized and became the **Palace-Museum of Serf Art**. Theater machinery of the late 18th century has been partly preserved, and invariably attracts the attention of visitors. Concerts of early Russian music are frequently held in the palace.

Next to the Ostankino Palace is the five-dome **Troitskaya** (Trinity) **Church**, an interesting example of late 17th-century architecture.

In 1967 a new Moscow landmark rose in Ostankino, the concrete **TV Tower**, 540 meters high (head designer Nikolai Nikitin, 1907-73)— the tallest structure in Europe. The tower is made of ordinary concrete, reinforced concrete, and metal. Its diameter at the base is 50 meters. At the 337-meter-level there is an observation platform to which visitors are taken by four elevators which operate at a speed of 7 meters per second. The observation platform provides a marvelous panoramic view of Moscow, and also serves as the foyer for the *Sedmoye nebo* (Seventh Heaven) **Restaurant**. Its three dining halls seating 288 guests are situated on three floors which encircle the tower beginning at the 325-meter-level. The floors slowly rotate one full revolution in 40 minutes, so that the diner sees a panorama of Moscow during the meal, including a clear view of the entire Exhibition grounds. Although the tower weighs 35,000 tons, it appears light and graceful, as if rising unbuttressed from the ground. In actuality, it has a foundation weighing 22,000 tons. Mounted along the perimeter of the tower's cavity are 150 taut steel cables 38 millimeters in diameter, with a tension force of 112 tons. Radio and TV equipment is installed on 44 storeys and 14 balconies inside and outside the tower. Television programs are broadcast from the tower over a radius of 120 kilometers.

Near the TV Tower is the huge **Television Center** (named after the 50th anniversary of the October Revolution). The building is over 400 meters long and 100 meters wide and houses 70 radio and 22 TV studios, as well as hundreds of offices and a conference hall seating 1,000. The TV Center is linked through cable, radio-relay and satellite communication systems with all the TV centers in the USSR and through Intervision and Eurovision with countries abroad.

Not far from the Television Center, at No. 2 *Shestoi Ostanskinsky pereulok* (6th Ostankino Lane), stands a two-storey cottage, now the Academician **Korolyov Museum**. Sergei Korolyov, the designer of the first spaceships, lived there from 1959 to 1966.

This completes our excursion. Our short sketch of the northern section of the city is also finished. Now we suggest that you reinforce your impressions by visiting the observation platform and the *Sedmoye nebo* Restaurant.

THE LENIN HILLS

If you would like to enjoy one more panorama of Moscow, then we suggest that you set aside two hours or so to visit the Lenin Hills. This is a favorite spot with Muscovites, who like to come here to rest and enjoy showing the fine view of the city to their guests. There is probably no better place for taking in all of Moscow at a glance. If you go there by car, which is the easiest way, your whole trip should not

Ostankino Palace

take more than an hour and a half.

The Lenin Hills are a high river bank which rises 85 meters above the Moskva River. The river itself is 115 meters above sea level. Up until 1924, the Lenin Hills were called Vorobyovy (Sparrow) Hills after the village that was once here. The shady avenue to the right leads to an observation platform a fifteen minutes' walk away. But let us first say a few words about the three buildings you can see on the left side of Vernadsky Avenue—the Palace of Young Pioneers, Children's Musical Theater, and the State Circus.

The **Moscow Palace of Young Pioneers** (named after the 40th Anniversary of the All-Union Pioneer Organization), was opened in June 1962. It is a large club covering an area of 138 acres. In the expanse of its lawn is the Parade Ground, where the crimson flag of the Pioneers flutters from a tall flagstaff. On festive occasions a Pioneer campfire burns in a great bowl there. The Parade Ground is the center of the whole architectural complex. The main building is a two-storey palace with glass walls

and a bright panel of colored tiles and smalt. It would be difficult to list all the halls and rooms of the palace's seven blocks. There are rooms where younger children can play games, sing and dance, rooms for noisy and quiet games of school-age children, the Lenin Hall, where children are admitted into the Young Pioneers organization, the Club of Fascinating Knowledge, a museum, etc.

Adjoining the main building are blocks with laboratories, workshops, and rooms for making various models, where young constructors come after school to make model planes, rockets, and ships. Well-equipped studios accept young painters, sketchers, amateur film makers, elocutionists, actors, musicians, dancers, cooks, and would-be motorists.

The palace has its own stadium with stands for 5,000 and gymnasiums, an artificial lake for learning to sail, row, and canoe, a large tract for young naturalists, agronomists, bee-keepers, and gardeners, a theater, and a concert hall. Many of the Pioneers are members of the International Friendship Club named after Yuri Gagarin, where children study foreign languages, meet with guests from abroad, and acquaint them with their school and Pioneer activities.

The 400 rooms of the palace are noisy and gay. Experienced teachers and activity leaders see to it that children get every opportunity from early childhood to develop their gifts and talents. All children are admitted here without restrictions. In addition to this palace there are 45 district Pioneer Houses in Moscow where children can attend various classes and group activities in their residential area. The Soviet state and trade unions allocate large sums for the development of children's creative abilities outside the school. The Young Pioneers Palace was designed by Igor Pokrovsky, Victor Yegerev, Vladimir Kubasov and Felix Novikov.

A bit further along Vernadsky Avenue, at No. 5 is a building of strikingly original architecture. It looks like an enticing toy—large and elegant. The building is crowned by a sculptural composition depicting the *Blue Bird of Happiness* soaring freely with outspread wings above a harp upraised to the sky (sculptor Vyacheslav Klykov). The *Blue Bird of Happiness*—the symbol of the dream of a happy life—"flew" here from the play written by the Belgian playwright Maurice Maeterlinck (this play has been performed in the Moscow Art Theater for over 75 years). The **Children's Musical Theater** (founded and directed by Natalya Sats) was opened in 1965. The theater's new building, with two halls seating 1,500, was built in 1980 to the design of architects Vladilen Krasilnikov and Alexander Velikanov.

A short distance beyond the theater is the large glass building of the new **Moscow Circus on the Lenin Hills** (near the *Universitet Metro Station*), opened in the spring of 1971 (architect Yakov Belopolsky). The building has 23 rows of seats extending to a height of 36 meters which can accommodate 3,400 spectators. The circus ring has four interchangeable floors that can be switched in a matter of five minutes. One is an ordinary circus ring, another is a pool for aquatic shows, a third, a rink for ballet and circus on ice, and the fourth, a special ring for illusionists. Two foyers, each 350 meters long, encircle the arena on two levels. Adjoining the main building are special quarters for the performing animals with exercise pens and a kitchen.

Muscovites are very fond of the circus. There is another circus in the center, on Tsvetnoy Boulevard (the old circus), which was closed

Children's Musical Theater

for major renovation in 1986, 100 years after its opening. In addition, in summer there is often a traditional circus in a tent in one of the city's parks.

The observation platform towards which we are heading is situated in front of the new building of the Lomonosov University (Moscow State University), which we have already mentioned during our walk along Marx Avenue. Over the years, the University has had a galaxy of famous teachers and alumni—world-renowned scientists who have founded many new scientific schools and fields, such as physicists Alexander Stoletov, Pyotr Lebedev, Sergei Vavilov, Igor Tamm, Pyotr Kapitsa, and Lev Landau; physiologist Ivan Sechenov; aerodynamist Sergei Chaplygin; chemists Nikolai Zelinsky and Alexander Nesmeyanov; geochemist Vladimir Vernadsky; linguist Filipp Fortunatov; mathematician Andrei Kolmogorov, and mathematician and mechanical engineer Mikhail Lavrentyev.

Since the Revolution Moscow

University has trained over 160,000 graduates in various fields; that is 50 per cent more than in its whole 150 years before the Revolution. The number of departments has grown from 4 during the pre-Revolutionary period to 17 departments, 280 sub-faculties and 4 scientific research institutes, with over 28,000 undergraduate students and 5,000 postgraduate students of 70 nationalities. The University's programs are geared towards providing students with a broad background in the fundamentals of knowledge combined with creative activity and participation in research work. Research work is carried out in all the main branches of contemporary science. The qualification level of the University's staff is the highest in the country, and includes 126 full and corresponding members of the USSR Academy of Sciences. Each year the University expands its international contacts, and its authority throughout the world grows. Over 1,500 undergraduate and

Circus on the Lenin Hills

postgraduate students from 100 countries complete the full course of study. Each year the University sponsors dozens of international seminars, conferences, and scientific symposiums.

These buildings were put up in 1949-53; construction was begun 4 years after the end of World War II in the area of the former Vorobyovo village. The University complex was built by some 20,000 workers in somewhat less than 4 years, and consists of 40 teaching blocks and research facilities, as well as botanical gardens, a sports stadium, and a big park, covering a total area of 791 acres. The architects of the main building, the center of the architectural ensemble, were Lev Rudnev, Sergei Chernyshev, Pavel Abrosimov, and Alexander Khryakov. The 32-storey main tower, with its spire crowned by a golden star set in ears of wheat, is 240 meters high. The diameter of the star is 5 meters. On the flanking 18-storey blocks there is a clock, a thermometer, and barometer with surface diameters around 9 meters. The buildings contain an assembly hall seating 1,500, a student club, 19 lecture halls and 140 auditoriums, dozens of teaching and research laboratories, a large library, hostels with 6,000 rooms for students, a **Museum of the Earth Sciences**, a swimming pool, and sports facilities.

The humanities departments, the last to move to the University campus, were housed in a simple

The Lomonosov University (new premises) on the Lenin Hills

and comfortable new building with laboratories equipped with the latest facilities.

A **Walk of Fame** leads up to the main building, and is flanked on both sides by granite busts of great Russian scientists and scholars.

If you approach the University along this walk you will see that sculpture has been widely used in its decoration. The statues include a unique one of a young man and woman by Vera Mukhina (in front of the main entrance) and a **statue of the founder, Mikhail Lomonosov**, by Nikolai Tomsky, which stands in the inner courtyard.

And now let us look at the view of Moscow from the **observation platform.** It seems that we are now relatively close to the center of the city. Before the Revolution its boundary ran along the Circular Railway, which you can clearly see from here. Behind it straight ahead are the gold domes of the Kremlin cathedrals and Ivan the Great Bell-Tower. To the left on the horizon are the new blocks of Kalinin Avenue, the building of the Council

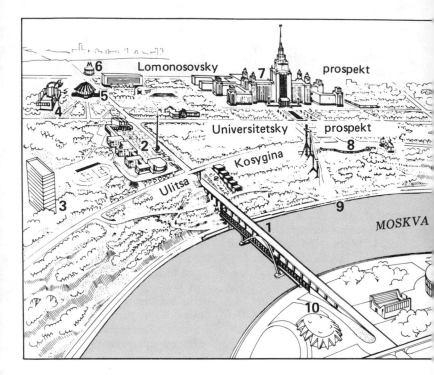

THE LENIN HILLS

1. *Metro Bridge*
2. *Palace of Young Pioneers*
3. Orlyonok *Hotel.* Sputnik *Youth Travel Bureau*
4. *Children's Musical Theater*
5. *Moscow Circus (on the Lenin Hills)*
6. *Universitet Metro Station*
7. *The Lomonosov University. New premises on the Lenin Hills*
8. *Observation platform*
9. *Motor-ship pier*
   Lenin Central Stadium at Luzhniki:

for Mutual Economic Assistance, and the *Ukraina* Hotel. On a clear day, you can see the TV Tower at Ostankino (to the left on the horizon). And down below the Moskva River flows quietly along between its granite embankments.

Between the river and the Circular Railway, surrounded by the river on three sides, are the white buildings of the **Lenin Central Stadium** in the midst of a green park. The whole thing was built amazingly quickly in fifteen months on an empty tract of marshy grounds and allotments. In the old days this area was called *Luzhniki* (the Marshes) because the meadows often used to be soggy after heavy rain or flooded when the

river overflowed its banks. The area set aside for the building of the stadium—462 acres—had to be first raised 1.5 meters. The big bowl in the center is the Large Sports Arena with stands for 100,000. The light masts are 56 meters in height. In front of the main entrance is a statue of Lenin by Matvei Manizer. Under the grandstands are around 1,000 premises—rooms for training and warming up, changing rooms, medical facilities, a hotel, a restaurant, cafés, two cinemas, and a unique **Museum of the Physical Culture and Sport.** To the right of the Large Sports Arena is a swimming pool with stands for 13,000 spectators. To the left is the indoor Small Sports Arena with stands for

10,000. Further to the left is *Dvorets sporta* (Palace of Sports), an indoor stadium which can seat up to 15,000 spectators. Here sports competitions, ice ballet performances, poetry readings, concerts, and New Year's theater presentations for children are held.

The most prominent new addition to the sports complex is the originally designed ***Druzhba*** (Friendship) **Universal Sports Hall**, which from the outside resembles a huge tortoise shell on 28 reinforced concrete legs. The glass-enclosed hall is 100 meters in length and 100 meters in width, and despite its heavy supports weighing many tons each, appears light and delicate in structure. The size and shape of the main arena can be altered to suit any of the twelve types of sports competitions which are held in it. There are stands which can seat from 3,000 to 4,000 spectators.

A total of 160,000 spectators can simultaneously watch competitions in any of 32 kinds of sports held in the stadium complex. There are 140 various sports facilities on the stadium's grounds, including football fields, and courts for tennis, volleyball, and basketball. These facilities are available not only for top class sportsmen and women but also for the rank-and-file members of Luzhniki's many sports sections and fitness classes. Everyday approximately 30,000 people from the ages of six to seventy use Luzhniki's facilities. Over 150,000 middle-aged and elderly Muscovites

belong to physical fitness groups.

During Luzhniki's more than 30-year history, a great number of important competitions have been held, including the 1980 Summer Olympic Games, many World and European championships, finals of all the summer Games of the Peoples of the USSR, and the "Friendship-84" International Competitions. During the latter, which were held under the motto of "Sports—Peace—Friendship", a flame burned in a bowl above the Large Sports Arena. In 1985 the opening and closing ceremonies of the 12th World Festival of Youth and Students were held here, and in 1986—the Goodwill Games.

Muscovites are great fans of sports, and there are nearly 5,000 various sports facilities in the city. One and a half million Muscovites go in for some kind of sport, and among them there are nearly 1,000 Honored Masters of Sport, over 1,000 Masters of Sport, more than 3,000 country champions, and over 1,000 World, European, and Olympic champions.

The Lenin Hills have much to offer all year round. In summer it's pleasant to sit beneath the shady trees or to stroll along the paths near the river bank. In winter the Lenin Hills are a favorite spot for skiing and tobogganing, and large winter sports competitions are held, such as ski-jumping (the spring-board is to the right of the observation platform).

The Lenin Hills have an interesting history. Before the Revolution workers' meetings and May Day demonstrations were held here. Lenin also came here. And earlier, in 1826, young Alexander Herzen and Nikolai Ogaryov, the advanced thinkers and leading revolutionary democrats of their time, swore a solemn oath here to devote their lives to the struggle for the people's freedom. "The sun lit up the whole of Moscow," Herzen recalled in his memoirs. "Moscow was looking at us... We took each other's hands and walked off together for life." They remained faithful to their pledge. On one of the slopes of the Lenin Hills in 1978 a **memorial monument** was erected consisting of a tall granite torch with an eternal flame symbolizing their faithfulness to their pledge which has become an inspiration to future generations.

All the buildings we have seen during our walk—the Palace of Young Pioneers, the Moscow University buildings, the Central Stadium at Luzhniki, and the new residential areas adjoining this region, were built according to a single urban development plan, and form a harmonious architectural ensemble. These buildings of great social value are spread out over a large territory with green parks and gardens—this is how Soviet architects and urban planners envisage all of Moscow in the future.

This completes our stroll on the Lenin Hills. The easiest way to return to your hotel is by the Universitet Metro Station, at the junction of Vernadsky and Lomonosov avenues.

IF YOU HAVE
AN EXTRA DAY ...

Moscow has many places of interest. We believe we have already described the most interesting ones that should be visited first. In choosing them we took into account that you may not have very much time for sightseeing; but if you should have an extra day to spare, here are some suggestions from among which to choose...

A TOUR OF THE METRO

We have already mentioned a number of Metro stations in describing walks around the city. We shall now tell you about the Metropolitan Railway as one of the city's major sights in itself, worth taking time to visit.

Plans to build an underground railway in Moscow were talked about before the Revolution. The City *Duma* looked into a project in 1902, but rejected it. "This project," the newspaper *Russkoye Slovo* wrote, "is a staggeringly impudent encroachment on everything Russian people hold dear in the city of Moscow. As the tunnel of the metropolitan railway will pass in places only a few feet beneath churches, the peace and quiet of these sacred places will be disturbed."

A Metro was begun in Moscow only in Soviet times. The first shaft was sunk in 1931 and the first train ran on May 15, 1935, when the first line, with thirteen stations, was opened. Steady building and extension continued, and did not stop even in the hard days of the war. The system which is still expanding, now has 138 stations, and is 218 kilometers long. According to the General Plan for the Development of the city, the length of the system when completed will be 360 kilometers.

The Metro is the quickest and most convenient way of getting around Moscow. It connects the center with all districts, including areas of intensive new housing development near the city limits, bounded by the Circular Motor Road. Its trains carry 7 million passengers daily. On some sectors their speed reaches 90 kilometers an hour, and during rush hour the interval between them is only 50 seconds. Nearly 8,000 trains a day are operated. An automatic train control system employing computers ensures punctuality and safety.

Most of the stations are deep underground, but there are sections of the line and some stations that are on the surface. The ventilation system of the tunnels and stations changes the air completely four times an hour.

The fare, which has remained unchanged since the day the Metro was opened, is 5 kopecks, regardless of the distance travelled.

No two stations are alike; most of them have their own unique appearance and architectural and artistic design. These "underground palaces" are light, spacious, and are kept immaculately clean. The architects, builders, artists and sculptors all strove to make each station a worthy extension of the new socialist city itself. Valuable stone and other fine new materials were used to face the halls, tunnels and escalators (some 45 kilometers in length) of the stations.

Although it is best to book your Metro excursion through the Service Bureau of your hotel, you may want to venture out on your own. In that case, simply enter the nearest Metro station and travel two or three stops, getting out at each station to look around the platform. This should take no more than an hour of your time. The best times for exploring the Metro are in the morning between 10 a. m. and 12 noon, in the afternoon between 2 p. m. and 4 p. m., or in the evening after 8 p. m. Rush hours, of course, should be avoided. The Metro operates from 6 a. m. to 1 a. m. Transfer from one station to another ends at 1 a. m. sharp.

In addition to the great store of experience of world metro construction utilized in the construction of the Moscow Metropolitan Railway, significant contributions were made by Soviet scientists, engineers, builders, architects and artists. The Metro is both a convenient mode of transport and a large, contemporary engineering structure, unique in the beauty of its architectural compositions and the harmonious combination of its technical and artistic execution. We feel we can safely say that the Moscow Metro has no analogies in the world. The underground halls of many stations are decorated with works of art executed of marble, metal, and glass. The interiors of some stations have entered into the history of world architecture: in 1938 at an international exhibition in New York the design of the **Mayakovskaya Metro Station** was awarded a gold medal, and twenty years later, at another international exhibition in Brussels the models of the **Kropotkinskaya and Komsomolskaya** (Circular Line) **stations** were judged worthy of the Grand Prix. The Kropotkinskaya Station was built in 1935 according to the design of architects Alexei Dushkin and Yakov Lichtenberg. Its architecture is simple and expressive, and it is so spacious and bright that it gives the impression of being filled with sunshine. Built in 1938 and also designed by Dushkin, the Mayakovskaya Station with its silvery steel columns has a festive, even cheerful air. The vaulting has mosaics executed to cartoons by the outstanding artist Alexander Deineka. Also of interest is the Komsomolskaya Station

"River trams" on the Moskva River

(Circular Line), built in 1952. It was designed by two men renowned in Soviet art, architect Alexei Shchusev and artist Pavel Korin. The vaults of the underground hall are supported on 72 pillars. It is decorated with eight large and colorful mosaic panels.

The station is 190 meters long and 9 meters high.

The more recent additions to the Metro are rather different in style, simpler in their architecture and more laconic and modest in their décor.

Here is a route that will enable you to visit the most characteristic of both the older and more recently built stations: **Ploshchad Revolyutsii** (Revolution Square) — **Arbatskaya** (Arbat) — **Kievskaya** (Kiev Railway Station) — transfer to the Circle Line **(Koltsevaya liniya)** — **Belorusskaya** (Byelorussian Railway Station) — transfer to the Gorky-Zamoskvoretskaya Line **(Gorkovsko-Zamoskvoretskaya liniya)** — **Mayakovskaya** — **Ploshchad Sverdlova** (Sverdlov Square) and exit at Revolution Square. The whole journey will take no more than an hour.

A BOAT TRIP ON THE RIVER

The Moskva River is 502 kilometers long and flows through the city for 80 kilometers. Motor ships, often called "river trams" make regularly scheduled trips, including excursion trips, along the river throughout the summer. We suggest you begin your trip at the **Kiev Pier, which is near the Kiev Railway Station** (*Berezhkovskaya naberezhnaya* — Berezhkovskaya Embankment), and a 10 minutes' walk from the Kievskaya Metro Station. The trip downstream will take you to the pier on **Moskvoretskaya Embankment** (nearest Metro Station Ploshchad Nogina). The trip will take about an hour and a half.

From a seat in the bow of the boat you will see many historical and cultural monuments on both banks, new residential areas, picturesque parks and gardens, beaches, embankments and bridges — many of which you will be seeing for the first time. You will pass close to the cathedrals and palaces of the Kremlin, the *Rossiya* Hotel, the Gorky Central Recreation Park, the Lenin Central

Stadium at Luzhniki, and the churches and towers of the Novodevichy Convent.

Comparative analyses of nearly all the navigable rivers of Europe running through large industrialized cities have shown that the Moskva River is one of the cleanest. This fact is borne out by the anglers you will see casting their lines directly from the parapet of the embankment. It's not just minnows they're fishing for, it seems, but for perch.

A river trip is a real treat and the best time is in the afternoon.

Near Spassky (Saviour) Cathedral in St. Andronicus Monastery

MASTERPIECES OF RUSSIAN CULTURE

The **Andrei Rublev Museum of Early Russian Culture and Art** is located inside the former **Andronikov** (St. Andronicus) **Monastery**, No. 10 *ploshchad Pryamikova* (Pryamikov Square), not far from the center to the east. The nearest **Metro Station** is **Proletarskaya.** It is not incidental that the museum should bear the name of the brilliant Russian painter, Andrei Rublev. Rublev was a monk at the St. Andronicus Monastery, and it was here that he worked and died (*circa* 1430 according to available data). Here, by the ancient walls of the Spassky (Saviour) Cathedral,

he was buried. Although his grave has not been preserved, the Museum of Early Russian Art established in the St. Andronicus Monastery has become a monument to the great artist. The museum was opened in September of 1960, at the time when, according to a decision of UNESCO, the 600-year anniversary of the Russian master was being commemorated the world over. Andrei Rublev is the founder of the Moscow School of icon painting. On display in the museum's six halls are icons from the 14th through the early 18th centuries, as well as fragments of

Statue of Andrei Rublev

wall paintings and various works of art executed in wood, metal and precious stones. The museum has a collection of 2,000 works of early Russian art.

The St. Andronicus Monastery, founded around 1360, stands on the high left bank of the Yauza River, which flows into the Moskva River. Its ancient structures tower above crenelated walls with tent-roofed towers: the white-stone Spassky (Saviour) Cathedral, built in the early 15th century, and one of the most ancient surviving stone edifices in Moscow; the Church of the Archangel Michael (1694); and the sloping roof of the Refectory Chamber (1504).

In 1947 the St. Andronicus Monastery was declared a state preserve, and since then it has undergone much restoration work. In April 1985 the **statue of Andrei Rublev** was erected in the garden

in front of the entrance to the museum. The monument consists of a granite pedestal surmounted by the 3-meter-high figure of the great icon-painter and was executed by sculptor Oleg Komov and architect Veniamin Nesterov.

The Church of the Intercession at Fili, branch of the Museum of Early Russian Art.

"Wonder of wonders" accurately describes this monument of Russian architecture, painting and decorative art. The Church of the Intercession is situated to the west of the city's center, and the nearest **Metro Station** is **Fili**. Fili was once the inherited estate of the Naryshkin *boyars*. The church was built in 1693-94 in the so-called "Naryshkin Baroque" style. This multi-tiered, beautifully proportioned church has a cruciform base and is crowned by an elegant bell-tower and a cupola. White-stone carving strikingly accents the red brick of the walls and gives the building a

Church of the Intercession at Fili

Novodevichy Convent viewed from the pond

forged flowers and leaves soldered to it is a unique work of 17th-century art.

Much restoration work has been undertaken by Soviet specialists in order to return the artistic riches of this unique monument of Russian culture to their original beauty.

The strains of old Russian music often resound beneath the vaults of the Church of the Intercession at Fili. Various choral and musical groups come to perform in the **concert hall** which has been opened

highly festive air. The term "Naryshkin Baroque" is mostly conventional in nature, and reflects the tendency towards the secularization of forms of church architecture characteristic of Russian 17th-century architecture. Together with decorative devices characteristic of the Baroque, Russian masters and architects of the time made bold use of Classical decorative elements such as columns, porticoes, and pediments. The interior of the church is also richly decorated. The iconostasis, arches, and window apertures are embellished with twining ornamentations of leaves, stalks, flowers and fruits carved of wood with subtle virtuosity. The faces on the icons which form the iconostasis are strikingly alive, and are believed to have been painted after the Naryshkin *boyars*, who funded the building of the church. An enormous chandelier suspended from a 15-meter-long chain in the form of a stalk with

Smolensky (Virgin of Smolensk) Cathedral viewed from the bell-tower

Folklore festival at Kolomenskoye

inside the church. Tickets for these concerts may be obtained through the Service Bureau of your hotel.

The Novodevichy Convent (Branch of the State Historical Museum).

The Novodevichy (New Maidens') Convent is located at Luzhniki, south-west of the center of the city at the end of *Bolshaya Pirogovskaya ulitsa* (Big Pirogov Street). The nearest **Metro Station** is **Sportivnaya.** The former convent has been an affiliate of the Historical Museum since 1934. Major restoration work has been undertaken on the territory of the convent and on its cathedral and churches, thus returning many monuments of Russian culture to their original aspect. On exhibit in the museum are materials relating to the history of Russia from the 16th–17th centuries, as well as works of art of

that period. Of especial interest are the unique collection of ancient weaponry, the wooden carved iconostases, the frescoes inside the cathedral, and a number of icons painted by outstanding ancient icon-painters.

The convent, founded in 1524, was an important defence bastion of Moscow. Its massive brick walls and towers, interconnecting inside passageways and embrasures are a splendid example of fortifications typical of the architecture of the time. Of the original 16th-century structures, the fortress walls and the five-dome Smolensk Cathedral named after the Icon of the Virgin of Smolensk (1524–25) have been preserved.

Additional building went on during the period from 1685–89, and it was then that it acquired the appearance which made it the most valuable monument of Russian architecture of the late 17th century. We would like to point out the convent's twelve towers and the two gate chapels, the Church of the Transfiguration and the Church of the Intercession, built in the "Naryshkin Baroque" style. The convent's ancient walls and cells have witnessed much. Long ago women of the tsar's family and distinguished *boyar* families took the veil in this convent. From here, in 1598, Boris Godunov was summoned to reign, an event poetically described in Alexander Pushkin's drama *Boris Godunov.* And it was here in 1689 that the Regent Sophia, sister of Peter I, was incarcerated after her attempt to seize the power from her brother, and it was near her chambers (which we see today) that the members of the *Streltsy* Corps who supported her were hanged.

The view of the Novodevichy Convent from the Moskva River is particularly striking. Rising up above the white-stone walls and towers decorated with red brick and cathedral domes is a slender 6-tier bell-tower. It was built in 1690 and is 72 meters tall.

On the territory of the convent are the burial sites of important public and political figures in Russia as well as writers and artists. In the **Novodevichye Cemetery** attached to the convent are buried the country's leading political and cultural figures.

Kolomenskoye. On the high right bank of the Moskva River in the southern section of the city is an area of unique charm—the Kolomenskoye architectural and historical preserve. When you visit Kolomenskoye (we hope you will follow our recommendation) you will marvel as you look at masterpieces of 16th–17th-century art and architecture and feel yourself a contemporary of that distant epoch, suddenly removed from the bustle and noise of the city blocks which surround you.

Even in the **Kolomenskaya Metro Station** you will see a large engraved metallic panel with depictions of an ancient town and Russian warriors in shirts of mail.

A fifteen minutes' walk will bring you to the grounds of the museum-preserve. The Kolomenskoye estate and surrounding territory were declared a state preserve in 1974. Kolomenskoye was first mentioned in the will of the Moscow Prince Ivan Kalita which dates to 1339.

Kolomenskoye's earliest architectural monument is the **Church of the Ascension**, an outstanding example of 16th-century Russian architecture. One of the first stone tent-roof churches to be built in Russia, it dates to 1532. Note the church's stone structural and decorative details—the three-tier upstretched *kokoshnik* gables, the white-stone window surrounds, and the high, eight-sided tent-roof—all contributing to the sensation of the structure's sweeping verticality. Reminiscing about his trips to Russia in 1847 and 1867, the renowned French composer Hector Berlioz wrote: "I have seen much in my life that I have admired and been astounded at, but the past, the ancient past of Russia which has left its imprint on this village, was for me something most miraculous. Here before my gaze stood the beauty of perfection and I gasped in awe. Here in the mysterious silence, amid the harmonious beauty of the finished form, I beheld an architecture of a new kind. I beheld man soaring on high. And I stood amazed."

Other interesting architectural monuments are the St. George Bell-Tower (16th century), the Water-Tower (17th century), and the

Kuskovo Palace

stone front gate (17th century). The Kolomenskoye Palace, known 300 years ago as the "eighth wonder of the world", deserves special mention. Neither it nor the other palaces built later on its site have been preserved. In 1667–71 Russian master craftsmen headed by senior carpenter Semyon Petrov and carpenter Ivan Mikhailov erected for Tsar Alexei Mikhailovich a palace of "wondrous intricacy and wondrous beauty". The palace consisted of several *terems* (tower chambers) connected by covered galleries and walkways, and had 270 rooms and 3,000 windows, and fanciful towers decorated with wood carving. For one hundred years it was a remarkable specimen of 17th-century wooden architecture. In 1768 the dilapidated palace was torn down, although the Kazan Church, the only stone structure in the palace ensemble, has survived to this day. A model of the palace, 1/40th of the original size, executed in 1868 by

the carver Dmitry Smirnov from 18th-century sketches, has also survived and is on display in the museum. After you've seen the model and the old Kazan Church, with a little imagination you can picture the way the "eighth wonder of the world" actually looked.

In 1930 a museum of Russian wooden architecture was organized in Kolomenskoye. Structures dating to the 17th-18th centuries were brought here, including a mead-brewery from the village of Preobrazhenskoye, the gateway-tower from the Nikolo-Korelsky Monastery, the Bratsk stockade tower from the Siberian taiga, and the house of Peter I from the northern city of Arkhangelsk. On display in expositions housed in the estate's

In Kuskovo park

old buildings are many valuable cultural and historical monuments. There are unique collections of early Russian painting, wood-carving, ceramic tiles, decorative metal-work, tower-clock mechanisms, and early printed books.

The Kolomenskoye ensemble is surrounded by an ancient park, where mighty 600-year-old oaks and lindens over one century old are still standing. In addition to these rarities there are old acacias which were transplanted to the site of the former palace; walks lined with 200 linden and birch trees, stretching from the front gate to the back gate; and elms, poplars, maples and lindens everywhere above ancient ravines.

The 18th-century palace-garden ensemble of **Kuskovo** is a treasure-house of Russian art, with masterpieces of architecture, sculpture, painting, landscaping, and decorative and applied arts. The Kuskovo ensemble, consisting of a palace, estate buildings, and a park, was built in the 1740s–70s by serf masters under the supervision of serf architects Fyodor Argunov (1732–68), Alexei Mironov (1745–1809), Yuri Kologrivov (1697–1754) and others, together with the Moscow architect Karl Blank (1728–93). The most ancient "witness to history" at Kuskovo is the pond. Erected on its banks was a palace, called the "summer country pleasure home of Count Sheremetev" at the time. Pyotr Sheremetev (1713–88), son of Field Marshal

In the Ceramics Museum

Boris Sheremetev, associate of Peter I, and one of the wealthiest people in Russia during the 18th century, began the construction of Kuskovo as a 23-year-old young man and abandoned it at his death at the age of 75. Kuskovo's uniqueness lies in the fact that it has never undergone significant reconstruction, so that the palace and estate have been preserved just as they were created by the craftsmen of Count Sheremetev, in the style of the 18th century.

The mirror-smooth surface of the big pond, the old palace with its elegant lattice-work gate, the shady walks lined with age-old trees, and the park pavilions all combine to create a picture of unique charm. The palace, built in 1769-75 under the supervision of Karl Blank, is the center of the architectural ensemble. The palace buildings are of wood. The Russian poet Gavriil Derzhavin (1743-1816) said of it that its exterior was distinguished neither by wood-carving nor gilding, and that the sophisticated taste of the old masters reflected in its majestic simplicity was its main virtue. Hidden behind the plain façade of the small palace building is a suite of magnificent rooms which make up a single harmonious ensemble. We would point out the Large Dance Hall and the Crimson Drawing-Room, one of the most elegant in the palace, with exquisite cut-glass chandeliers, carved furniture, and porcelain vases.

The 18th-century Kuskovo estate ensemble includes the Church of the Icon of the Saviour (Veronica) (1739), the Italian House (1755), the Conservatory (1764), the Dutch House (1751), and the Hermitage (1767). The interior décor of these structures harmonizes with their exteriors, and gives a broad conception of 18th-century Russian decorative art.

Also housed in the estate building is the **Ceramics Museum**, with a rich collection of over 20,000 works of porcelain, faience, majolica, and glass of various periods. The museum takes pride in its collection of Russian porcelain, which includes dinner and tea services, plates and dishes of so-called Kuznetsov porcelain with elegantly simple paintings, articles by Gzhel masters and an extensive collection of ceramics of the Soviet period—decorative vases, painted tea services, and figurines—which show the birth in the 1920s of new emblems and symbols and the craftsmanship of contemporary masters. The Kuskovo formal park is beautifully laid out, with straight alleys, a colorful parterre, decorative statues—sculptural groups on high pedestals—on its lawns, and with a grotto—a large stone summer-house reminiscent of an underwater cavern.

In the past ten years restorers have done a great deal of work to return the architectural ensemble to its original 18th-century aspect.

Kuskovo is situated to the east of the city center. The quickest and most convenient way to get there is by **Metro** to the **Vychino** or **Ryazansky prospekt stations**, and then by bus (Nos. 197, 208, 620, or 615). You can also arrange for an excursion to Kuskovo through Intourist.

Spassky (Saviour) Cathedral in St. Andronicus Monastery

Kuskovo Museum-Estate. "Dutch House" pavilion

Kuskovo Museum- Estate. "Grotto" pavilion

Novodevichy Convent

Moscow. New regions
Autumn in Moscow

The Kremlin. Day is breaking ...

At a bus stop …

Arkhangelskoye Museum-Estate. Park

COUNTRYSIDE AROUND MOSCOW

Moscow is surrounded by picturesque forests, fields, oak woods, and meandering rivers. The countryside has much to offer besides its natural beauty alone—there are many memorable places just outside Moscow associated with Russian history and culture. The Moscow countryside was the home of many great Russians who brought fame to their country through their contribution to world culture. In addition to being interesting and informative, a trip to these memorable places will give you an opportunity to relax away from the bustle and noise of a city.

It is not easy to describe all the areas around Moscow in limited compass, so we shall confine ourselves to a few spots that are especially worth visiting.

ARKHANGELSKOYE ESTATE

The Arkhangelskoye estate, situated in a picturesque spot on the bank of the Moskva River, is a monument of 18th-19th-century Russian culture. It is located 9 kilometers from the city's boundary (along Volokolamsk Highway and then along the road to Petrovo-Dalneye).

The whole ensemble of Arkhangelskoye—palace, park, theater, and service buildings—took forty years to build and lay out. The first gardens were laid out at the end of the 17th century. In 1810, the land passed into the hands of Prince Yusupov, who owned much valuable property throughout the land and was the master of tens of thousands of serfs. Yusupov was the director of the imperial theaters and the Hermitage. When purchasing works for the Hermitage, Yusupov kept himself in mind, and turned his palace near Moscow into a real museum displaying many works by talented painters, sculptors, and folk artists.

The centerpiece of the estate is the palace built in the Classical style to the design of Osip Bovet and other well-known Russian architects. The whole ensemble was built by Yusupov's serfs, headed by the serf architects Vasily Strizhakov and Ivan Borunov.

The palace stands at the highest point of the estate and its south façade overlooks the park, which slopes down to the Moskva River in terraces. The main courtyard of Arkhangelskoye is framed by wing colonnades of the central part of the palace. The palace's many halls are sumptuously decorated and furnished with antique sculptures, tapestries, and porcelain, incrusted furniture, cut-glass chandeliers, numerous mirrors, murals, and a multi-pattern parquet.

The palace is surrounded by a splendid park, its walks embellished with sculptures, decorative stairways, colonnades, pavilions, and summer-houses. A triumphal arch, built in 1818, stands at the entrance to the estate. After the October Revolution, Arkhangelskoye was nationalized and taken under state protection as a valuable monument of Russian culture. Restoration work, begun in 1933, returned the palace and the park to their original appearance. A new phase of restoration work was begun in 1986.

Today Arkhangelskoye is a splendid museum with a valuable collection. In the building of the theater, constructed in 1817, there is an exposition entitled "The Serf Theater in Arkhangelskoye". Opposite the main entrance to the estate is the *Arkhangelskoye* **Restaurant**, where you can sample traditional Russian cuisine. A visit to Arkhangelskoye is a fine outing. The road to it is picturesque and passes through forests of conifers, nut groves, and glades, and in places runs very close to the Moskva River.

BORODINO

If you visited the Panorama Museum of the Battle of Borodino, then you know that on August 26, 1812, a tremendous battle took place on a field near the village of Borodino between Napoleon's troops and the Russian army commanded by Mikhail Kutuzov. Napoleon put 135,000 soldiers and 587 guns into battle against the

Russian army, which had 132,000 men and 624 guns on the eve of the battle. The battle lasted 15 hours.

The village of Borodino is 124 kilometers from Moscow on Minsk Highway. Monuments to the courage and heroism of the Russian soldiers have been erected on the historic battlefield, most of them in 1912, to mark the centenary of the battle, from funds contributed by officers and men of Russian army units that had fought there. A monument to Field Marshal Kutuzov was erected on the spot from where he directed the operations of the Russian army. It is a granite obelisk, crowned with a bronze eagle with outspread wings and a laurel wreath. Above the bas-relief portrait of Kutuzov are the words from his dispatch on the results of the battle: "The enemy was repulsed at all points." Some 150 meters from the Shevardinsky redoubt, where on August 24, two days before the Battle of Borodino, there was fierce fighting between an advanced post of the Russian army and the advancing French regiments, there is a grey granite obelisk to the fallen of the Grande Armée. This obelisk was also erected in 1912 with funds raised in France. At the entrance to the memorial chapel to the soldiers of the 1st and 19th Chasseur Regiments of the Russian Army who were killed in action, there is an inscription in gold: "We pledged to die and we kept our oath of loyalty at the Battle of Borodino" (lines taken from a poem by Mikhail Lermontov).

On the Borodino battlefield is the **Borodino State Military History Museum** with a collection of documents and exhibits relating to the events in the 1812 War and the Battle of Borodino. Lev Tolstoy visited the battlefield in September 1876, when working on his novel *War and Peace.* While there, he drew up a plan of the battle between the two armies that he described so authentically in his novel.

In the autumn of 1941 Borodino was once again in the center of military activities. The battlefield was covered with trenches and anti-tank ditches. For five days and nights the outnumbered Soviet soldiers fought the enemy. Only two houses in the large village of Borodino were left standing after the fighting. Near the monument to Kutuzov is the common grave of Soviet Guardsmen who fell in action against Nazi troops.

Lenin Museum in Gorki Leninskiye State Historical Preserve

Today Borodino field is a unique open-air museum where visitors can see the open expanse of fields and meadows dotted with groves and copses, the sites of the defence fortifications of the War of 1812, as well as those of 1941—trenches and pillboxes, command posts, and the common grave with a *T-34* tank on a pedestal.

Gorki Leninskiye. Park

Lenin's study in Gorki Leninskiye

GORKI LENINSKIYE

About 13 kilometers south of Moscow on Kashira Highway is the Gorki Estate, a mansion on a high hill in an extensive park of old trees. From September 1918 Lenin frequently went there to rest and relax, and lived there from March 1923 until his death on January 21, 1924. On the 25th anniversary of Lenin's death a memorial museum was opened in the Gorki Estate, and everything was preserved as it was in his day: the two-storey wing, where he lived upstairs with his family; the central building where he lived the last months of his life; and his favorite spots, in particular the round summer-house not far from the house, where he would sit and admire the lovely view of the surrounding fields and villages.

An area of 865 acres has been turned into the **Gorki Leninskiye State Historical Preserve**, with a protected zone of nearly 24,710 acres surrounding it.

The room in which Lenin lived and died is very simply furnished, with an upholstered armchair and a small table with an inkstand, letter opener, spectacles, and several books. One of the books is a volume of stories by Jack London— *Love of Life*, the story that his wife, Nadezhda Krupskaya, was reading to him two days before he died. In the left-hand corner is a wooden bed. Between the window and the bed is a mirror with a glass shelf on which stands a lamp, a small nickel-plated bell, and some medicine bottles. One is struck by Lenin's exceptionally simple tastes.

Despite his illness, at Gorki, as his secretary Lidiya Fotieva recalled, Lenin "worked literally to the limits of the humanly possible". Here he carefully worked out problems related to the Party and Government, and wrote a number of major theoretical works. Delegates from the workers and peasants of Soviet Russia used to come to see him at Gorki. In November 1923 he was visited by a delegation of textile workers, who brought him a gift of a calico shirt made by their finest weavers, and 18 cherry saplings. In their accompanying letter they wrote: "May these cherry trees freshly planted in your garden bring you speedy recovery." On New Year's Eve, 1923-24, Lenin asked for a New Year's tree to be set up in Gorki for the children of the local peasants; and he saw the New Year in with them, cheerfully watching them singing and dancing. Three weeks later, at 6.50 p. m. on January 21, he passed away. A man thus died who, as Henri Barbusse wrote, "was the embodiment of the whole Russian Revolution, who conceived it in his mind, prepared it, carried it through, and saved it—Lenin, the greatest, and in every way the most honest of the creators of history, a man who did more for the people than anyone else". In the orchard stands the sculpture "The Burial of the Leader" by Sergei Merkurov.

At the entrance to the Gorki Estate stands a **statue of Lenin**—a strikingly dynamic 6-meter-high sculpture, by Isaac Brodsky. The effect is such that Lenin seems to be striding swiftly towards those gathered. Thousands of people from all corners of the earth come to Gorki Leninskiye to immerse themselves in the atmosphere of the final years in the life of the brilliant leader of the proletariat.

ZAGORSK

Seventy kilometers north of Moscow on Yaroslavl Highway is the **Zargorsk Museum of Art and History**, which contains magnifi-

Trinity Cathedral in the Trinity Monastery of St. Sergius

cent relics of Russian culture of the 15th- to 17th centuries. Located here is the Troitse-Sergiyev (Trinity and St. Sergius) Monastery, built in the 1340s, and one of the oldest around Moscow. The monastery played a major role in the history of Moscow and the Russian State. It was a stronghold that more than once defended the principal city of old Russia from foreign invaders. Its stone fortifications, erected in 1540-80, are 12 meters high. In 1608-10 the defenders of the monastery, around 3,000 strong, heroically withstood a 16 months' siege by 15,000 well-armed Polish soldiers. The young Tsar Peter I took refuge here in 1689 during the rebellion of the *Streltsy* Corps led by his sister, the Regent Sophia. From the 14th to the 17th centuries the monastery was a major cultural center where master icon-painters, copyists,

wood-carvers, silversmiths, and other craftsmen worked. Wonderful treasures were accumulated in its churches.

In 1920 a museum was opened on the monastery's grounds. Today the Moscow Theological Academy and Seminary are housed in the monastery.

The USSR Constitution guarantees its citizens the right of conscience, i.e. the right to practise any religion or none at all, to perform religious cults or to conduct atheistic propaganda. The Church in the USSR is separated from the state and school. Around 200 Orthodox societies and churches operate in Moscow and Moscow Region. In addition, there are over 60 other religious societies in existence, each with separate places of worship (churches, cathedrals,

Uspensky (Dormition) Cathedral in the Trinity Monastery of St. Sergius

mosques, synagogues, prayer-houses, etc.) To coincide with the Millennium of the Baptism of Russia (988-1988) the Danilov Monastery on the Moskva River has been turned into the Patriarch's residence. Buildings in the monastery (founded in the 13th century if not earlier) dating from the 16th to the beginning of the 19th centuries have been restored. (The nearest Metro Station is **Tulskaya**).

In the USSR citizens are not classed according to their faith—believers enjoy the same rights as all citizens and participate in the country's political, economic and social life. Religious societies take an active stand in support of peace, the prevention of nuclear war, and fair relations between nations.

The whole ensemble of the Troitse-Sergiyev Monastery is of exceptional value. Here some of the finest and most characteristic examples of early Russian architecture and painting have been preserved. The most important among them is the white-stone **Troitsky** (Trinity) **Cathedral**, built in 1422-25. Its façade is adorned with pilasters and a horizontal band of carved stone. The building is crowned by a huge dome. The paintings on the iconostasis and murals, fragments of which have been preserved to this day, were executed by Andrei Rublev and other artists of his school in 1425-27, and were subsequently painted over. The Church of the Descent of the Holy Spirit *(Dukhovskaya tserkov)* built in 1476-77, is an archi-

tecturally striking building with a two-tier tower. Bells hang on the lower tier, while the upper serves as a watch-tower.

In 1559-85, the monumental five-dome Cathedral of the Dormition *(Uspensky sobor)* was built on the monastery grounds by order of Ivan the Terrible, and came to be considered the principal cathedral of the monastery. Its architectural forms are similar to those of the Cathedral of the Dormition in the Moscow Kremlin. 17-century frescoes and a finely carved and gilded 18th-century iconostasis, and paintings by Russian artists have been preserved inside.

There are other interesting architectural monuments in the monastery, including the Hospital Wards with the tent-shaped Church of Sts. Zosima and Savvaty (1635-38), the Tsar's Chambers and the Refectory (1686-92), the private chambers of the Metropolitan, and others. The bell-tower, built in 1741-70 by architects Ivan Michurin and Dmitry Ukhtomsky; the well-chapel, built at the end of the 17th century, with its small carved white-stone columns intertwined with grape vines; and the elegant Smolensk Church, erected in 1745-48, are all beautiful monuments of 18th-century architecture.

This excursion will acquaint you with the landscapes of the contemporary Moscow countryside.

On the way, 43 kilometers from Moscow, is the *Russkaya skazka* (Russian Fairy-tale) **Restaurant**.

Monastery in Novy-Yerusalim (New-Jerusalem), Voskresensky (Resurrection) Cathedral

ISTRA

The small town of Istra is situated to the north-west of Moscow, 37 kilometers from the Moscow Circular Motor Road on Volokolamsk Highway. It is situated in a picturesque locale on the bank of the meandering Istra River, from which the town took its name. The town arose in the 16th century and became famous in the 17th century in connection with the creation of the New-Jerusalem (Novoiyerusalimsky) Monastery. At that time, under the audacious plan of the powerful and ambitious Patriarch Nikon, the imposing Cathedral of the Resurrection was built. It was erected "in the image and likeness" of the Jerusalem Cathedral of the Resurrection with a rotunda of the Church of the Holy Sepulchre in Palestine. According to Nikon's plan, the monastery was to become the center of the "holy spots" in the outskirts of Moscow.

The **Cathedral of the Resurrection at Istra** was built from 1658 to 1685 (with a 13-year interval). Russian masters created a majestic and unique structure, reminiscent in layout to the cathedral in ancient Jerusalem, but entirely different in external appearance and décor. The multi-volume composition of the New-Jerusalem Monastery's Cathedral of the Resurrection unfolds from an underground church sunk five meters into the ground to an enormous stone tent-shaped roof and a 75-meter-high bell-tower.

This remarkable monument of Russian culture has a tragic history. In 1723 the tent-shaped roof collapsed, and three years later the cathedral was damaged by fire. It was restored in the mid-18th century, and its interiors regained their original splendor. Stucco mouldings in the Baroque style, dominant at the time, created a strikingly festive appearance, a vivid gold and white counterpoint to the blue of the walls. Restoration work which imparted new beauty to the cathedral was carried out by the renowned architect Bartolomeo Rastrelli (1700-71) of St. Petersburg together with Moscow architects Karl Blank and Matvei Kazakov.

In December 1941 Istra became the site of fierce fighting between Soviet troops and the German fascist aggressors. During the short time Istra fell under enemy occupation, irreparable damage was done to this priceless monument of Russian culture. Retreating beneath the onslaught of the Soviet Army, the Germans blew up the New-Jerusalem Monastery.

Large-scale, complex, and costly restoration work was begun on the monastery in 1958. If you go to Istra you will see how much has already been done. The Moscow Museum of Regional Studies, founded back in 1920, has been reopened in the restored buildings of the Refectory, the chambers of the senior

Monastery in Novy-Yerusalim (New-Jerusalem). Underground church

priests, and the hospital wards.

Restoration work on the Cathedral of the Resurrection is not yet completed, but when you see it we think you will agree with Academician Igor Grabar (1871-1960), one of the leading figures involved in restoration work in the USSR, who asserted that the New-Jerusalem Monastery was a genuine marvel of national Russian art, and one of the most captivating architectural fairy-tales ever created by man.

KLIN

Klin is an old Russian town 84 kilometers north-west of Moscow on Leningrad Highway. It was founded in 1318 on the high bank of the Sestra, a tributary of the Volga. A church built on the grounds of the former Dormition Monastery in the early 16th to the

mid-17th centuries, and the Church of the Assumption on the main square of the town, built in 1712 in the Moscow Baroque style with a tent-shaped bell-tower of the 17th-18th centuries are reminiscent of the town's past.

But Klin is known first and foremost for another reason: it was the home of Tchaikovsky (1840–1893). Thousands of tourists and music-lovers come here to pay tribute to the great composer's memory. The house in which he last lived in Klin has been turned into a **museum**. In the center of the spacious drawing-room stands Tchaikovsky's grand piano. It was here that Tchaikovsky composed many of his romances, the ballet *The Sleeping Beauty*, the *Hamlet* overture, his Fifth and Sixth Symphonies, and worked on *The Nutcracker* ballet.

On a writing table are Tchaikovsky's last notes, and in the corner are shelves with his favorite books, including works by Pushkin, Gogol, Lev Tolstoy , and Chekhov. On other shelves there are collections of Russian folk songs which the composer loved so well. In the bedroom stands a rustic birch table at which Tchaikovsky sat to write the Sixth Symphony, a masterpiece of world symphonic music.

Tchaikovsky was very fond of Klin, of its tranquility and landscape. "I can't say how terribly attached I have become to Klin," he wrote, "and I just can't imagine myself anywhere else. I find no words to express how much I feel the charm of the Russian countryside, the Russian landscape, and this stillness that I need more than anything else."

Visiting composers and musi-cians from various countries often come to Klin and pay honor to Tchaikovsky's great contribution to the treasure-house of world music. Twice a year, on the anniversaries of Tchaikovsky's birth and death, leading Soviet and foreign musicians sit down at his piano there and play his music. In 1958 Van Cliburn, the American pianist who won the First International Tchaikovsky Piano Competition in Moscow, visited Klin. Since then, the winners of this important contest have been given the privilege of playing on Tchaikovsky's piano.

The house is surrounded by a garden with large, tall trees that form shady walks along which Tchaikovsky used to enjoy strolling. Every bough and every twig here seems to sing.

This house has an interesting history. After the composer's death, his servant, Alexei Sofronov, bought it from the merchant who owned it, so that it could be kept intact. In 1920 a society of Friends of the Tchaikovsky Museum was organized. During the war the house underwent a terrible ordeal. German fascist troops who had occupied Klin in 1941 ravaged it. Following liberation of the town on December 15, 1941, the house was restored and on May 7, 1945, Tchaikovsky's birthday, the museum was reopened to endless visitors who find inexhaustible joy and inspiration in his music.

INFORMATION
AND ADDRESSES

INFORMATION

HOW TO GET TO MOSCOW

Moscow is the terminus of eleven railways and twelve highways. The Moscow Canal connects the capital with the ports of five seas: the Black Sea, the Sea of Azov, the Caspian, the Baltic, and the White Sea. Aeroflot's aircraft serve 122 major cities in 97 countries. Foreign airlines, both those of the socialist countries and Alitalia, Finnair, Air India, Air France, British Airways, KLM, Lufthansa, SAS, Japan Airlines, and Pan American, have regularly scheduled flights to Moscow.

Those who plan to travel by rail can use the Soviet through trains and coaches which connect Moscow with the capitals and cities of 27 countries of Europe and Asia. For example, the Berlin–Moscow train covers a distance of 1,889 kilometers in 28 hours and 42 minutes; the Paris–Moscow express coach (2,969 km) arrives at its destination 45 hours and 14 minutes after departure; and the London–Moscow express coach (3,061 km), is en route for 49 hours and 38 minutes.

People who enjoy car holidays can drive to Moscow from or through Finland (Torfyanovka–Vyborg–Leningrad–Novgorod–Kalinin–Moscow; 930 km), Poland (Brest–Minsk–Smolensk–Moscow; 1,060 km), Hungary and Czechoslovakia (Chop–Uzhgorod–Lvov–Kiev–Bryansk–Kaluga–Moscow; 1,670 km), or Romania (Porubnoye–Chernovtsy–Vinnitsa–Zhitomir–Kiev–Bryansk–Kaluga–Moscow; 1,464 km).

Aeroflot flights from Moscow to various Soviet tourist spots have the following durations: Alma-Ata—4 hours 15 minutes, Baku—2 hours 45 minutes, Volgograd—1 hour 35 minutes, Yerevan—2 hours 35 minutes, Kiev and Leningrad—1 hour 20 minutes, Irkutsk—7 hours, Riga—1 hour 30 minutes, Samarkand—3 hours 40 minutes, Tashkent—3 hours 50 minutes, Simferopol—2 hours 15 minutes, Khabarovsk—7 hours 45 minutes. As an interesting comparison—the journey from Moscow to Khabarovsk on the *Rossiya* Express takes 150 hours, i. e., more than six days. Aeroflot has regularly scheduled flights from Moscow to 175 Soviet cities.

MOSCOW TIME

The USSR has 11 time zones, ranging from zone 2 through zone 12. Moscow is situated in time zone 2, known as Eastern European time, but is one hour ahead of Eastern European time as the result of a decree passed in 1930.

Daylight savings time begins at 2 a. m. on the last Sunday in March when clocks are moved up one hour, and ends at 3 a. m. on the last Sunday in September.

Moscow time operates in most of the western part of the USSR, for example, in Leningrad, Kiev, Yalta, and Sochi. But when it is 12 a. m. in Moscow, it is 5 p. m. in Irkutsk, 3 p. m. in Tashkent, and 1 p. m. in Tbilisi.

SOME USEFUL HINTS

There is a Service Bureau in all hotels catering to foreign tourists and visitors. It is usually open from 9 a. m. until 9 p. m. The service personnel are fluent in foreign languages. The Service Bureau can give you the information you need about your stay in the USSR, make reservations for you for visits to exhibitions, museums, art galleries, theaters, the circus, concert halls, sports competitions, and can arrange special excursions and trips to the Moscow countryside and other cities. The Service Bureau has pamphlets with the repertoires of theaters and concert halls for the current ten day period. Tickets can be ordered in advance through the Service Bureau. Questions concerning your travel documents and arrangements, trains, routes, and departure times, hotel and restaurant services, and so on can be referred to the Service Bureau; and they can tell you where shops are located and when they are open. The Service Bureau can help you with plane or train reservations and tickets, car rentals, and ordering taxis.

The monetary unit in the Soviet Union is the rouble. It is equal to 100 kopecks. The coinage consists of one-, two-, three-, five-, ten-, 15-, 20-, and 50-kopeck pieces, and one rouble coins. Paper money consists of one-, three-, five-, ten-, 25-, 50-, and 100-rouble notes.

Stores dealing in consumer goods usually open at 10 a.m. and close at 8 p.m. Large department stores open at 8 a.m. and close at 9 p.m. They are usually closed on Sundays. Food stores are open daily from 9 a.m. to 8 p.m. (several shops work until 10 p.m.). On Sundays and holidays they close two hours earlier.

Factory and clerical workers in the Soviet Union have a five-day-work week (41 hours) with Saturdays and Sundays off, with the exception of those working in enterprises with continuous production processes. In factories and mills the working day usually begins at 8 a.m. and in offices at 9 a.m. The working day is 8 hours, with a lunch interval of one hour except on the days before national holidays when the closing time is one hour earlier. The lunch break is usually taken between 12 noon and 1 p.m.

The national holidays (non-working days) of the USSR are January 1 (New Year's Day), March 8 (International Women's Day), May 1 and 2 (Holiday of International Solidarity of Working People), May 9 (Victory Day over German fascism), October 7 (Constitution Day), and November 7 and 8 (the Anniversary of the Great October Socialist Revolution).

Evening theater and concert performances begin respectively at 7 p. m. and 7.30 p. m. It is customary to check your hat and coat at the theater. There is no charge for this service. Opera glasses can be hired for a small charge (30 kopecks).

Cinemas are open from 9 a.m. until about midnight. Ticket holders are only admitted in the intervals between programs. The program usually consists of a newsreel, or a short film, and a full-length feature film, and lasts about two hours. Smoking is not permitted in the auditorium. Seats are numbered and reserved.

There are no night clubs in Moscow. Restaurants close at 11 p.m. (a few at midnight). Certain hotels have bars that are open until 2 a. m. Most restaurants and cafés have orchestras and dance floors. The *Arbat* Restaurant, and *Zvyozdnoye nebo* Restaurant in the *Intourist* Hotel and others have evening floor-shows.

Check-out time in hotels is 12 noon. The length of your stay is determined according to this time. On the day of departure guests are ordinarily expected to free their rooms by noon.

CITY TRANSPORT

Metro. The single fare is 5 kopecks, which covers any distance and all transfers to other lines. After depositing a 5 kopeck piece into the automatic entry gate, you may proceed to the boarding platform. If you don't have the correct change, you can use the automatic change machines situated at the entrance of every station. The Metro begins operation each day at 6 a.m. and ends at 1 a.m. (on holidays at 2 a.m.).

Trolleybuses, Buses, and Trams. Services begin at 6 a.m. and end at 1 a.m. The single fare (no transfers), regardless of distance, is 5 kopecks. Please bear in mind that there are no conductors or fare boxes on Moscow's trams, trolleybuses or buses and that the ticket-punch system is employed. Therefore, we recommend that you purchase tickets in advance. These are sold in booklets of ten (cost 50 kopecks) at newsstands, stores, pedestrian underpasses, and can also be purchased directly from bus, trolley and tram drivers.

Taxis. Taxis are easily recognizable by the black and white checkered ban on both sides of the car and a green light in the top right-hand corner of the windshield. When the green light is burning, the taxi is free. There are some 250 taxi stands in the city. You can also order a taxi by phone from your hotel (we advise you to do this through the Service Bureau). You can hail a taxi anywhere in the street by raising your arm, but not near a taxi stand if there is a line. The fare is registered on a taximeter. The rate is 20 kopecks per kilometer, plus a 20-kopeck service charge (regardless of the number of passengers).

Fixed-route taxis. There are many fixed-route taxis (mini-buses) which run between the main squares and main thoroughfares of the city, at intervals of ten to fifteen minutes. They have definite stops along their route, but if they are not full, they will stop at any point to pick up passengers. The single fare, regardless of distance, is 15 kopecks per person.

POST, TELEGRAPH AND TELEPHONE

Postal arrangements in the Soviet Union are much the same as anywhere else in the world. A letter or postcard can be posted from Moscow to any part of the world. There is a post office in practically every hotel, where you can buy envelopes, postcards, stamps, and writing paper.

Overseas Postage Rates*

	Letters	Postcards
Ordinary mail	20 kopecks	15 kopecks
Air mail	45 kopecks	35 kopecks
Registered mail	80 kopecks	75 kopecks
Registered air mail	1.05 roubles	95 kopecks

---

* Postal rates for mail to Albania, Bulgaria, Vietnam, the GDR, Korean People's Democratic Republic, Mongolian People's Republic, Hungary, Poland, Romania, Czechoslovakia, Yugoslavia, Chinese People's Republic, and Cuba do not differ from USSR international postage rates.

Both ordinary and express telegrams can be sent to any city in the world. Express telegrams are charged at double the ordinary rate.

Telegraph Rates (charge per word for ordinary telegrams)

Great Britain	40 kopecks
Belgium	40 kopecks
Canada	1 rouble
USA	1 rouble
France	40 kopecks
Sweden	40 kopecks
Japan	80 kopecks

Telephone calls can easily be put through to most cities in Europe and many cities in America, Asia, Africa, and Australia. You can book a call from your hotel or from special trunk-call offices. **The charges for a one-minute conversation with selected countries are as follows:**

Great Britain	3 roubles
Belgium	3 roubles
Canada	6 roubles
USA	6 roubles
France	3 roubles
Japan	4 roubles

In the building of the *Intourist* Hotel, 3 Gorky Street, there is a **post restante office**, K-600, which you can use as a forwarding address. It is convenient to use this service as tourists and visitors do not always know their address in advance. The address is simple, just Moscow, K-600.

REMINDER FOR PEDESTRIANS

Traffic in Moscow streets is heavy and fast, and at rush hours it is difficult to cross certain streets because of the number of vehicles. It would be well therefore, in order to avoid accidents, to know Moscow's main traffic regulations and highway code.

Here are some of the basic rules:

—walk only on the pavements (sidewalks) and keep to the right;

—cross streets only at pedestrian crossings, on the green "cross" sign;

—remember that Moscow drives on the right side of the road. Before crossing, look left, and then, when you have reached the middle, look right;

—if you get caught by oncoming traffic when you are crossing, stand still to make it easier for drivers to go round you;

—remember that many streets have one-way traffic only;

—only pass behind stationary buses and trolleybuses, but in front of stationary trams, otherwise you may not notice oncoming traffic;

—remember that it is prohibited for drivers to blow their horns in the city;

—even when you are crossing the street on the green light, watch out for traffic coming from the left and turning right.

It is useful to remember that the buildings' numbers on streets radiating from the Kremlin, as with all radial roads in Moscow, have even numbers on the right and odd numbers on the left, and begin the numbering from the center.

SOME HINTS FOR MOTORISTS

Here are a few suggestions to help you drive confidently through Moscow's streets and squares, observing the city's traffic regulations.

As you already know, Moscow drives on the right side of the street. Remember, too, not to drive if you have had a drink (alcoholic).

Please also remember:

—to drive at a speed that ensures your own safety, and that of pedestrians. The speed limit in Moscow is 60 kilometers an hour (about 35 m.p.h.); however on the city's main thoroughfares a speed of 80 kilometers is permitted.

—horns and hooters may only be used outside the city limits, or in an emergency situation to prevent an accident;

—listen for the sirens of special service vehicles (fire engines, ambulances, etc.) and give way to them;

—reduce speed before crossroads and "zebra" crossings.

If you did not insure your car at the Soviet border, you may do so in Moscow at the offices of **Ingosstrakh (Insurance Company of the USSR).** It has branches at all the border stations and in many large cities. You may insure all forms of transport against third party risks (person and property) and accident on the territory of the USSR. Policies are made out in any currency. Premiums are payable and claims are met in currency used in making out the policy.

AN ABC OF MOSCOW'S MAIN STREETS AND THOROUGHFARES

All of Moscow's main thoroughfares are numbered in order to help the motorist find his way around the city. The ring roads have an alphabetical index number: the Boulevard Ring is "A", the Garden Ring is "Б", the inner city circular road (Begovaya ulitsa—ulitsa Nizhnyaya Maslovka—ulitsa Sushchevsky val) is "B", and the outer Circular Motor Road is "K".

The avenues and streets radiating from the center have a numerical index number. If such a radial street is a continuation of a major highway, the letter "M" is added to its number. For instance, the road to Leningrad is No. 10. Within Moscow it becomes Leningrad Highway, then Leningrad Avenue, which is therefore numbered M 10.

Here is a list of Moscow's major radial highways and their destinations:

M 1—Kutuzovsky prospekt, Minskoye shosse (Kutuzov Avenue, Minsk Highway)—to Smolensk, Minsk, and Brest

M 4—Varshavskoye shosse (Warsaw Highway)—to Kharkov, Simferopol, and Yalta

M 8—shosse Entuziastov (Enthusiasts' Highway)—to Vladimir and Suzdal

M 9—prospekt Mira (Peace Avenue)—Yaroslavskoye shosse (Yaroslavl Highway)—to Zagorsk and Yaroslavl

M 10—Leningradsky prospekt, Leningradskoye shosse (Leningrad Avenue, Leningrad Highway)—to Leningrad.

SOUVENIRS

In Moscow you will find a large selection of souvenirs, including handicrafts and manufactured goods.

Handicrafts make splendid souvenirs: wood carvings, ivory figurines, painted wooden articles, ceramics, stamped leather, chased, enamelled and filigree metalwork, embroidery, and rugs.

Palekh lacquer miniatures are very popular. The work of Palekh artists (Palekh is the village where this style of miniature painting was developed) is noted for its finesse, rich range of colors and highly decorative effect. There are caskets, cigarettecases, powder boxes, and brooches among other things, all painted on a *papier mâché* base.

Articles made in the villages of Mstera and Fedoskino are of a similar type. Their miniatures usually depict characters from Russian fairy-tales, scenes from rural and urban life and Russian scenery.

Russian lace makes an elegant souvenir. You will find a good selection of lace tablecloths, bedspreads, pillow cases, napkins, collars, and shawls.

Craftsmen from the village of Khokhloma have been practising their art for over 300 years. The bright red and black wooden articles, with an attractive pattern on a golden background, invariably attract the attention of souvenir shoppers. Khokhloma ware includes wooden cups and spoons, all kinds of goblets, trays and furniture, all painted in this unique and traditional style. Khokhloma ware is durable and can be washed in warm water.

Bone carvings (from walrus ivory) by Northern craftsmen make unusual and interesting souvenirs. There are filigree brooches, picture frames, letter openers, caskets, and figurines of various size, depicting animals and scenes from the life of the peoples of the North.

Nearly all tourists are attracted by the *matryoshka* wooden dolls, painted in bright colors and lacquered. Sometimes there are as many as twelve dolls, one inside the other. These original *matryoshka* dolls are made near Moscow in Khotkovo and in the town of Semyonovo near Gorky. Bright and colorful, they make a delightful present, and are very inexpensive.

A bar of chocolate or a bottle of perfume, such as *Krasnaya Moskva* (Red Moscow) also make good souvenirs.

A Soviet camera is a splendid gift. Moscow stores have a wide range of good cameras at reasonable prices. Soviet watches, known for their reliability and precision, also make excellent keepsakes.

If you are a music lover you will not go wrong in buying records of Russian folk and classical music. And last, but not least, there is the *balalaika*, created about 300 years ago in the Russian peasant's cottage, that has gained recognition in the concert halls of many countries.

NATIONAL DISHES OF THE USSR

When you are in Moscow, don't miss the chance to sample the variety of Russian cooking.

Russian snacks and appetizers—salads, cold fish, and aspics—are well known. Dishes we recommend are cucumbers and tomatoes with sour cream, herring *à la russe*, salmon, sturgeon, jellied pike or sterlet, jellied tongue, and *studen* (meat jelly). Caviar hardly needs advertising; but try it on buttered rye bread.

As for the soup course, such stand-byes as *borshch*, *shchi*, and *solyanka* are worth sampling. You might try *borshch* with mushrooms, Russian noodle soup, or *rassolnik* (pickled cucumber soup with fish balls). In the summer Russians are very fond of cold vegetable or meat *okroshka* (*kvass* soup) and cold *borshch*.

Your impression of Russian cuisine will not be complete without tasting Siberian *pelmeni* (meat dumplings, rather like ravioli); with butter or sour cream, in bouillon or fried. You might also try *blini* (Russian pancakes), *oladyi* (raised pancakes), and *blinchiki* (fritters) with meat, cottage cheese, or apples.

Russians are very fond of cereals, especially buckwheat and semolina pudding. They are very nutritious and tasty with milk or butter. Some prefer them with sugar or jam. *Kisel* (kind of blancmange) is also a traditional part of a Russian dinner. We suggest a cup of tea, very popular in Russia, as a wonderful complement to your meal, especially with pastries or homemade cookies.

You probably already know Russian vodka. There are various brands of different strength, but we recommend either *Pshenichnaya*, *Stolichnaya*, or *Starka*. Some like to wash down a cup of vodka with a glass of *kvass*—a fermented Russian beverage made from rye bread.

Russian cuisine, of course, is only a part of our country's cuisine, which includes many dishes of all the nationalities that live in the USSR. Equally delicious are Russian meat pies, Ukrainian *borshch*, Uzbek pilau, Georgian *shashlik* (kebab), Armenian *dolma* (stuffed grape leaves), Azerbaijan *piti*, and many other superb national dishes and snacks. Moscow has many national restaurants where experienced chefs prepare a wide range of delicacies bound to delight the most refined tastes. One of the best of these is the **Aragvi**, which serves around thirty of the main Georgian dishes, including *shashlik*, chicken *satsivi*, grilled sturgeon, *suluguni* cheese, and chicken *tabaká*. The table wines of sunny Georgia are served. Among them are Tsinandali and Gurdjaani (white), Mukuzani (dry red), and Kakheti (white and red).

People who like eastern cuisine will enjoy the ***Uzbekistan*** and ***Baku* restaurants**.

A feature at the Uzbekistan is *tkhum-dulma* (hard boiled egg in a fried meat patty), *mstava* (a rice soup with specially prepared meat), *logman* (a spiced soup with meat and noodles) and Uzbek pilau. But the tastiest dish of all is probably *maniar*—a spiced broth, with minced meat, egg, and bits of pastry. There is also a wide choice of main dishes in Uzbek cuisine, prepared from poultry, meat and vegetables. Their *shashliks* are very tasty.

The bread deserves mention; it is baked on the premises, in a special oven, Uzbek style. The oven is made of clay in the shape of a cupola, with burning charcoal inside. Raw dough is rolled into flat loaves and tossed upward so that they stick to the red-hot inside of the oven. The temperature must be exactly 275 °C. If it is not, the flat loaves will fall into the burning coals.

The best Uzbek dessert wines are Aleatiko and Uzbekiston.

The *Baku* is an Azerbaijanian restaurant famous for its choice of pilaus. You may order pilau with chicken or stuffed spring chicken, with mutton or beef, milk or eggs; and there are many sweet pilaus. The soups are also delicious. *Piti*, for example, is prepared and served in a clay pot. Or you may try a nut soup with chicken, or *dovta*—a sour milk soup with meat. The restaurant is also known for its *shashlik, basturma*; *golubtsy* (chopped meat and rice in grape leaves), pot roast with pomegranates, broiled spring chicken, and many other national Azerbaijanian dishes. Two excellent red Azerbaijanian wines are Matrassa and Shamkhor; Akstafa is a delicious dessert wine.

The *Yerevan*, an Armenian restaurant, has an equally diversified menu of some 40 Armenian specialties. We recommend Armenian style *solyanka*, Yerevan *bozbash* (lamb and potato soup), steamed, fried, or broiled trout, "Ararat" *shashlik*, roast lamb, and pilau with raisins. The restaurant serves delicious *chebureki* (meat pastries fried in deep fat). Armenia is famed for its brandies. The best are Yubileiny (Jubilee), Armenia, Yerevan, and Dvin. Many people prefer "ordinary" three-star Armenian brandy. Armenian muscats are good and Armenian sherry is well known. It has a delicate fruit bouquet with a slight nutty flavour. Of the dessert wines, Aigeshat is recommended.

Of the other restaurants specializing in national dishes, the *Ukraina* is interesting for its famous Ukrainian *borshch, galushki*, and wines. The best of these are the Massandra wines (from the south coast of the Crimea) and the dessert wines, the rose, white and black muscats and the tokay. *Krasny Kamen* (Red Stone) is a world famous Crimean muscat. Its bouquet captures the delicate fragrance of alpine pastures with a slight hint of citrus.

Moscow has many other restaurants with fine cuisine (see p. 272 for addresses). There are large restaurants in all Moscow hotels. If you would like to sample the delicacies of the national cuisines of other countries, you should visit *Praga, Sofia, Belgrad, Savoy, Budapesht, Bukharest, Varshava,* and *Gavana* restaurants. The Intourist restaurants in the *National, Intourist, Kosmos, Savoy, Metropole,* and *Sevastopol* hotels offer superb European cuisine. But if you want to sample delicacies prepared according to old Russian recipes, then you should make an effort to visit the *Slavyansky bazar* (Slavic Bazaar) Restaurant, the restaurants of the *Rossiya* and *Tsentralnaya* hotels, as well as the *Rus* and *Arkhangelskoye* restaurants in the environs of Moscow.

FOR FACT COLLECTORS

—every day about 300 boys and girls are born in Moscow;

—in Moscow there are 100,000 Ivanovs, and 90,000 Kuznetsovs which are the most common surnames in Moscow;

—every day the theaters and concert halls are attended by 41,000 people, the cinemas by 320,000, and on Sundays by as many as 500,000 people;

—every day Muscovites receive and send three million letters and postcards;

—on fine days the USSR Economic Achievements Exhibition in visited by as many as 180,000 people;

—every day over 15,000 taxis are in operation in Moscow;

—there are more than 8,000 elks in the woods of Moscow's green belt;

—the Moskva River has over 600 tributaries, and is spanned by 16 bridges; there are 220 bridges (including flyovers) in Moscow;

—there are 8,000 amateur art and drama groups in Moscow, including 1,000 choirs, 2,000 musical ensembles and 700 dance groups, in which a total of 250,000 people participate;

—there are swans (including the black Australian variety) on 14 lakes in Moscow, and wild geese and ducks; sparrows and pigeons are the most common birds in Moscow;

—there is a mighty oak on Tverskoy Boulevard that was already considered old in 1775;

—Muscovites are very fond of ice-cream, eating more than 170 tons a day (around 1,800,000 portions) winter and summer alike;

—river trips are a favorite way of relaxing; there are over 100 large pleasure boats in Moscow and more than 800,000 people take trips on the river and the Moscow Canal every summer;

—fishing in the Moskva River within city limits is permitted year round. In winter anglers catch perch, roach, and ruff; in summer—goby, bream, pike-perch, and pike as well. There are over 20 varieties of fish in the Moskva River;

—in winter the skating rinks in Moscow parks cover more than 250,000 square meters;

—the city has around 100 parks and over 600 gardens;

—the trees on Moscow streets, squares, boulevards, and courtyards include chestnuts, larch, blue spruce, rowan-trees, bird-cherry and jasmine as well as pines, birches, poplars, limes, oaks, and maples—altogether 114 varieties of trees and shrubs;

—on Saturdays brass bands play in 50 Moscow's squares, parks, and gardens, such as the square in front of the Bolshoi Theater (from May till the end of September);

—there are 8,300 cafeterias, cafés, restaurants, buffets, snack bars, and special cafés selling meat pastries, *pelmeni*, tea, curd dumplings, pancakes, *shashliks* and *chebureki*;

—in order to clear the streets and squares of the city of snow 10 centimeters thick, dump trucks must make 150,000 journeys; in 1966 the heaviest snowfall in Moscow was 28 centimeters;

—in winter 19,000 people fly into Moscow each day; in summer the number reaches 35,000;

—during the summer 305 long-distance trains depart daily from Moscow's 9 railway stations;

—Moscow city transport carries around 8,5 million passengers a day; the city's tram, trolleybus and bus routes cover a distance of over 6,000 kilometers;

—there are 28,000 telephone booths on Moscow's streets and squares;

—most of Moscow's new buildings are nine-, twelve-, or eighteen-storey high;

—around 600 young couples are married each day.

ADDRESSES

STATE AND PUBLIC ORGANIZATIONS

Executive Committee of the Moscow City Soviet—13 ulitsa Gorkogo
USSR Ministry of Foreign Affairs—32 Smolenskaya-Sennaya ploshchad
USSR Ministry of Foreign Economic Affairs—32 Smolenskaya-Sennaya
ploshchad
18 Ovchinnikovskaya naberezh-
naya
Bank for Foreign Economic Affairs of the USSR—37 ulitsa Plyushchikha
USSR State Bank—12 ulitsa Neglinnaya
All-Union Chamber of Trade and Commerce—6 ulitsa Kuibysheva
World Trade Center (WTC)—12 Krasnopresnenskaya naberezhnaya
Council for Mutual Economic Assistance—56 prospekt Kalinina
USSR State Commitee for Foreign Travel (the Intourist)—16 prospekt Marksa
USSR Company for Foreign Travel (Moscow Branch)—11 Stoleshnikov pereu-
lok
Intourist Travel Bureau—1 ulitsa Gorkogo
International Youth Travel Bureau "Sputnik"—15 ulitsa Kosygina
Insurance Company of the USSR (Ingosstrakh) Ltd.—12 Pyatnitskaya ulitsa
Diplomatic Corps Administration—20 Kropotkinskaya ulitsa
Central International Aeroflot Agency—29 Leningradskoye shosse
All-Union Central Council of Trade Unions (ACCTU)—42 Leninsky prospekt
Union of Soviet Friendship Societies for Cultural Relations with Foreign
Countries—16 prospekt Kalinina
Soviet Peace Committee—36 prospekt Mira
Soviet Committee for Relations of Peace-loving Forces—36 prospekt Mira
Soviet Women's Committee—6 ulitsa Nemirovicha-Danchenko
Committee of Soviet Youth Organizations—7 ulitsa Bogdana Khmelnitskogo
Soviet Peace Fund—10 Kropotkinskaya ulitsa
Soviet Culture Fund—6 Gogolevsky bulvar
Soviet Committee for Cultural Relations with Compatriots Abroad—10 Bolshoi
Kharitonyevsky pereulok
USSR Union of Red Cross and Red Crescent Societies—5 Pervy Cheryomush-
kinsky proyezd
Soviet War Veterans' Committee—4 Gogolevsky bulvar
Soviet Committee for European Security and Cooperation—3 Kropotkinskaya
ulitsa
Soviet Afro-Asian Solidarity Committee—10 Kropotkinskaya ulitsa
Soviet Latin American Solidarity Committee—9 Krivokolenny pereulok
"Znanye" (Knowledge) Society—4 proyezd Serova
Committee for Physical Culture and Sport of the USSR Council of Minis-
ters—8 Luzhnetskaya naberezhnaya
Central Council for Tourism and Excursions of the ACCTU—50 Ozerkovskaya
naberezhnaya
USSR United Nations Association—36 prospekt Mira

House of Friendship with Peoples of Foreign Countries—16 prospekt Kalinina
Union of Soviet Architects—3 ulitsa Shchuseva
Union of Soviet Journalists—4 Zubovsky bulvar
Union of Soviet Composers—8 ulitsa Nezhdanovoy
Union of Soviet Writers—52 ulitsa Vorovskogo
Union of Soviet Film Workers—13 Vasilyevskaya ulitsa
Union of Soviet Artists—10 Gogolevsky bulvar
All-Russia Theatrical Society—16 ulitsa Gorkogo
Union of Theater Workers of the USSR—12 ulitsa Gorkogo
All-Union Organization of War and Labor Veterans—8 ulitsa Shchepkina
USSR Cultural Fund—35 ulitsa Arbat
All-Union Musical Society—13 ulitsa Gertsena
All-Union Volunteer Anti-Alcoholic Society—18 ulitsa Chekhova

PRESS, RADIO, TELEVISION AND NEWS AGENCIES

Newspapers
Izvestia—5 Pushkinskaya ploshchad
Komsomolskaya Pravda—24 ulitsa Pravdy
Literaturnaya Gazeta—13 Kostyansky pereulok
Moskovskaya Pravda—7 ulitsa Tysyacha Devyatsot Pyatogo goda
Moskovskiye Novosti (Moscow News)—2 Pushkinskaya ploshchad
Pravda—24 ulitsa Pravdy
Sotsialisticheskaya Industriya—24 ulitsa Pravdy
Sovetskaya Kultura—73 Novoslobodskaya ulitsa
Sovetskaya Rossiya—24 ulitsa Pravdy
Sovetsky Sport—8 ulitsa Arkhipova
Trud—4 Nastasyinsky pereulok
Vechernyaya Moskva—7 ulitsa Tysyacha Devyatsot Pyatogo goda
Magazines
Inostrannaya Literatura—41 Pyatnitskaya ulitsa
Kommunist—5 ulitsa Marksa i Engelsa
Mezhdunarodnaya Zhizn (International Affairs)—14 Gorokhovsky pereulok
Moskva—20 ulitsa Arbat
Nauka i Zhizn—24 ulitsa Kirova
Novoye Vremya (New Times)—1/2 Maly Putinkovsky pereulok
Novy Mir—1/2 Maly Putinkovsky pereulok
Ogonyok—14 Bumazhny proyezd
Puteshestviye v SSSR (Travel in the USSR)—8 Neglinnaya ulitsa
Rabotnitsa—14 Bumazhny proyezd
Sovetskaya Literatura (Soviet Literature)—7 naberezhnaya Shevchenko
Sovetskaya Zhenshchina (Soviet Woman)—6 Miusskaya ploshchad
Sovetsky Soyuz (Soviet Union)—8 ulitsa Moskvina
Turist—14 Bolshoi Kharitonyevsky pereulok
Vneshnyaya Torgovlya (Foreign Trade)—11 Minskaya ulitsa

* * *

TASS (Telegraph Agency of the USSR)—2, 10, 12 Tverskoy bulvar
Novosti Press Agency (APN)—4 Zubovsky bulvar
State Committee for Television and Radio Broadcasting *(Gosteleradio)*—25 Pyatnitskaya ulitsa
State Committee for Publishing, Printing, and Book Trade *(Goskomizdat)*—5 Strastnoy bulvar

FOREIGN EMBASSIES

Afghanistan, Democratic Republic of—3/2 Sverchkov pereulok
Algeria (Algerian People's Democratic Republic)—1a Krapivinsky pereulok
Angola, People's Republic of—54 Mosfilmovskaya ulitsa
Arab Emirates, United—12 Krasnopresnenskaya naberezhnaya (*Mezhdunarodnaya* Hotel)
Argentina, Republic of—4 Sadovaya-Triumfalnaya ulitsa
Australia, Commonwealth of—13 Kropotkinsky pereulok
Austria, Republic of—1 Starokonyushenny pereulok
Bangladesh, People's Republic of—6 Zemledelchesky pereulok
Belgium, Kingdom of—7a Stolovy pereulok
Benin, People's Republic of—4a Uspensky pereulok
Bolivia, Republic of—5 Lopukhinsky pereulok
Brazil, Federative Republic of—54 ulitsa Gertsena
Bulgaria, People's Republic of—66 Mosfilmovskaya ulitsa
Burkina Faso—17 Meshchanskaya ulitsa
Burma (Socialist Republic of the Union of Burma)—41 ulitsa Gertsena
Burundi, Republic of—7 Uspensky pereulok
Cameroon, United Republic of—40 ulitsa Vorovskogo
Canada—23 Starokonyushenny pereulok
Cape Verde Islands, Republic of—9 Bolshaya Spasskaya ulitsa
Central African Republic—20 ulitsa Gilyarovskogo
Chad, Republic of—10 ulitsa Yelizarovoy
China, People's Republic of—6 ulitsa Druzhby
Colombia, Republic of—20 ulitsa Burdenko
Congo, People's Republic of—12 Kropotkinsky pereulok
Costa Rica, Republic of—7/4 Kutuzovsky prospekt
Côte d'Ivoire, Republic of—7 Dobryninskaya ulitsa
Cuba, Republic of—40 Mosfilmovskaya ulitsa
Cyprus, Republic of—51 ulitsa Gertsena
Czechoslovakia (Czechoslovak Socialist Republic)—12/14 ulitsa Yuliusa Fuchika
Denmark, Kingdom of—9 pereulok Ostrovskogo
Ecuador, Republic of—12 Grokholsky pereulok
Egypt, Arab Republic of—56 ulitsa Gertsena
Ethiopia (Socialist Ethiopia)—6 Orlovo-Davydkovsky pereulok
Federal Republic of Germany—17 Bolshaya Gruzinskaya ulitsa
Finland, Republic of—15/17 Kropotkinsky pereulok
France, Republic of—45 ulitsa Dimitrova

Gabon, Republic of—16 ulitsa Vesnina
German Democratic Republic—95a Leninsky prospekt
Ghana, Republic of—14 Skatertny pereulok
Great Britain and Northern Ireland, United Kingdom of—14 naberezhnaya Morisa Toreza
Greece (Hellenic Republic)—4 ulitsa Stanislavskogo
Guinea, People's Revolutionary Republic of—6 Pomerantsev pereulok
Guinea-Bissau, Republic of—35 ulitsa Bolshaya Ordynka
Guayana, Co-operative Republic of—7 Vtoroi Kazachiy pereulok
Hungary (Hungarian People's Republic)—62 Mosfilmovskaya ulitsa
Iceland, Republic of—28 Khlebny pereulok
India, Republic of—6-8 ulitsa Obukha
Indonesia, Republic of—12 Novokuznetskaya ulitsa
Iran, Islamic Republic of—7 Pokrovsky bulvar
Iraq, Republic of—12 Pogodinskaya ulitsa
Ireland, Republic of—5 Grokholsky pereulok
Italy, Republic of—5 ulitsa Vesnina
Jamaica—flat 70-71, 7 Dobryninskaya ulitsa
Japan—12 Kalashny pereulok
Jordan, Hashemite Kingdom of—3 pereulok Sadovskikh
Kampuchea, People's Republic of—16 Starokonyushenny pereulok
Kenya, Republic of—70 ulitsa Bolshaya Ordynka
Korea, Democratic People's Republic of—72 Mosfilmovskaya ulitsa
Kuwait—13/5 Tretiy Neopalimovsky pereulok
Laos (Lao People's Democratic Republic)—18/1 ulitsa Bolshaya Ordynka
Lebanon, Republic of—14 ulitsa Sadovaya-Samotechnaya
Liberia, Republic of—58 Mosfilmovskaya ulitsa
Libya (Socialist People's Libyan Arab Jamahiriya)—38 Mosfilmovskaya ulitsa
Luxembourg, Grand Duchy of—3 Khrushchevsky pereulok
Madagascar, Democratic Republic of—5 Kursovoi pereulok
Malaysia, Federation of—50 Mosfilmovskaya ulitsa
Mali, Republic of—11 Novokuznetskaya ulitsa
Malta, Republic of—flat 219, 7 Dobryninskaya ulitsa
Mauritania, Islamic Republic of—66 ulitsa Bolshaya Ordynka
Mexico (United Mexican States)—4 ulitsa Shchukina
Mongolia (Mongolian People's Republic)—11 ulitsa Pisemskogo
Morocco, Kingdom of—8 pereulok Ostrovskogo
Mozambique, People's Republic of—20 ulitsa Gilyarovskogo
Nepal, Kingdom of—14/7 Vtoroi Neopalimovsky pereulok
New Zealand—44 ulitsa Vorovskogo
Nicaragua, Republic of—50 Mosfilmovskaya ulitsa
Niger, Republic of—7 Kursovoi pereulok
Nigeria, Federal Republic of—13 ulitsa Kachalova
Norway, Kingdom of—7 ulitsa Vorovskogo
Netherlands, Kingdom of the—6 Kalashny pereulok
Pakistan, Islamic Republic of—17 Sadovaya-Kudrinskaya ulitsa
Palestine (Palestine Liberation Organization)—23 Trubnikovsky pereulok
Peru, Republic of—22 Smolensky bulvar

Philippines, Republic of—6 Karmanitsky pereulok
Poland (Polish People's Republic)—4 ulitsa Klimashkina
Portugal, Republic of—1 Botanichesky pereulok
Romania, Socialist Republic of—64 Mosfilmovskaya ulitsa
Rwanda, Republic of—72 ulitsa Bolshaya Ordynka
Senegal, Republic of—12 Donskaya ulitsa
Sierra Leone, Republic of—4 ulitsa Paliashvili
Singapore, Republic of—5 pereulok Voyevodina
Somalia (Somali Democratic Republic)—8 Spasopeskovskaya ploshchad
Spain—50/8 ulitsa Gertsena
Sri Lanka, Democratic Socialist Republic of—24 ulitsa Shchepkina
Sudan, Democratic Republic of—9 ulitsa Vorovskogo
Sweden, Kingdom of—60 Mosfilmovskaya ulitsa
Switzerland (Swiss Confederation)—2/5 pereulok Stopani
Syria (Syrian Arab Republic)—4 Mansurovsky pereulok
Tanzania, United Republic of—33 Pyatnitskaya ulitsa
Thailand, Kingdom of—3 Yeropkinsky pereulok
Togo, Republic of—1 ulitsa Shchuseva
Tunisia, Republic of—28/1 ulitsa Kachalova
Turkey, Republic of—7/37 Vadkovsky pereulok
Uganda, Republic of—5 pereulok Sadovskikh
United States of America—19 ulitsa Tchaikovskogo
Uruguay, Oriental Republic of—38 Lomonosovsky prospekt
Venezuela, Republic of—13 ulitsa Yermolovoy
Vietnam, Socialist Republic of—13 Bolshaya Pirogovskaya ulitsa
Yemen Arab Republic—3 Kropotkinskaya naberezhnaya
Yemen, People's Democratic Republic of—14 ulitsa Alexeya Tolstogo
Yugoslavia, Socialist Federal Republic of—46 Mosfilmovskaya ulitsa
Republic of Zaïre—12 pereulok Ostrovskogo
Zambia, Republic of—52a prospekt Mira
Zimbabwe, Republic of—6 Serpov pereulok

FOREIGN AIRLINES

AIR FRANCE—7 Dobryninskaya ulitsa
AIR INDIA—7 Dobryninskaya ulitsa
ALIA (Jordanian Airlines)—3 pereulok Sadovskikh
ALITALIA—7 Pushechnaya ulitsa
AUA—(Austrian Airlines)—room 1805, 12 Krasnopresnenskaya naberezhnaya
BAKHTAR (Afghan Airlines)—room 628, Sheremetyevo-2
BALKAN (Bulgarian Civil Airlines)—3 ulitsa Kuznetsky most
British Airways—room 1905, 12 Krasnopresnenskaya naberezhnaya
Choson Minhang (Korean Airlines)—72 Mosfilmovskaya ulitsa
ČSA (Czechoslovak Airlines)—21/27 Vtoraya Brestskaya ulitsa
CUBANA—7 Dobryninskaya ulitsa
Ethiopian Airlines—6 Serpov pereulok (Embassy)
FINNAIR—6 proyezd Khudozhestvennogo teatra
GUGAK (General Administration of Civil Aviation of China)—8 ulitsa Druzhby

INTERFLUG (German Democratic Republic)—33 Kalanchevskaya ulitsa
Iraqi Airways—37 Pyatnitskaya ulitsa
JAL (Japan Airlines)—3 ulitsa Kuznetsky most
JAT (Jugoslovenski Aerotransport)—3 ulitsa Kuznetsky most
KLM (Royal Dutch Airlines)—room 1307, 12 Krasnopresnenskaya naberezhnaya
LAA (Libyan Arab Airlines)—7 Dobryninskaya ulitsa
LOT (Polish Airlines)—flat 161, 13/21 Smolenskaya ploshchad
LUFTHANZA (Federal Republic of Germany)—3 ulitsa Kuznetsky most
MALEV (Hungarian Airlines)—6 proyezd Khudozhestvennogo teatra
PAN-AMERICAN—12 Krasnopresnenskaya naberezhnaya
SAAL (Syrian Arab Airlines)—7 Dobryninskaya ulitsa
SAS (Scandinavian Airlines)—3 ulitsa Kuznetsky most
SWISSAIR (Switzerland)—12 Krasnopresnenskaya naberezhnaya
TAAG (Angola Airlines)—7 Dobryninskaya ulitsa
TAROM (Rumanian Air Transport)—64 Mosfilmovskaya ulitsa
YEMENIA (Yemen Arab Republic)—Sheremetyevo-2

TRADE DELEGATIONS OF SOCIALIST COUNTRIES

Bulgaria, People's Republic of—52 Mosfilmovskaya ulitsa
Czechoslovakia (Czechoslovak Socialist Republic)—12/14 ulitsa Yuliusa Fuchika
Hungary (Hungarian People's Republic)—1-7 ulitsa Krasnaya Presnya
Mongolia (Mongolian People's Republic)—7/1 Spasopeskovsky pereulok
Poland (Polish People's Republic)—4 ulitsa Klimashkina
Romania, Socialist Republic of—64 Mosfilmovskaya ulitsa

REPRESENTATIVES OF FOREIGN TOURIST FIRMS AND ORGANIZA-TIONS

American Express (USA)—21-a Sadovaya-Kudrinskaya ulitsa
Balkantourist (Bulgaria)—66 Mosfilmovskaya ulitsa
Čedok Travel Office (Czechoslovakia)—35 Chetvyortaya Tverskaya-Yamskaya ulitsa
Ibusz Travel Office (Hungary)—26/1 ulitsa Gorkogo
Orbis Travel Office (Poland)—flat 88, 56 ulitsa Gorkogo
Reisebüro der DDR (GDR)—33 Kalanchevskaya ulitsa
Yugotours—flat 55, 7 Kutuzovsky prospekt

TELEPHONE NUMBERS TO REMEMBER

01—Fire
02—Police
03—Ambulance
05—General Inquiries about Moscow
07—Inter-city telephone
09—Directory Inquiries
100—Time

MUSEUMS

Museums of the History of the Revolution
Central Lenin Museum—2 ploshchad Revolyutsii
Central Museum of the Revolution—21 ulitsa Gorkogo
Central Museum of the Soviet Armed Forces—2 ulitsa Sovetskoi Armii
Kalinin Museum—21 prospekt Marksa
Karl Marx and Friedrich Engels Museum—5 ulitsa Marksa i Engelsa
Krasnaya Presnya Museum—4 ulitsa Bolshevistskaya
Museum of the Defence of Moscow—3 ulitsa Pelshe
Underground Printing Press of the Central Committee of the RSDLP
(Branch of Central Museum of the Revolution)—55 Lesnaya ulitsa

Historical Museums
State Historical Museum—1/2 Krasnaya Ploshchad
Branches:
Vasily the Blessed Cathedral (the Cathedral of the Intercession)—Krasnaya Ploshchad
Novodevichy Convent—1 Novodevichy proyezd
Church of the Intercession of the Virgin at Fili—6 Novozavodskaya ulitsa
Trinity Church at Nikitniki—3 Nikitnikov pereulok
Chambers of the 16th-17th Centuries in Zaryadye—10 ulitsa Razina
Panorama Museum of the Battle of Borodino—38 Kutuzovsky prospekt
Branch:
Izba Kutuzova—38 Kutuzovsky prospekt
Museum of the History and Reconstruction of Moscow—12 Novaya ploshchad
Museum of the Decembrists—23 ulitsa Karla Marksa

Art, Theatrical and Literary Museums
Kremlin Museums, Armoury Chamber, and USSR Diamond Fund—the Kremlin
Tretyakov Art Gallery—10 Lavrushinsky pereulok
State Picture Gallery of the USSR—10 ulitsa Krymsky val
Pushkin Museum of Fine Arts—12 ulitsa Volkhonka
Museum of Folk Art—7 ulitsa Stanislavskogo
All-Russia Museum of Decorative and Folk Art—3 Delegatskaya ulitsa
Museum of Oriental Art—12 Suvorovsky bulvar
Andrei Rublev Museum of Early Russian Culture and Art—10 ploshchad Pryamikova
Museum of Tropinin and Other Artists of His Time—10 Shchetininsky pereulok
Shchusev Museum of Architecture—5 prospekt Kalinina
Donskoy Monastery (Branch of Museum of Architecture)—1 Donskaya ploshchad
Ostankino Palace-Museum of Serf Art—5 Pervaya Ostankinskaya ulitsa
Kuskovo 18th-Century Estate and Ceramics Museum—4 ulitsa Yunosti
Kolomenskoye Museum-Preserve—39 prospekt Andropova
Bakhrushin Theatrical Museum—31/12 ulitsa Bakhrushina
Glinka Music Museum—4 ulitsa Fadeyeva
Museum of Literature—28 ulitsa Petrovka (Soviet section—17 Trubnikovsky pereulok)
Pushkin Museum—12/2 Kropotkinskaya ulitsa

Tolstoy Museum—11 Kropotkinskaya ulitsa
Tolstoy Museum (branch)—12 Pyatnitskaya ulitsa

Memorial Museums
Chaliapin House-Museum—25 ulitsa Tchaikovskogo
Chekhov House-Museum—6 Sadovaya-Kudrinskaya ulitsa
Dostoyevsky Apartment-Museum—2 ulitsa Dostoyevskogo
Golubkina Studio-Museum—12 ulitsa Shchukina
Gorky Apartment-Museum—6 ulitsa Kachalova
Herzen House-Museum on Arbat—27/9 pereulok Sivtsev Vrazhek
Konenkov Studio-Museum—17 ulitsa Gorkogo
Korolyov House-Museum—2 Shestoi Ostankinsky pereulok
Lermontov House-Museum—2 ulitsa Malaya Molchanovka
Mayakovsky Museum—3 proyezd Serova
Nemirovich-Danchenko Apartment-Museum—5/7 ulitsa Nemirovicha-Danchenko
Nikolai Ostrovsky Apartment-Museum—14 ulitsa Gorkogo
Alexander Ostrovsky House-Museum—9 ulitsa Ostrovskogo
"Pushkin's Apartment on Arbat" Museum—53 ulitsa Arbat
Scriabin Apartment-Museum—11 ulitsa Vakhtangova
Stanislavsky Apartment-Museum—6 ulitsa Stanislavskogo
Lev Tolstoy Mansion-Museum—21 ulitsa Lva Tolstogo
Vasnetsov House-Museum—13 pereulok Vasnetsova
Yermolova House-Museum—11 Tverskoy bulvar

Science and Polytechnic Museums
State Polytechnic Museum—3 Novaya ploshchad
Planetarium—5 Sadovaya-Kudrinskaya ulitsa
Zoological Museum—6 ulitsa Gertsena
Memorial Museum of Cosmonautics—prospekt Mira, alleya Kosmonavtov
Frunze Central House of Aviation and Cosmonautics—4 Krasnoarmeiskaya ulitsa
Alexander Fersman Museum of Mineralogy—18 Leninsky prospekt
Kliment Timiryazev Biological Museum—15 Malaya Gruzinskaya ulitsa
Paleonthological Museum—123 Profsoyuznaya ulitsa

Museum of Physical Culture and Sport—Lenin Central Stadium in Luzhniki, Eastern Sector

Main Botanical Gardens of the USSR Academy of Sciences—4 Botanicheskaya ulitsa
The Zoo—1 Bolshaya Gruzinskaya ulitsa

EXHIBITIONS AND EXHIBITION HALLS

USSR Economic Achievements Exhibition (VDNKh)—Prospekt Mira
Building Section of the USSR Economic Achievements Exhibition—30 Frunzenskaya naberezhnaya
Exhibition of Urban Development—4 Berezhkovskaya naberezhnaya

Central Exhibition Hall (former Manège)—ploshchad Pyatidesyatiletiya Oktyabrya
Krasnaya Presnya Exhibition Complex—Krasnopresnenskaya naberezhnaya
Exhibition Hall of the USSR Academy of Arts—21 Kropotkinskaya ulitsa
Exhibition Hall of the Soviet Culture Fund—15 ulitsa Karla Marksa
Exhibition Hall of the All-Russia Society for the Preservation of Monuments of
History and Culture—12 ulitsa Razina
Exhibition halls of the USSR Union of Artists—10 ulitsa Krymsky val, 25 ulitsa
Gorkogo, 20 ulitsa Kuznetsky most
Exhibition Hall of the USSR Union of Journalists—8 Gogolevsky bulvar
Exhibition halls of the RSFSR Union of Artists—46 ulitsa Gorkogo, 11 ulitsa Kuznetsky most
Exhibition pavilions of the All-Russia Society for the Preservation of Nature—5 ulitsa Vorovskogo, 4 ulitsa Razina
Fashion exhibitions—14 ulitsa Kuznetsky most, 21 prospekt Mira
Children's Book Exhibition—43 ulitsa Gorkogo

THEATERS, CONCERT HALLS AND CIRCUSES

Bolshoi Theater (the USSR State Academic Bolshoi Theater of Opera and Ballet)—2 ploshchad Sverdlova
Central Children's Theater—2/7 ploshchad Sverdlova
Central Puppet Theater—3 Sadovaya-Samotechnaya ulitsa
Central State Concert Hall (*Rossiya* Hotel)—1 Moskvoretskaya naberezhnaya
Central Theater of the Soviet Army—2 ploshchad Kommuny
Chamber Music Theater—71 Leningradskoye shosse
Children's Musical Theater—5 prospekt Vernadskogo
Circus (new)—17 prospekt Vernadskogo
Circus (old)—13 Tsvetnoy bulvar
Concert Hall of the Central House of Art Workers—9 Pushechnaya ulitsa
Concert Hall of the Central House of Tourists—146 Leninsky prospekt
Concert Hall of the Izmailovo Tourist Complex—71 Izmailovskoye shosse
Drama Theater on Malaya Bronnaya—2/4 Malaya Bronnaya ulitsa
Durov Animal Theater—4 ulitsa Durova
Film Actors' Studio Theater—33 ulitsa Vorovskogo
Gogol Drama Theater—8a ulitsa Kazakova
House of Trade Unions *(Dom Soyuzov)*, Hall of Columns and October Hall—1 Pushkinskaya ulitsa
Lenin Komsomol Theater—6 ulitsa Chekhova
Maly Theater—1/6 ploshchad Sverdlova; branch—6 ulitsa Bolshaya Ordynka
Mayakovsky Theater—19 ulitsa Gertsena
Mime Theater—39 Izmailovsky bulvar
Moscow Art Theater (*MKhAT*)—3 proyezd Khudozhestvennogo theatra; branch—3 ulitsa Moskvina
Moscow Puppet Theater—26 Spartakovskaya ulitsa
Moscow *Hermitage* Theater—3 ulitsa Karetny ryad
Moscow Theater on Taganka—Taganskaya ploshchad
Mossovet Theater—16 Bolshaya Sadovaya ulitsa
Novorossiisk Cinema-Concert Hall—47 ulitsa Chernyshevskogo

Novy Drama Theater—2 ulitsa Prokhodchikov
Oktyabr Cinema-Concert Hall—42 prospekt Kalinina
Olympic Village Large Concert and Chamber halls—Michurinsky prospekt, Olympic Village
Operetta Theater—6 Pushkinskaya ulitsa
Palace of Congresses—the Kremlin
Peoples' Friendship Theater—22 Tverskoy bulvar
Pushkin Drama Theater—23 Tverskoy bulvar
Romen Gipsy Theater—32 Leningradsky prospekt
Satire Theater—2 ploshchad Mayakovskogo
Satiricon Theater—8 Sheremetevskaya ulitsa
Sfera Theater-Studio—3 ulitsa Karetny ryad
Sofia Cinema-Concert Hall—31 Sirenevy bulvar
Sovremennik Theater—19-a Chistoprudny bulvar
Stanislavsky and Nemirovich-Danchenko Musical Theater—17 Pushkinskaya ulitsa
Stanislavsky Drama Theater—23 ulitsa Gorkogo'
Tchaikovsky Concert Hall—4/31 ploshchad Mayakovskogo
Tchaikovsky State Conservatoire (Large and Small halls)—13 ulitsa Gertsena
Vakhtangov Theater—26 ulitsa Arbat
Variety Theater—20/2 Bersenevskaya naberezhnaya
Varshava Cinema-Concert Hall—10 Leningradskoye shosse
Yermolova Theater—5 ulitsa Gorkogo
Young Spectators' Theater—10 pereulok Sadovskikh

CINEMAS

Cyclorama—in the USSR Economic Achievements Exhibition
Kosmos—109 prospekt Mira
Gorizont—21 Komsomolsky prospekt
Khudozhestvenny—14 Arbatskaya ploshchad
Metropole—1 prospekt Marksa
Mir—11 Tsvetnoy bulvar
Moskva—2 ploshchad Mayakovskogo
Oktyabr—42 prospekt Kalinina
Rossiya—2 Pushkinskaya ploshchad
Udarnik—2 ulitsa Serafimovicha
Zaryadye—1 Moskvoretskaya naberezhnaya

RECREATION PARKS AND GARDENS

Aquarium Gardens—16 Bolshaya Sadovaya ulitsa
Dzerzhinsky Recreation Park—7 Pervaya Ostankinskaya ulitsa
Friendship Park (Park Druzhby)—Leningradskoye shosse
Garden of the Central Club of the Soviet Army—2 ploshchad Kommuny
Gorky Central Recreation Park—9 Krymsky val
Hermitage Gardens—3 Karetny ryad

Izmailovo Recreation Park—17 Narodny prospekt
Krasnaya Presnya Recreation Park—5 Mantulinskaya ulitsa
Sokolniki Recreation Park—1 Sokolnichesky val

STADIUMS AND SPORTS FACILITIES

Aquatic Sports Palace—27 Mironovskaya ulitsa
Dynamo Sports Palace—32 ulitsa Lavochkina
Dynamo Stadium—36 Leningradsky prospekt
Dynamo Swimming Pool—36 Leningradsky prospekt
Equestrian Center at Bitsa Forest-Park—33 Balaklavsky prospekt
Hippodrome—22 Begovaya ulitsa
Krylatskoye Olympic Sports Complex—10 Krylatskaya ulitsa
Lenin Central Stadium—Luzhniki
Lokomotiv Central Stadium—125 Bolshaya Cherkizovskaya ulitsa
Moskva Swimming Pool—37 Kropotkinskaya naberezhnaya
Olympic Center for Rowing Sports—2 Pyataya Krylatskaya ulitsa
Olympic Center for Aquatic Sports—25 Tkatskaya ulitsa
Olympic Sports Complex—16 Olimpiisky prospekt
Olympic Village Sports Complex—Michurinsky prospekt, Olympic Village
Sports and Fitness Complex of the Lenin Komsomol Auto Plant—46 Volgogradsky
prospekt
Sports Complex of *TsSKA* (Central Army Sports Club)—39 Leningradsky prospekt
Young Pioneers Stadium—31 Leningradsky prospekt

HOTELS
(with nearest Metro stations)

Aeroflot—37 Leningradsky prospekt, *Dynamo, Aeroport*
Altai—41 Botanicheskaya ulitsa, *VDNKh*
Belgrad-I*—5 Smolenskaya ploshchad, *Smolenskaya*
Belgrad-2*—8 Smolenskaya ploshchad, *Smolenskaya*
Savoy*—3 ulitsa Rozhdestvenka, *Dzerzhinskaya, Kuznetsky most*
Bukharest—1 ulitsa Balchug, *Novokuznetskaya, Tretyakovskaya*
Budapesht—2 Petrovskiye linii, *Prospekt Marksa, Kuznetsky most*
Druzhba—53 prospekt Vernadskogo, *Prospekt Vernadskogo*
Intourist*—3 ulitsa Gorkogo, *Prospekt Marksa*
Kosmos*—150 prospekt Mira, *VDNKh*
Leningradskaya—21/40 Kalanchevskaya ulitsa, *Komsomolskaya*
Metropole*—1 prospekt Marksa, *Ploshchad Revolyutsii, Prospekt Marksa*
Mezhdunarodnaya—12 Krasnopresnenskaya naberezhnaya, *Ulitsa 1905 Goda*
Minsk—22 ulitsa Gorkogo, *Mayakovskaya, Gorkovskaya*
Mir—9 Bolshoi Devyatinsky pereulok, *Krasnopresnenskaya, Barrikadnaya*
Molodyozhnaya—27 Dmitrovskoye shosse, *Savyolovskaya*
Moskva—7 prospekt Marksa, *Prospekt Marksa, Ploshchad Revolyutsii*
National*—14 prospekt Marksa, *Prospekt Marksa*
Orlyonok—15 ulitsa Kosygina, *Leninsky prospekt*

Ostankino — 29 Botanicheskaya ulitsa, *VDNKh*
Pekin — 1 Bolshaya Sadovaya ulitsa, *Mayakovskaya*
Rossiya — 6 ulitsa Razina, *Ploshchad Nogina*
Salyut — 158 Leninsky prospekt, *Yugo-Zapadnaya*
Sevastopol* — 1a Bolshaya Yushunskaya ulitsa, *Kakhovskaya*
Severnaya — 50 ulitsa Sushchevsky val, *Rizhskaya*
Sovetskaya — 32 Leningradsky prospekt, *Dynamo*
Soyuz — 17 Levoberezhnaya ulitsa
Sport — 90 Leninsky prospekt, *Universitet*
Sputnik — 38 Leninsky prospekt, *Leninsky Prospekt*
Tourist — 17 Selskokhozyaistvennaya ulitsa, *VDNKh*
Tsentralnaya — 10 ulitsa Gorkogo, *Gorkovskaya, Pushkinskaya*
Ukraina — 2/1 Kutuzovsky prospekt, *Kievskaya*
Ural — 40 ulitsa Chernyshevskogo, *Ploshchad Nogina*, *Kirovskaya*
Vostok — 8 Gostinichny proyezd, *VDNKh*
Varshava — 2 Oktyabrskaya ploshchad, *Oktyabrskaya*
Yaroslavskaya — 8 Yaroslavskaya ulitsa, *VDNKh*
Yunost — 34 ulitsa Khamovnichesky val, *Sportivnaya*
Yuzhnaya — 87 Leninsky prospekt, *Leninsky Prospekt*
Zarya — 5 Gostinichnaya ulitsa, *VDNKh*
Zolotoi kolos — 15 Yaroslavskaya ulitsa, *VDNKh*
Camping Sites, Motels
Mozhaisky* — 165 Mozhaiskoye shosse
Solnechny* — Varshavskoye shosse (21st km)

Hotels and motels marked with an * belong to Intourist

RESTAURANTS

Abkhaziya — 44 Novocheryomushkinskaya ulitsa
Aragvi (Georgian cuisine) — 6 ulitsa Gorkogo
Arbat — 29 prospekt Kalinina
Baku (Azerbaijanian cuisine) — 24 ulitsa Gorkogo
Belgrad* — 5 and 8, Smolenskaya ploshchad
Savoy* — 6 Pushechnaya ulitsa
Bombey — 91 Rublyovskoye shosse
Bukharest — I Sadovnicheskaya naberezhnaya
Budapesht — 2 ulitsa Petrovskiye linii
Gavana — 88 Leninsky prospekt
Hanoi — 20 prospekt Shestidesyatiletiya Oktyabrya
Deli — 23 ulitsa Krasnaya Presnya
Intourist* — 3 ulitsa Gorkogo
Kontinental — 12 Krasnopresnenskaya naberezhnaya
Labirint — 29 prospekt Kalinina
Metropole* — 1 prospekt Marksa
Minsk (Byelorussian cuisine) — 22 ulitsa Gorkogo
Mir — 9 Bolshoi Devyatinsky pereulok

Moskva—7 prospekt Marksa
National*—1 ulitsa Gorkogo
Pekin—1 Bolshaya Sadovaya ulitsa
Praga (Czechoslovakian cuisine)—2 ulitsa Arbat
Rossiya (Russian cuisine)—6 ulitsa Razina
Sedmoye nebo—Ostankino TV Tower
Severny luch—16 Olimpiisky prospekt
Slavyansky bazar (Russian cuisine)—17 ulitsa Dvadtsat Pyatogo Oktyabrya
Sofia (Bulgarian cuisine)—32 ulitsa Gorkogo
Sovetsky—22 Leningradsky prospekt
Sputnik—38 Leninsky prospekt
Stolichny—4 ploshchad Sverdlova
Tsentralny (Russian cuisine)—10 ulitsa Gorkogo
Ukraina (Ukrainian cuisine)—2 Kutuzovsky prospekt
Varshava (Polish cuisine)—2 Oktyabrskaya ploshchad
Volga—51 Leningradskoye shosse (Northern River Port)
Yakor—49 ulitsa Gorkogo
Yubileiny—prospekt Mira, *VDNKh* (North Entrance)
Zolotoi kolos—*VDNKh*
Zvyozdnoye nebo*—3 ulitsa Gorkogo
Dubrava*
Galaktika*
Kalinka* } —150 prospekt Mira, in the *Kosmos* Hotel
Lunny*

---

* Restaurants marked with an * belong to Intourist

STORES

Art Shops
Artist of the RSFSR—54 ulitsa Dimitrova
Moscow Art Salon—12 ulitsa Petrovka
Russky suvenir (Russian Souvenir)—9 Kutuzovky prospekt
Russkiye uzory (Russian Pattern)—16 ulitsa Petrovka
Art Fund Salon—6 Ukrainsky bulvar
Books
Dom knigi (The House of Books)—26 prospekt Kalinina
Druzhba (Friendship) (books from socialist countries)—15 ulitsa Gorkogo
Foreign Books—18 ulitsa Kuznetsky most
Foreign Second-hand Books—16 ulitsa Kachalova
Iskusstvo (Art)—4 ulitsa Arbat
Knizhny mir (Book World)—6 ulitsa Kirova
Moskva—8 ulitsa Gorkogo
Progress (books in foreign languages)—17 Zubovsky bulvar
Sovetskaya Rossiya (Soviet Russia)—4 Kutuzovsky prospekt
Cameras and Photographic Supplies
Jupiter—27 prospekt Kalinina

Kinolyubitel—62 Leninsky prospekt, 25 ulitsa Gorkogo, 15 ulitsa Petrovka, 44 Komsomolsky prospekt
Computers
Vychislitelnaya tekhnika—6 proyezd Khudozhestvennogo teatra
Cut Glass
Dom farfora (House of Porcelain)—36 Leninsky prospekt,
18 Bolshaya Dorogomilovskaya ulitsa,
8 ulitsa Kirova
Khrustal (Crystal)—15 ulitsa Gorkogo
Komissionny magazin (Second-hand Store)—46 ulitsa Gorkogo
Podarki (Gifts)—29 prospekt Kalinina
Department Stores
TsUM—2 ulitsa Petrovka
Detsky mir (Children's World)—2 prospekt Marksa
GUM—3 Krasnaya Ploshchad
Moskovsky—6 Komsomolskaya ploshchad
Moskva—54 Leninsky prospekt
Moskvichka—23 prospekt Kalinina
Vesna (Spring)—27 prospekt Kalinina
Film Strips ans Slides
Diafilmy i diapozitivy—5 Stoleshnikov pereulok, 27 prospekt Kalinina
Gifts
Podarki—29 prospekt Kalinina, 4 and 37 ulitsa Gorkogo, 13 Stoleshnikov pereulok
Instruments and Tools
Instrumenty—15 ulitsa Kirova, 25 Tsvetnoy bulvar
Jewelry
Agat (Agate)—16 Bolshaya Kolkhoznaya ploshchad
Almaz (Diamond)—14 Stoleshnikov pereulok
Beriozka—12 ulitsa Gorkogo
Malakhitovaya shkatulka (Malachite Casket)—24 prospekt Kalinina
Samotsvety (Precious Stones)—35 ulitsa Arbat
Sapfir (Sapphire)—120 prospekt Mira
Zhemchug (Pearl)—22 Olimpiisky prospekt
Perfumery and Cosmetics
Siren (Lilacs)—44 prospekt Kalinina,
7 prospekt Marksa, 8 ulitsa Gorkogo
Radio Equipment
Radiotovary—14 Bolshaya Kolkhoznaya ulitsa, 78 Leninsky prospekt
Records
Melodia—40 prospekt Kalinina, 11 Leninsky prospekt
Television Equipment
Elektronika—87 Leninsky prospekt
Era—27 ulitsa Gorkogo
Rubin—10 Kutuzovsky prospekt
Orbita—7 Smolenskaya ulitsa
Tobacco
Gavana—17 Komsomolsky prospekt
Tabak—14 Stoleshnikov pereulok, 17 ulitsa Kuznetsky most, 34 ulitsa Arbat

Toys
Detsky mir (Children's World)—2 prospekt Marksa
Dom igrushki (House of Toys)—28 ulitsa Dimitrova
Podarki (Gifts)—29 prospekt Kalinina
Watches
Chasy (Watches)—8 ulitsa Petrovka
Sekunda—29 ulitsa Arbat,
4 ulitsa Gorkogo,
11 Stoleshnikov pereulok
Wines and Spirits
Novoarbatsky—21 prospekt Kalinina,
Rossiiskiye vina (Russian Wines)—4 ulitsa Gorkogo,
7 Stoleshnikov pereulok

A SHORT PHRASE-BOOK

Greetings

Hello	Zdrástvuit'e
Good morning	Dóbraye útra
Good day	Dóbry d'én'
Good evening	Dóbry v'écher
It's good to see you	Rad vas v'éed'et'
Good-bye	Da sveedániya
Good-night	Spakóynoy nóchee
Have a good trip	Shchastl'éevava poot'ée

Introductions

Hello	Zdrástvuit'e
Very glad to meet you	Óchen' rad(-a)* s vám'ee paznakómitsa
Let me introduce myself. My name is ...	Razreshéet'e predstávitsa. Yah ...
May I ask your name	Razreshéet'e ooznát' váshoo fam'ée-liyoo
I arrived from ...	Yah priyékhal(-a) iz ...
I've come to the Soviet Union as a tourist	Yah priyékhal(-a) v Sav'étskiy Sayóoz kak tur'éest(-ka)
I've wanted to visit the Soviet Union for a long time	Yah davnó khatél(-a) pabyvát' v Sav'étskom Sayóoz'e

Forms of Address

Comrade	Tavár'eeshch
Citizen(ess)	Grazhdan'-éen(-ka)

Requests

Please	Pazháhlsta
Please call a translator	Pazavéet'e, pazháhlsta, pirivódchika

---

* In instances where two forms are given, the latter is the feminine equivalent.—**Ed.**

Stop, please	Astanavéet'es', pazháhlsta
Help me, please	Pamagéet'e, pazháhlsta
Could you see me off (meet me)	Prashóo vas pravad'éet' (vstréht'eet') min'á
Can you help me call the embassy (trade delegation, consulate, my friend …)	Pamagéet'e mn'e pazvan'éet' v pasól'stva (v torgprédstva, v kónsool'stva, dróogoo)

Acknowledgement of Thanks

Thank you	Spas'éeba
I'm grateful to you	Yah vam pr'eeznátel'-en(-na)

Apologies

I beg your pardon	Eezv'een'éet'e
Excuse me	Prast'éet'e
It's my fault	V'eenavát

Wishes

I'd like to look round the city (the exhibition)	Yah khachóo asmatrét' górad (výstavkoo)
I want to go to the theater (a concert, the circus, the movies, the museum, the park, the club, the stadium)	Yah khachóo payt'ée v tiátr (na kantsért, v tséerk, v k'eenó, v mooz'áy, v párk, v kloob, na stadión)
I want to meet with you	Yah khachóo vstréteetsa s vám'ee
I want to rest (eat, drink, sleep)	Yah khachóo otdakhnóot' (yest', peet', spat')
I'd like to buy a souvenir	Yah khatyél(-a) bi koopéet' shtó-neebóod' na pámyat'
I need to buy …	Mnye nóozhna koopéet' …
I want to call a taxi	Yah khachóo výzvat' taks'ée

Affirmation

I agree	Yah saglás-en(-na)
I have no objection	N'e vazrazháyoo
Yes, of course	Da, kan'éshna
With pleasure	S oodavól'stv'eeyem
You're right	Vy právy

Refusal, Diagreement

I don't want	Yah n'e khachóo
No, thank you	N'et, spas'éeba
Unfortunately, I'm busy	K sazhal'én'eeyoo, yah zán'at(-a)
You're wrong	Vy n'e právy
You're mistaken	Vy asheebáyet'es'
I disagree with you	Yah n'e saglás-en (-na) s vám'ee
I can't, I don't have time	N'e magóo, oo m'in'á n'et vrémin'ee

Congratulations and Good Wishes

Congratulations	Pazdravl'áyoo vas

Happy birthday (New Year)	Pazdravl'áyoo vas s dn'óm razhd'éne-eya (s Nóvym gódom)
I'd like to propose a toast to our friendship	Yah khachóo predlazhéet' tost za ná-shoo dróozhboo
To your health	Za váshe zdaróv'e
I wish you happiness (health, success)	Zheláyoo shchást'a (zdaróv'a, oo-spékha)
I wish you success in your work	Zheláyoo vam oospékha v rabót'e
My best regards to your spouse	Nayeelóocheeye pazhelán'eeya vásh-ei(-emu) soopróog-e(-oo)

Language

I don't speak Russian	Yah n'e gavar'óo pa-róosk'ee
I only speak English (French, German)	Yah gavar'óo tól'ka pa-angl'éesk'ee, (pa-frantsóosk'ee, pa-nim'étsk'ee)
I want to learn to speak (read, write) Russian	Yah khachoo nauchéetsa gavar'éet' (cheetát', peesát') pa-róosk'ee
I don't understand you	Yah n'e pan'eemáyoo vas
Repeat once more, please	Pavtar'éet'e, pazháhlsta, yishchó ras
Speak more slowly	Gavar'éet'e m'édlin'iye

Days of the Week

What day is it?	Kakóy sivódn'a d'en?
Monday	Panid'él'nik
Tuesday	Ftórnik
Wednesday	Sridá
Thursday	Chitv'érk
Friday	P'átn'eetsa
Saturday	Soobóta
Sunday	Vaskris'én'e
Working day	Rabóchei d'en'
Non-working day	N'erabóchei d'en'
Day off	Vykhadnóy d'en'
Week	Nid'él'a

Months of the Year

Month	M'és'its
January	Yanvár'
February	Fevrál'
March	Mart
April	Apr'él'
May	Mai
June	Eeyóon'
July	Eeyóol'
August	Ávgoost
September	S'intyábr'
October	Aktyábr'
November	Nayábr'
December	Dikábr'

Seasons of the Year

Winter	Zeemá
Spring	V'esná
Summer	L'éta
Fall	Ósin'
Holiday	Prázneek
New Year	Nóvy God

Time

What time is it?	Katóry chas?
Nine o'clock in the morning (evening)	Dév'at' chasóf ootrá (v'échera)
Morning, in the morning	Óotra, óotrom
Evening, in the evening	V'écher, v'écherom
Night, in the night	Noch', nóchyoo
Day, in the day	D'en', dn'óm
Noon, midnight	Póld'en', pólnoch
Minute	Minóota
Quarter hour	Chétv'ert' chása
Half hour	Polchasá
Hour	Chas
Today	Sivódn'a
Tomorrow	Záftra
Yesterday	Vcherá
Day before yesterday	Pazavcherá
Day after tomorrow	Posl'ezáftra
Now	Seichás

Numbers

How much?	Skól'ka
1—one	adéen
2—two	dva
3—three	tr'ee
4—four	chitýre
5—five	p'at'
6—six	shest'
7—seven	s'em'
8—eight	vósim'
9—nine	d'évit'
10—ten	d'ésit'
11—eleven	adéenatsat'
12—twelve	dvenátsat'
13—thirteen	tr'eenátsat'
14—fourteen	chitýrnatsat'
15—fifteen	pitnátsat'
16—sixteen	shisnátsat'
17—seventeen	s'imnátsat'
18—eighteen	vosimnátsat'
19—nineteen	d'ivitnátsat'

20—twenty	dvátsat'
30—thirty	tr'eetsat'
40—forty	sórok
50—fifty	pit'dis'át
60—sixty	shisdis'át
70—seventy	sémdis'at
80—eighty	vósimdis'at
90—ninety	divinósta
100—one hundred	sto
200—two hundred	dv'ésti
300—three hundred	tr'eésta
400—four hundred	chitýrista
500—five hundred	pitsót
600—six hundred	shissót
700—seven hundred	s'imsót
800—eight hundred	vosimsót
900—nine hundred	divitsót
1,000—one thousand	týsicha

Money

One kopeck	Adná kap'éika
Two, three, four kopecks	Dv'e, tree, chitýre kapéikee
Five kopecks (and up)	Pyat' kapéyik (d'ésit' … pitnátsat' …)
One rouble	Adéen róobl'
Two, three, four roubles	Dva, tree, chitýre roobl'á
Five (and up) roubles	Pyat' roobléi (d'ésit' … stó …)
How much does it cost?	Skól'ka stóyit?
Please write down the cost	Nap'eeshéet'e, pazháhlsta, tsénoo
Please change this hundred rouble note	Razmin'áit'e, pazháhlsta, storubl'óvkoo
Change	Zdácha
How much do I owe you?	Skól'ka yah vam dólzh-en (-ná)
Have I paid for everything?	Yah rasplat'éel-s'a (-as')

Attributes

Good	Kharósh-eei (-aya, -aiye)
Bad	Plakh-óy (-aya, -oye)
Beautiful	Kras'éev-y (-aya, -oye)
Ugly	N'ekras'éev-y (-aya, -oye)
Interesting	Interésn-y (-aya, -oye)
Uninteresting	N'einterésn-y (-aya, -oye)
Expensive	Darag-óy (-aya, -oye)
Inexpensive	D'eshóv-y (-aya, -oye)
High	Vysók-eei (-aya, -oye)
Thin, fine	Tónk-eei (-aya, -oye)
Full, stout	Póln-y (-aya, -oye)
Slow	M'édlenn-y (-aya, -oye)
Cheerful	V'es'ól-y (-aya, -oye)
Boring	Skóochn-y (-aya, -oye)

Signs

Attention	Vn'eemáneeye
Stop	Stop
Crossing	Pirikhót
Bus stop (trolleybus, tram)	Astanófka aftóboosa (traléyiboosa, tramváya)
Caution, vehicle passage	Birigées' aftamabéel'a
Taxi stand	Stayánka taks'ée
Telephone booth	Tilifón-aftamát
Information bureau	Správachnaye b'uró
Men's Room	Moozhskóy tooal'ét
Ladies' Room	Zhénsk'ei tooal'ét
Drugstore	Apt'éka
Post Office	Póchta
Telegraph Office	Tiligráf
Hairdresser's	Pareekmákherskaya
Theater Box Office	Tiatrál'naya kássa
Restaurant	Ristarán
Cafeteria	Stalóvaya
Snack Bar	Zakóosachnaya
Café	Kafé
Bakery	Bóolachnaya
Confectioner's	Kand'éeterskaya
Grocery Store	Gastronóm
Florist's	Tsv'etý
Perfumer's Shop	Parf'umériya
Tobacco Shop	Tabák
Book Store	Kn'eég'ee
GUM Department Store	Oon'eevermák Goom
TsUM Department Store	Oon'eevermák Tsoom

In the Metro

Entrance	Vkhot
Exit	Výkhot
No exit	Výkhoda n'et
Deposit 5 kopecks	Appoost'éet'e pyát' kapéyik
Proceed to the left	Prakhad'éet'e sl'éva
To the trains	K payizdám

On the Street

Can you tell me ...	Skazhéet'e, pazháhlsta ...
how to get to my hotel?	Kak prayt'ée k gast'éenitse?
the name of this street?	Kak nazyváyetsa éta óoleetsa?
which bus (trolley-bus, tram) I can take to the center?	Kak'éem aftóboosom (traléiboosom, tramváyem) yah magóo payékhat' da tséntra górada?
where is the bus stop?	gd'e astanófka aftóboosa?
where is the taxi stand?	gd'e stayánka taksée?

Can you give me directions to ...	Kak mn'e dayékhat' da ...?
Straight	Pr'áma
To the left	Nal'éva
To the right	Napráva
I've lost my group	Yah atstál(-a) ot svayéi gróopy
I have lost my way	Yah zabloodéel-s'a (-as')
Help me	Pamag'éet'e mn'e
I'm late	Yah apázdyvayoo
Police officer	Militsion'ér

Hotel Accommodations

At which hotel will we be staying?	V kakóy gast'éen'eetse mi asta-nóv'eems'a?
What is the room charge per day?	Skól'ka stóyit nómir v sóotk'ee?
Where is the elevator (restaurant, service bureau, café?)	Gd'e nakhód'eetsa l'éeft (ristarán, b'uró apslóozheevan'iya, kafé?)
Please reserve me two theater tickets for tomorrow's performance	Zakazhéet'e mn'e, pazháhlsta, na záftra dva bil'éta v tiátr
Please arrange for an excursion tomorrow around the city (to the museum, to *VDNKh*)	Zakazhéet'e, pazháhlsta, na záftra, eks-kúrs'eeyoo pa góradoo (v moos'éi, na Ve-De-N-Khá)
Please wake me tomorrow at ... o'clock	Razbood'éet'e min'áh, pazháhlsta, v ... chasóf
Is my hotel account settled?	Yah pólnost'oo rasplat'éels'a za nómir?

Dining Out

Please bring us ... the menu (beer, wine, pepsi-cola, juice, mineral water)	Pasháhlsta, prinis'éet'e nam ... min'óo (p'éeva, v'eenó, pepsi-cólu, sok, mine-rál'nooyo vódu)
We would like to order some Russian national cuisine	Mi khat'éem zakazát' shto-n'eebóod' iz róoskoy natsionál'noy kóokhn'ee
I'd like some caviar (salmon, Russian salad)	Yah khachóo papróbavat' eekró (laso-séenoo, salát pa-roósk'ee)
The check, please	Dáit'e, pazháhlsta, shchot
Thank you for the prompt service	Spaséeba, vy nas býstra apsloozhéel'ee

First Aid

I am ill	Yah n'izdoróv(-a)
I'm feeling bad	Yah plókho sib'á choóstvooyoo
Please, call the doctor (an ambulance)	Výzav'eet'e, pazháhlsta, dóktara (skó-rooyoo pómashch)
I have a temperature (a fever)	Oo min'á timperatóora (min'á l'eekha-rád'eet)
I'm feeling better	Mn'e oozhé lóochshe
I'm feeling fine	Yah sib'áh chóostvooyoo kharashó

Departure

| I'm leaving tomorrow at ... o'clock | Yah ooyezháyoo záftra v ... chasóf |

Please prepare my bill	Pr'eegatóvt'e mn'e, pazháhlsta, shchot
When does the train depart for Paris?	Kagdá atkhód'eet póyizt v Parish?
Where is the train (plane, ship) schedule?	Gd'e mózhna pasmatrét' rasp'eesániye poyizdóf (samal'ótof, parakhódof)?
When does the flight leave for London? Flight number?	Kagdá výlit samal'óta v Lóndon? Nómir réisa
Where do I board train number ... to ...?	Gd'e pasádka na póyizt nómir ... da ...?
Where is the departure gate for flight number ... to ...?	Gd'e pasádka na samal'ót reiys nómir ... da ...?

Customs

Where do I pass through customs?	Gd'e bóod'et tamózhennoye afarmlén'eèye?
This is all my baggage	V'es' état bagázh móy
This is my suitcase	Éta moy cheemadáhn
I have nothing to declare	Oo min'áh n'et n'eechevó shto sl'édooyet abyav'éet'
Permitted (Not permitted)	Razrisháyetsa (N'e razrisháyetsa)
How much duty must I pay?	Kakóoyoo póshl'eenoo yah dólzhen(-na) ooplatéet'?
I have an import license	Oo min'áh litsénz'eeya na vvoz
Is the inspection finished?	Dasmótr akónchen?
You're very kind	Vy óchen' l'oob'ézny
Here's my passport	Vot moy pásport
I'm a tourist	Yah tooréest(-ka)
I want to come back to your country	Yah khachóo pr'eeyékhat' v váshoo stranóo yishchó raz

SUBJECT INDEX

STREETS AND SQUARES INDEX

ТРИ ДНЯ В МОСКВЕ
Путеводитель на английском языке
Изд. № 11/3-8526: (5.00)